# THE UFO PHENOMENA

*Also by Edward Ashpole*

The Search for Extraterrestrial Intelligence

# *THE* UFO PHENOMENA

A Scientific Look at the Evidence for
Extraterrestrial Contacts

Edward Ashpole

HEADLINE

First published in 1995
by HEADLINE BOOK PUBLISHING

10 9 8 7 6 5 4 3 2

British Library Cataloguing in Publication Data

Ashpole, Edward
UFO Phenomena
I. Title
001.942

ISBN 0-7472-1246-5

Typeset by Keyboard Services, Luton, Beds

Printed and bound in Great Britain by
Mackays of Chatham PLC, Chatham, Kent

HEADLINE BOOK PUBLISHING
A division of Hodder Headline PLC
338 Euston Road
London NW1 3BH

To all ETs, wherever they may be: on their planets, transmitting radio messages across the light-years for our astronomers to detect; or here in flying saucers, studying the latest civilisation in the Galaxy for a million years.

# CONTENTS

# ACKNOWLEDGEMENTS

---

Much of the science supporting the extraterrestrial hypothesis of the UFO phenomena is at the frontiers of knowledge. Many discussions with highly specialised scientists have therefore been needed to gain a balanced perspective on that science. I will not name them here because few would wish me to do so. The science community has to be vigorously sceptical of untested ideas, and it is inadvisable for professional scientists to give serious attention to the subject of UFOs. But I am deeply grateful to them for their willingness to engage in detailed discussions, often in areas of science where there are no accepted answers.

I will now turn to those helpful people actively engaged with the UFO phenomena who will not mind being named. My thanks therefore to:

Roy Dutton for many discussions over the years about his Astronautical Theory which, if confirmed, would confirm the extraterrestrial hypothesis of the UFO phenomena (the ETH).

Erling Strand, Head of Project Hessdalen in Norway, and his colleague Odd-Gunnar Roed, for providing much information on the Hessdalen phenomena and for checking my account of their research findings and the strange phenomena which they have been studying.

Vincente-Juan Ballester Olmos of Spain, who has contributed greatly to the rational understanding of the UFO phenomena, for his generous help in supplying much useful material.

Dr Richard Haines of California for his generous help in assessing my view of the role of photography in investigating the UFO phenomena, and for some of the photography in this book.

Mark Rodeghier in Chicago, Scientific Director at the J. Allen Hynek Center for UFO Studies, for his detailed and helpful correspondence.

Harry Godfrey for his letters, sketches, photographs and video on the apparatus he builds in his garage in Rosanna, Australia, to test the physics of his hypothesis on how motor vehicles are immobilised by close encounters with UFOs.

Dr J. J. Velasco, Head of SEPRA, a group of the Centre National d'Etudes Spatiales (France's equivalent of NASA), the group responsible for investigating unexplained aerial phenomena in French airspace.

Philip Mantle, Director of Investigations for BUFORA (British UFO Research Association), and some of his colleagues for numerous discussions about the problems of investigating the UFO phenomena.

Dr Erol Faruk for his help in my account of the Delphos incident.

Those at Quest International for chats about the UFO phenomena and for much material which has been invaluable in the preparation of this book.

Those scientists in astronomical SETI who have for many years sent me their papers and publications, including those at the SETI Institute in California which is now running the most powerful and comprehensive observational search for evidence of other world civilisations.

Also, I have to thank many people whose writings have been invaluable to me, but with whom I have not had the opportunity to communicate. They include Professor Frank Tipler whose brilliant articles in the science journals have contributed enormously to making some of us more realistic in our thinking about SETI, although perhaps not in the way he intended. The writings of Bill Chalker and James McCampbell have been valuable. Chalker in Australia has worked to get UFO landing sites investigated with science and rigour while McCampbell has looked closely at the possible physics of UFOs.

Lastly, moving from science to publishing, I must thank my editor at Headline, Lorraine Jerram, who has shown patience and understanding in the face of the editorial difficulties which arose during the production of this book.

# INTRODUCTION
## *From Mythology to Science*

A few days ago, as I was completing this book, a letter of considerable significance arrived from Dr J. J. Velasco, Head of SEPRA [Service d'Expertise des Phénomènes de Rentreés Atmosphériques], part of the Centre National d'Etudes Spatiales, the French space agency. Since 1977 SEPRA has been ready to investigate all unidentified aerospatial phenomena, including the most interesting UFO events in France, and it has achieved a level of scientific investigation not matched in any other country.

As Head of SEPRA, Dr Velasco has been ideally placed to make an objective assessment of the UFO phenomena. He writes:

> Relations between UFO Phenomena and Extra-earthly intelligence are not yet definitely established as of to-date. However, researches on French cases such as the Trans-en-Provence case, or some aerospace cases such as Teheran in 1976, indicate that we are face to face with artificial objects having an intelligent behaviour that we cannot control and which are superior to our present technology.

This provisional view is similar to that held by numerous scientists who are familiar with the most interesting aspects of the UFO phenomena. And it is a view which is in line with the scientific rationale that justifies astronomical SETI [search for extraterrestrial intelligence] which has been scanning the skies for ET's broadcasts since 1960. The search for evidence of our counterparts in the universe has therefore taken on a new dimension.

The discovery of ET would be a great event. There would be world-wide interest in the discovery itself, but the nature of the evidence might rather affect our reaction to it. If the nearest

1

extraterrestrial civilisation is hundreds of light-years away among the stars and we pick up its broadcasts, we would feel excitement and curiosity at the discovery. If we find evidence that ET is here, in the Solar System, studying us from UFOs, we might feel something more than excitement and curiosity. I hope to show in this book that we would have nothing to worry about. If UFOs are currently here, they have not just arrived. For statistical reasons, they must have been coming here for thousands of years – perhaps for millions of years.

We are faced today with an impressive problem because the sophistication of modern civilisation has led to so many UFOs being observed – by pilots, radar, the military, the police as well as the public. UFOs have been recorded on films and video tapes and have left traces behind at landing sites. But hardly any of these observations have been treated scientifically. Instead, a remarkable mixture of media hype and mythology has been created in which the most interesting aspects of the UFO phenomena are smothered. Scientists interested in discovering other intelligent life have concentrated on searching across the light-years for ET's radio broadcasts. The gullibility and lack of intellectual rigour which we find in too many accounts of flying saucers and cosy chats with extraterrestrials have alienated the scientific mind. The scientific establishment has developed an irresistible avoidance reflex to anything ufological.

So, while most scientists nervously avoid the subject of UFOs for fear of being labelled a touch wacky, perfectly sane astronomers search for broadcasts from other worlds with the full approval of the science establishment – and have been doing so since 1960. But the astronomers engaged in the search for extraterrestrial intelligence skip the fact that the same science which justifies their searches also supports the hypothesis that some UFOs (let us say just 1 per cent of those reported) may have an extraterrestrial origin.

We must review astronomical SETI in this book because *it* and the extraterrestrial hypothesis [ETH] of ufology are two faces of the same coin. This analogy is appropriate because those two faces never look directly at each other, although some SETI astronomers have looked for extraterrestrial probes parked in appropriate orbits in nearby space. The thinking is that they would be ancient probes, relics of missions completed millions of years ago. The longer the period ETs have had to send their probes, the more likely they are to be here. But this research opened up astronomical SETI – just a little. With their attempts to detect alien probes, astronomers in SETI have unintentionally moved next door to the extraterrestrial hypothesis of ufology. This hypothesis suggests that at least a small proportion of

UFO reports indicate the possible presence of alien probes. If it is scientifically respectable to search for such probes in orbit, then it should also be respectable to investigate the most credible reports of flying saucers in our immediate environment.

Actually, scientists in general don't know much about the UFO phenomena, except for the sensational stories they read in newspapers. It all seems nonsense to them – and rightly so, because most of what they read *is* nonsense. A contributing factor to this ignorance could be university libraries. In my experience, no British university library takes any of the few scholarly journals that are available on the UFO phenomena.

Not long ago, I was told that a certain professor of physics was about to give a lecture on UFOs and the paranormal at a conference in Edinburgh. I thought he might have a new angle to disclose, so I phoned him. He was kind enough to say that our conversation was the most rational he had had on the subject of UFOs, but I gained nothing from our chat, since he was unaware of the main lines of research and the leading researchers in ufology. I could understand why. I had the same experience many years ago when an editor asked me to write a science article about flying saucers. If your first contact is with a 'true believer', as mine was, you are helped with information and passed on to other 'true believers'. It is like entering a new-age religion as a possible convert. You can find yourself in a vague and gullible atmosphere far removed from the rigours of science. It is a culture shock. But if you stay with it (and the perplexed professor didn't have time before his lecture), you may eventually find able researchers, and even a number of scientists – they do exist, though vastly outnumbered by 'true believers'.

Journalists on the whole don't put UFOs into their proper perspective. They tend to mix UFOs with ghosts and the paranormal into one big mystery. They fail to mention that there is no accepted science to support the possible existence of ghosts and the paranormal, whereas the existence of UFOs, as extraterrestrial spacecraft, could be predicted from what we already know about life and the universe. If UFO reports did not exist, we could still predict that a phenomenon which could be explained as extraterrestrial activity might be observed from time to time.

Another problem, which would not exist if ufology stayed closer to science, is that many ufologists have drifted off into areas of thought more akin to a new mystical religion than a rational investigation of apparently physical phenomena. In the literature you can find some ufologists speculating on the links between UFOs and the psychical world – even on the 'healing power of UFOs'. They do not actually mention ghosts, but they are in the same mythical territory as ghosts, which is not very promising since the nature of ghosts has defied explanation for rather a long time.

This drift towards the psychical and paranormal has been ruinous for those who want to persuade scientists to give UFOs a chance. We do not yet know the nature of UFOs, nor the nature of the paranormal and psychical. We can therefore hardly expect to be able to explain phenomena which we do not understand (UFO phenomena) by reference to yet other phenomena which we do not understand (paranormal and psychical phenomena) and arrive at an answer which we *do* understand. Yet many attempts to do so can be found in the UFO literature.

But back to that conservative 1 per cent of UFO reports. What makes them interesting is the scientific rationale for astronomical SETI which has justified spending millions of dollars searching for ET's broadcasts. I have been writing on this science since 1963, and if it did not exist I would not be writing this book – I would probably have thought that all UFO reports were work for the psychologists and sociologists. But the scientific rationale for SETI is convincing and if applied can offer explanations for some otherwise unex-plainable aspects of the UFO reports.

Most of us are familiar with the popular scenarios of extra-terrestrial contact offered in fiction, but if we speculate on the basis of past discoveries in science, the first detected manifestation of extraterrestrial intelligence is more likely to be very different from what we expect. The unexpected is what we should expect. And this, in a way, is what a small proportion of reported UFOs provide.

That is not to say that ET is out there in flying saucers, monitoring our world. It is to say that the relevant science is not inconsistent with the extraterrestrial hypothesis for some UFO reports.

## CURIOUS CONTRADICTION
There exists an inconsistent combination of beliefs in science today which is directly relevant to the ETH for some UFOs. Scientists and engineers in astronautics are convinced that space technology will one day take us to the stars, that our descendants in centuries to come will explore other planetary systems and discover other civilisations. No one in the science community rubbishes that dream. Also, scientists agree that extraterrestrial technological civilisations will be more advanced than us, since we have only just arrived on the technological scene.

There is a curious contradiction in believing that, though other civilisations in the Galaxy are more advanced than us, they will *not* have had our dream about exploring other worlds and will *not* be arriving here before we travel to the stars to discover them.

This position is especially unsatisfactory when we have indications, though vague and often unreliable, that other civilisations may have realised our dream long before we even evolved on this planet. *They* may be here or they may not be here, but the theory justifies expert attention. UFOs should cease to be a no-go area for professional scientists.

What I wish to demonstrate in this book is that the extraterrestrial hypothesis for some UFOs is a reasonable one in the light of current science, and seemingly irresistible following certain reported events. A lifetime of work as a science correspondent has set me firmly in the scientific camp, which, I think, can provide the only way we have of getting reliable and acceptable information, if it is there to be obtained. But I am not tied to the science establishment and can write freely on this contentious subject. I can explore the possibility of what is unmentionable in scientific circles, and, I hope, encourage a more open approach to a major mystery of our time. We do not want to be blinkered by the currently accepted paradigm of science, nor do we want to be carried away by uncritical belief. We are in an area where the maximum scepticism is not only justified but also essential.

# CHAPTER 1
## *The Best UFO Report*

The UFO was a little late for Christmas, but its lights made the season's illuminations look rather dull. Its persistent performance in Rendlesham Forest at the end of December 1980 is arguably the best manifestation of any UFO. Senior officers and other ranks of the United States Air Force and the RAF confronted the UFO for several hours. Tape recordings were made, though only one tape was released – four years after the event! The military personnel involved have since publicly confirmed all we know of the event, but because this UFO was observed and studied by the military, the physical evidence that it may have provided was not investigated by any civilian authority.

According to the air force staff, a greater than normal number of officials visited the base after the UFO's visit. Government scientists may therefore have investigated the event, but their findings, if they exist, are hidden from public view for the present. No one in an official position to disclose research data will do so, except to say that the event posed no threat to the security of British airspace. Yet no one who supports the hypothesis that some UFOs are extra-terrestrial artifacts would think that there was any threat to British airspace. One can understand the need to keep everything under wraps at the time. Think of the headlines! 'Air Force Colonel Chases UFO in Woods.' But the Ministry of Defence could come clean now.

So what happened? The bare bones are stated in Colonel Charles Halt's memo to the Ministry of Defence in London. Halt was then a deputy commander at the twin air force bases of Bentwaters and Woodbridge, which are separated by three miles of Rendlesham Forest. As one would expect from a military man reporting a UFO's visit to a top-security military base, the memo is brief and to the point. A much fuller picture of what happened has come from Halt's tape recording, made while his patrol pursued the UFO in Rendlesham Forest, and from the subsequent interviews with those involved, including Halt himself. Halt was later promoted to base commander where he served for a further four years.

What the Halt memo tells us is that at about 3.00 a.m. on 27 December 1980 three USAF patrolmen, including two sergeants, investigated brilliant lights just outside the east gate of the Woodbridge air base in Suffolk. Leaving the base and entering the forest, the patrol discovered a highly luminous object, triangular in shape, about nine feet wide and six feet high and seemingly metallic. As the men approached the UFO it moved away through the forest and eventually took off and disappeared, but was reported again an hour later on the perimeter of the base. All the UFO left behind that night were three depressions in the ground and some broken branches.

On the night of 29/30 December, Colonel Halt was interrupted at a dinner by the duty officer who told him that the UFO had returned. He assembled a team and led them into the forest to investigate.

What they saw seems to have amazed everyone present. Halt mentions a red sun-like light which moved and pulsed. It appeared to drip luminous particles. It broke into separate white objects which disappeared. Halt and his men then observed three star-like objects in the sky that moved 'rapidly in sharp angular movements and displayed red, green and blue lights... The objects to the north remained in the sky for an hour or more. The object to the south was visible for two or three hours and beamed down a stream of light from time to time.' These events kept them in the forest for several hours.

Such was the essence of the Colonel's report to the Ministry of Defence, a report to which Halt says he never received a reply.

The Rendlesham UFOs displayed behaviour and visual characteristics which had been reported many times before, but what interests a sceptic is that in this case it was all witnessed and reported by senior officers and other ranks responsible for one of the most important and sensitive military bases in Britain. We can dismiss the accounts of such strange events by single witnesses, by claiming that they are so soaked in UFO mythology that any unusual light or object becomes a flying saucer. Even small groups of civilian witnesses can be doubted. But two patrols of competent military men investigating a UFO in Rendlesham Forest, initially for a short period and later for several hours, while taking readings of relatively high radiation levels and other effects, are not so easily dismissed. Geiger-counter readings in places were twenty-five times the background level, and the night-vision scope saw an unusual amount of heat radiating off the trees.

Several members of the two patrols, including Halt himself, have added further credibility to the case in television interviews. Sergeant Jim Penniston, who thought an aircraft might have crashed, was in the first patrol to investigate the UFO:

I started to see a defined shape, and at that point I realised it wasn't an aircraft, a fire or anything of that sort. The air was filled with electricity. You could feel it on your skin as we approached the object. It was about the size of a tank. It was triangular in shape. Underneath the craft was a high-intensity light radiating from it, and it was bordered by red and blue lighting – alternating. On the upper left side of the craft was an inscription. It measured six inches high, in symbols. They looked familiar but I couldn't ascertain why. It slowly started to move away, weaving in and around the trees. It got about forty feet away and then it shot off as fast as you could blink.

That was the best account of the first encounter.

Colonel Halt was told about the UFO the next day. 'I personally knew the individuals,' he said. 'I knew they were very credible people.'

On the night of 29/30 December, when the UFO returned, Halt assembled a small team of experts

. . . we set off into the forest really to debunk it. I certainly wasn't convinced it was a UFO, but I didn't know what it was and I wanted a logical explanation for what was going on. I'm certainly glad we made the tape, because if we hadn't made the tape even I would have trouble in believing what happened that night.

Huge portable floodlights called lightalls had been erected in the forest, but the night the UFO returned they didn't work. Halt said:

It's very unusual to have a problem with a lightall. That night the lightalls wouldn't work. Even when we swapped them and got others from the base. In addition we had trouble with our radios. All three frequencies we were using were intermittent and did not work properly that night.

Halt has seemed almost apologetic for what he witnessed in the forest:

> It pulsated as though it were an eye winking at you, and around the edges it appeared to have molten metal dripping off it and falling to the ground. But I didn't see any evidence of it on the ground. I just couldn't believe what I was seeing. None of us could. Here I am a senior official who routinely denies this sort of thing and I'm involved in the middle of something I cannot explain.

The end of the encounter didn't come quickly. According to Halt:

> The object suddenly exploded, a silent explosion, and broke into 3 to 5 white objects and rapidly disappeared. As we moved out of the forest we noticed three objects in the sky. The objects in the sky were moving about – sharp angular movements, very high speed, as if they were looking for something. I kept getting on the radio and called the Command Post. I wanted to know if they were finding anything on the radar scope. One of the objects in the sky was sending down beams – beams of light, beams of energy, I'm not sure what they were. But at the same time I could hear on the radio voices talking about the beams coming down on the base.

It was at that time that a brilliant beam of light shone down on the patrol. 'At this stage my scepticism had definitely disappeared,' said Halt. 'I was really in awe.'

Staff at the base later spoke of secret visits and unscheduled flights coming in about which they were supposed to keep quiet. Was this the expected scientific investigation of the site? Clifford Stone, a former US military intelligence officer, has said that some of his colleagues were involved:

> There was a total blackout of any information leaving the base. Even the senior officials on the base were not told about these flights coming in and leaving. These flights contained teams of specialists. They were to gather specific data in their fields of expertise. All of that information then was to be sent to Washington DC where it would be assessed and accumulated for a finalised, highly classified report.

10

And what did that highly classified report have to say? According to Stone, it would have confirmed the extraterrestrial hypothesis of some UFOs:

> That finalised report concluded that real objects were seen; that those objects were the result of a highly advanced technology, so advanced that we cannot replicate it. That there was an intelligence involved and that that intelligence did not originate on Earth.

We could not have anything more conclusive than that, but we would need the report and all the scientific evidence on which it was based to convince the science community. To try to obtain that report could be a real challenge for some of the UFO groups.

Critics have offered mundane explanations for what the airmen reported: a meteor and spacecraft debris were witnessed by inhabitants in eastern England in the early hours of 26 December; the ever-present lighthouse at Orford Ness, several miles away, sweeps its beam through Rendlesham Forest. But the men at the base were familiar with the lighthouse and maintain they could not possibly have mistaken its light for the UFO they witnessed. Over-excited UFO believers might have so deceived themselves, but would patrols of experienced military personnel? Halt had some thirty men in Rendlesham Forest investigating the second UFO event.

There is also the physical evidence of the UFO's presence to speculate upon. As in the Trans-en-Provence case in southern France, which we will consider later, a proper scientific investigation could have demonstrated that *something* had landed. Perhaps one day a full scientific analysis of the evidence will be released.

One cannot but wonder why it is now that distinguished military men like Charles Halt are willing to describe the Rendlesham event in detail for all the world to hear. And why Colonel Sam Morgan, who succeeded Halt as commander at the base in 1984, released the tape of what happened in Rendlesham Forest that night in December 1980. Are they being encouraged in this? Is it part of a strategy to move the public towards some future revelation?

## MYSTERIOUS COVER-UP
Halt's memo to the British Ministry of Defence, sent seventeen days after the visitation, seems to have been somewhat delayed in the writing. Did Christmas put the United States Air Force so far

behind in its correspondence? One would have thought, bearing in mind the impact the UFO had made, that immediate reports to London and Washington would have been appropriate. An unknown craft landed just outside a top-security air base stocked with nuclear weapons. A patrol led by a deputy commander at the base had spent several hours tracking a weird and wonderful luminous phenomenon in the adjacent forest. It all happened on British soil, yet the Ministry of Defence in London was not told until seventeen days later! Does this need an explanation? Maybe Halt and his immediate superiors decided that their pursuit of a UFO in the woods just after Christmas would be too much for top generals and politicians to take just after their own celebrations. Such news is hardly likely to enhance one's career prospects in the military. So it may have been wise to wait a couple of weeks.

When the Halt memo was released in America to UFO investigators three years after the event, Members of Parliament questioned the Minister of Defence, Michael Heseltine. It looks as if he tried to tell the truth within the limitations imposed upon him. He said that the incident posed no threat to Britain – which is obviously so if ETs have been visiting our planet since eternity. As to the pertinent questions – What investigations had the British government carried out? Would the minister publish the results of such investigations? – MPs got nowhere.

If there was no threat, as the minister stated, then what reason could there be for not publishing the results of the government's investigations – apart from an innate fixation on secrecy? Unless, of course, the ministry would have to face embarrassment because no scientific investigations *had* been carried out.

Some critics of the Halt memo suggest it was part of a cover-up for a catastrophe at the base. Ralph Noyes, who worked in the Ministry of Defence, retiring from the Civil Service in 1977 on a grade equal to that of an Under-Secretary of State, takes an active interest in UFO phenomena. It is therefore gratifying to have his authoritative opinion on this idea:

As a former Defence official, who had responsibilities for designing and frequently reviewing the procedures for handling major mishaps (possible loss of nuclear contraptions, the crash of aircraft, the going spare of other troublesome items), I have no doubt at all that we and our American allies would never have been so foolish (or irresponsible) as to conceal our problems by propagating peculiar stories of a kind hard to believe. We would either have kept the whole thing secret (if

12

the public hadn't heard of it and we were also satisfied that no public damage would ensue), or we would have conspicuously cordoned off the area and braced ourselves for the inevitable questions.[1]

Ralph Noyes believes that government ministers and civil servants are as puzzled by the UFO phenomena as the rest of us. Actually their understanding may be less because most politicians and civil servants will not have lived in close proximity to the science of SETI, as some scientists and ufologists have done. So the partially informed may be pressing for answers from the embarrassingly uninformed.

That governments are defensive is understandable. If any one of us were Minister of Defence, or his top civil servant, when something like the Rendlesham UFO turned up, what would we do? Having no overwhelming interest in extraterrestrials, we would keep the event as quiet as possible and get on with real life. Far from appreciating the significance of what may have happened, we would not know what the hell had been going on! And none of the military men present could provide answers that made any sense. What a situation! But no harm was done, so better forget the whole business and deny it ever happened. We then live in relative peace for a few years until those dreadful people in the UFO societies get hold of the Halt memo through their colleagues in America. We are in an embarrassing position again. If at this late stage we tell the truth, we would say that a UFO landed outside the gates of a top-security air base where it manifested itself for several hours in the presence of senior officers and other ranks, but that no one had any idea what it was and how it came to be there. The military were powerless. All they could do was follow the UFO through the forest, making notes and recordings. But we could add that the UFO was relatively well behaved, breaking only a few branches as it moved among the trees. We would then have to explain that we didn't mention the event at the time for these reasons and because there was nothing anyone could do about it anyway. We could then add that because of public interest due to the leaked Halt memo, we were setting up an on-going scientific group to investigate the whole subject of UFOs, and that its findings would be made public on a regular basis.

If Michael Heseltine had said that at that time, the media in Britain would have erupted, along with most of the Commons and the House of Lords. The minister would have shown himself converted to ufology, a transformation too shocking to contemplate. So, being a professional at replying to unanswerable questions, the minister gave answers which, although intellectually inconsistent, did the trick.

We can imagine what the civil servants were told after the release of the Halt memo:

> If those persistent ufologists keep digging away for more details about Rendlesham, keep explanations concrete and ordinary – and keep extraterrestrials out of the picture. We don't want the electorate thinking we can't defend them against extra-terrestrials.

And so we have those never-ending arguments about space debris and the flashing light from the lighthouse and what Halt and his men really did witness in Rendlesham Forest. We might have been saved from them if the site had been investigated by professional scientists with the right equipment soon after the event and their findings made public. We might then have had something like the Trans-en-Provence case in which university scientists established as a fact that *something* had landed. Such scientific confirmation added to the military reports would have been difficult to brush aside.

Nevertheless, bearing in mind what the United States military have publicly revealed, there may be a stack of reports somewhere to shake up the science community. All the detective work and investigative journalism by ufologists have not been nearly enough to do that.

The difficulty is that when a range of ufologists investigate major UFO cases, some with a scientific approach and some without it, and then go on to write articles for the UFO magazines, distortions and gullibility can get incorporated into the accounts of the events. The literature may then seem phoney, and this discredits serious attempts to appraise the original investigations and information. As a result UFO events get a bad press.

The Rendlesham case, however, is too good to be written off by a bad press. And what was reported is not inconsistent with numerous other UFO events. But we need to follow the well-tested methods of science to make progress. Ralph Noyes, a cautious student of ufology, says about the Rendlesham case:

> It confirms what some of us have long felt – that the UFO phenomenon is utterly *real*, but something other than wholly nuts-and-bolts; that it is, indeed, a phenomenon at the very edge of human comprehension, more analogous to the appari-tions and poltergeists of psychical research...

Here I would like to remind Noyes of the comment by Arthur C. Clarke that our technology in a thousand years' time might appear as magic to anyone of us transported into that future. *In fact it might look somewhat psychical.* If some UFOs are extraterrestrial, we could be facing a technology not a thousand but hundreds of thousands of years beyond our own. And the biological element must also be considered. Not only is the technology going to appear 'psychical', but, to make comprehension near impossible, the intelligences behind that technology may be several orders of magnitude greater than our own.

Such differences in intelligence are, in theory, possible from what we currently know of biology. Put these two factors together (super technology and super intelligence) and we would have something to face which would indeed be 'at the very edge of human comprehension'.

## TOP BRASS ON RENDLESHAM

Lord Peter Hill-Norton, Admiral of the Fleet and Britain's former Chief of Defence Staff in the 1970s, has taken a keen interest in the Rendlesham event:

> It seems to me that something physical took place, that something landed at this US Air Force base. And I have no doubt that it got the people concerned at the base, including the Commanding General, into a very considerable state.
>
> My view is that the Ministry of Defence, who were repeatedly questioned about this, not only by me but by other people, have doggedly stuck to their normal line, which is that nothing of defence interest took place on that occasion.
>
> My position about this has always been quite clear, and I have said this both in public and on the television and radio. Either large numbers of people, including the Commanding General at Bentwaters, were hallucinating, and for an American Air Force nuclear base this is extremely dangerous, or what they say happened did happen. In either of these circumstances there can only be one answer and that is that it was of extreme interest to the United Kingdom.

There is, of course, a lot more involved than the security of the United Kingdom, but there was no danger in what Colonel Halt and his men reported, if it did happen. Only if they were all totally misled in their observations was there an element of danger at that time, during the Cold War. In any case there is nothing we can do about it, except try to understand what is happening. And that is what this book is all about.

# CHAPTER 2
## A Question for Everyone

The basic consideration of this book is the most fundamental question of all – and the UFO phenomena might provide the answer we seek. It is a question for everyone, though only science can address it with any hope of finding an answer. Our view of ourselves within this universe, if it is to be based on fact, depends upon an answer. But only a positive answer will do. We cannot prove a negative. And until we find that positive answer – if indeed it is there to be found – we have to rest upon speculation and belief.

The question is: Is life a universal phenomenon or are we, and all life on Earth, the result of a once-in-eternity chance event with no rightful place in the scheme of things?

In this book we will consider the hypothesis that life *is* a universal phenomenon and we will examine the ways being tried to test this hypothesis. It is not a claim or a belief, but a hypothesis which indirect evidence from several different scientific disciplines indicates may be correct. Although our question has been of major concern in philosophy throughout history (the ancient Greeks and Chinese are frequently quoted on the subject), it is only in our time that it has become a scientific hypothesis. Our society is the first to possess the science and technology to test it – and perhaps find an answer.

I do not want to mislead you into thinking that an answer is imminent. That it may come some time during the next decade or two is possible, but it is also possible that an acceptable answer may elude us. Confirmation of our hypothesis would be of such great importance, however, that we are justified in pursuing a difficult search. As Robert Burns said two hundred years ago: 'That a man's reach should exceed his grasp or what's a heaven for.'

The foremost (though not the only) scientific approach so far uses

17

existing radio telescopes to which specially developed computer-receivers are connected. These receivers can scan millions of frequencies simultaneously, searching for the broadcasts of other world civilisations, or for evidence of technology among the stars which betrays its presence by the radiation of certain frequencies in the electromagnetic spectrum. Such searches have been in progress since the 1960s, but current continuous programs are millions of times more powerful than those which searched during the 1960s and 1970s, when the scale of the task ahead was only beginning to be appreciated. Nowadays, however, the combination of radio astronomy and computer technology does look advanced enough to stand a chance of detecting evidence of universal life. If astronomers could detect just one civilisation within a few hundred light-years of our planetary system, it would mean that other life and civilisations must exist within the thousands of light-years spanning our Galaxy – and also in the millions of other galaxies in the universe.

This search for extraterrestrial intelligence is a bold adventure, involving observatories and universities in several countries. Some of the cleverest people around are contributing to astronomical SETI, and the astronomical approach has provided the scientific thrust in the search for evidence. In recent years it has gained for itself a Section within the International Astronomical Union, a sign of approval and acceptance by the scientific establishment.

Professor Frank Drake, the pioneer of astronomical SETI and President of the SETI Institute in California, has said that:

Commission 51 gave SETI the same status as the study of stars and galaxies in the eyes of the world's astronomers. There could no longer be any question that our pursuit was legitimate astronomical science.

The Astronomy Survey Committee of the National Academy of Sciences in the United States reported in 1991:

Ours is the first generation that can realistically hope to detect signals from another civilization in the Galaxy. The search for extraterrestrial intelligence [SETI], involves, in part, astronomical techniques and is endorsed by the Committee as a significant scientific enterprise. Indeed, the discovery of highly complex organic molecules in the interstellar medium lends even greater scientific support to this enterprise. Discovery of intelligent life beyond the Earth would have profound effects for all humanity.

This sounds fine, but SETI has its critics. John Barrow, Professor of Astronomy at Sussex University, has called the participating astronomers 'blindfolded men searching a darkened room for a black cat that isn't there'. Harsh words, but one cannot help but remember that it was Columbus who discovered the natives of North America and not the other way round. So could Barrow's 'black cat', if it does exist out there in space, know about us already?

We have to consider this possibility, while Barrow's criticism does not give credit for the rich synthesis of knowledge that those in astronomical SETI have assembled since the 1960s to provide theoretical support for their searches. The rationale for SETI arguably provides the best perspective on the human situation – what we are, where we are and where we may be going – that science has so far given us. SETI has not yet found ET, *even if ET has found us*, but it has contributed immensely to the discovery of ourselves.

## EVER PRESENT BROADCASTERS

The basic problem for astronomical SETI is that it is precariously dependent on the assumption of a *constant* supply of extraterrestrial broadcasters throughout the long history of our Galaxy. As the Galaxy is about three times the age of the Earth, according to the most reasonable astronomical estimates, the first civilisations could have started to transmit their messages across space more than five billion years ago, given that the rate of evolution on Earth, from single living cells to complex intelligent life, has been roughly the same on a proportion of Earth-like planets. The first messages could, therefore, have been crossing space before the Earth even existed – and we have only been listening for a few decades! Thus the business of broadcasting information across interstellar space must have been a common activity for world civilisations throughout the past few billion years, otherwise we cannot expect a sufficient number to be broadcasting in the vastness of the Galaxy in our epoch.

Civilisations would have to be remarkably stable and persevering by our standards to transmit their messages for many thousands of years, but this may be the sort of period needed for a signal to stand a chance of being received and acknowledged. We can expect extraterrestrial broadcasters to want to be understood – and to want a reply.

Astronomer Patrick Moore once provided the good analogy of a dark room with two electric light bulbs, each of which lit up at random for a second once every twenty-four hours (the light of technological intelligence shining in the darkness of the Galaxy). Communication could take place when the two bulbs lit up in the same second. It is more complicated than this – other factors have to be considered when estimating the probability of detecting evidence – but the analogy does show the basic problem facing the radio astronomers. One SETI experimentalist, Harry Godfrey in Australia, wrote in a letter to me: 'This suggests a person sitting near a phone, waiting for it to ring – and it may never ring!'

It is a probability to be faced. Yet this objection does not apply to the use of astronomy to detect certain frequencies which could proclaim the presence of ET's technology among the stars. I would suggest that we accept astronomical SETI as only one approach to testing the hypothesis of universal life, although it has pioneered the field experimentally. It has set the scientific standards and has stimulated some of the best brains in a wide range of scientific disciplines to synthesise a convincing rationale for SETI.

## THE CONCLUSION SETI SCIENTISTS AVOID

Thus we come to the underlying conclusion of this book: that if the scientific rationale justifiably supports the astronomical approach (and the astronomical establishment thinks it does), then it also supports what for the moment we might call the 'local approach' to SETI. We have to accept that evidence of ET, if such exists, is as likely to be within the Solar System as among the stars, though not necessarily living evidence.

The reason for this is relatively simple. We can assume that civilisations that could broadcast across the Galaxy for, say, many thousands of years, may also have the astronomy and technology to detect life-bearing planets in other systems and to send intelligent probes to explore. The obvious way they could do this would be to detect Earth-like planets by the oxygen and ozone lines in their spectra, as astronomers here are already planning to do. From the study of biology, geology and palaeontology we know that for the past 350 million years at least the Earth has been what amounts to a beacon of life beckoning life. But no one seems to want to look at that fact. I have yet to find it discussed in the scientific literature. No one in astronomical SETI and planetary detection has wanted to turn their research around and push it forward a century or two to speculate on what astronomically minded ETs might have done millions of years ago. I find it very odd that when people in SETI were challenged some years ago about the wisdom of advertising our presence by transmitting a message to a vast cluster of stars, they said: 'There's no point in worrying because leakages from radio and television have already been advertising our presence for the past seventy years.' This line has often been repeated in the literature of astronomical SETI. But seventy years is insignificant. The ETs may not detect us in seventy years, or in 700 years, but given 350 million years their chances of doing so are somewhat greater.

We definitely know that from about 350 million years ago the Earth has had an atmosphere with an oxygen content comparable to that of today. This atmosphere and its ozone layer were created by life, by the photosynthesis of plants. And not until enough free oxygen was present in the atmosphere could the ozone layer form, which then shielded life from damaging radiation as it emerged from the protection of water and began to evolve and colonise the land. The main beneficiaries of the newly formed ozone shield were the fishes which came ashore and evolved into the first amphibians. We know that arachnids [mites and spiders] began to colonise the land earlier, but these may not have been so dependent on the ozone shield.

## THE FREQUENCIES OF LIFE

A few years ago, astronomers at the University of Arizona designed an infra-red telescope with a sixteen-metre mirror to be placed in Earth orbit at some time in the future. It cannot be built yet because the necessary money is not available, but it is obvious future technology. Its main purpose would be the detection of the oxygen and ozone lines of Earth-like planets. Oxygen provides a very prominent line at 7,600 angstroms (in the near-infra-red, just outside the visual spectrum) and ozone a strong absorption line at 96,000 angstroms (in the mid-infra-red). But these two elements produce numerous other spectral lines. Other astronomers are already working out what may be done to detect them from bases on the Moon, which will surely be available in the next century.

My purpose in this book, though, is not to forecast what we will do in the next century in astronomy but to guess what would be easily possible for more advanced civilisations than our own. And to make the point that our planet has been detectable as a life-bearing planet for the past 350 million years, a shining target for any neighbourly ETs with an interest in alien biologies.

Michael D. Papagiannis, Professor of Astronomy at Boston University, is a leading figure in SETI with an interest in the detection of the planets of other stars. And he has worked out what may be done from a Moon base:

21

Assuming that we will be able to make spectroscopic observations to a distance of sixty-seven light-years [the distance possible with the proposed Lunar Infra-Red Array facility] we may be able to study close to one hundred Sun-like stars. This number would be reduced significantly by eliminating stars younger than about 3,500 million years.

If we want to find Earth-like planets inhabited by technological civilisations with a capacity to make their existence known, we should concentrate on Earth-like planets at least as old as the Earth, which means finding Sun-like stars at least as old as the Sun. According to Papagiannis:

Ultimately, we may start with the nearest Sun-like stars that are older than 3,500 million years, and try to obtain spectroscopic evidence for the presence of oxygen and/or ozone in the atmospheres of some of their planets. The technical means to attempt such a major project are not yet available, but in the twenty-first century we may be able to establish a Lunar Infra-Red Array on the Moon to look for habitable planets in other solar systems.

## ALIEN PROBES

As we can plan such astronomy for the next century, other civilisations which have preceded ours may have carried it out many times in the history of our Galaxy. What would then be their next step, if some of those civilisations had detected the Earth during the past 350 million years? Given that they had the necessary technology to cross interstellar space, they would probably send investigative probes rather than begin broadcasting in the hope that fully evolved radio astronomers were on the planet ready to receive their messages.

Successful probes, arriving in working condition, homing in on planets with oxygen and ozone lines, would provide results, as our probes have in the unmanned explorations of the Solar System. You would need to be a long-lived species and civilisation to enjoy the results of such exploration, but that seems a reasonable expectation for highly advanced beings. The extraterrestrials would not then have to rely on the primitive inhabitants of other worlds having invented radio and being tuned into the right frequencies at the right times in galactic history. Probes arriving here a hundred million years ago would have found the dinosaurs, who were not noted for their expertise in radio technology, yet probes at that time could

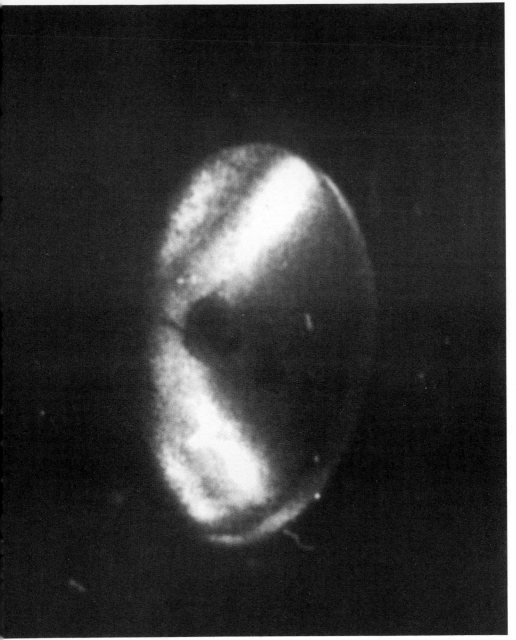

1. An aerial survey in Costa Rica, Central America, on 4 September 1971, from an altitude of 10,000 feet, photographed this UFO in just one of its frames. What is seen here is an enlargement made by Richard F. Haines and Jacques F. Vallee in their detailed analysis of the complete photograph – see Reference Section. (© *Dr Richard F. Haines*)

2. A typical UFO-light seen above a mountain in Hessdalen, Norway. Arne P. Thomassen, one of the research team, took this photograph in October 1982.

3. The Hessdalen field station in the winter of 1985.

4. When Leif Havik took this photograph the strange light was stationary, but it moved away during the exposure. (*Project Hessdalen*)

5. Harry Godfrey's experimental saucer. Godfrey has spent his retirement investigating various aspects of the physics behind the UFO phenomena, building experimental apparatus in his garage in Rosanna, Australia. The saucer was built to test the Earth's magnetic field as a possible source of lift. (*Harry Godfrey*)

6. A twenty-first century space colony. It would be 19 miles long and 4 miles in diameter, and would revolve on its long axis to provide gravity equal to that of Earth. Research has been in progress in the USA, at Princeton University and elsewhere, on the feasibility of establishing such colonies. No technical obstacles appear to exist, although a new system of propulsion would be needed to put equipment into Earth orbit and to mine the Moon for building materials. Today, space scientists eagerly plan such developments but ignore the possibility that other civilisations could have passed through this stage long ago, and then gone on to cross the light-years – and even visit the Earth.

have collected a vast amount of information about our planet and its life and the rest of the Solar System.

It seems certain that planetary systems would be the most interesting places in the universe for intelligent beings with the technology to explore them, and especially so where life is present. Yet we have to allow that the flourishing biospheres of most life-supporting planets may not include a technological species with a civilisation.

So, will civilisations with the desire to know about their neighbouring planetary systems go ahead and explore with intelligent probes rather than trying to make contact by radio? It would seem an obvious decision, especially if near speed-of-light spaceflight becomes possible for small automated craft. And as the communications technology of such craft is going to exceed anything we could provide, even if we detected their signals, they are going to receive better quality information from their own intelligent probes than they could hope to get from us.

What may surprise most of us is the possible life expectancy of interstellar probes. Take our own probes, the earliest and most primitive products of space technology, to illustrate the point. NASA's Pioneers One and Two and Voyagers One and Two will all become interstellar spacecraft (two already have) journeying from the Solar System into the Galaxy. NASA's engineers reckon these craft will be almost unchanged in a billion years. Interstellar space, with a constant temperature, very low levels of radiation and no erosion, is so benign towards spacecraft that only in rare circumstances would an interstellar craft suffer damage, if it came too near a star or dense clouds of matter.

This durability in the interstellar medium is important because if our first steps in space technology can build such long-lasting probes, a more advanced technology might make probes that would last more or less for ever. Relate this to the enormous expanse of time available for visits to the Solar System and we have to be open-minded about the possible arrival of probes. We cannot rule out the possibility that a few ancient probes may be in orbit somewhere, even though parking in the Solar System would make them more liable to damage from dust and radiation than journeying through the emptiness of interstellar space. Several astronomers have searched for them – and will do so again. Intelligent probes might switch off and remain in orbit indefinitely, whereas biological beings would have a relatively short shelf-life. Interstellar spaceflight does not seem compatible with flesh and blood.

The possible presence of ET's interstellar probes in the Solar System was widely discussed in the early days of astronomical SETI. The thinking then was that the purpose of such probes might be to wait in orbit until the inhabitants of our world woke up and invented radio. The probes would report this great news to their home planets and try to contact us in the meantime. This always seemed an odd idea to me because of the unimaginably long period during which the Earth has been visitable compared to the period during which we have been broadcasting. However, this does not change the probability of probes arriving to explore a fascinating planet full of life, and astronomers have already made several attempts to detect them orbiting in nearby space. And with this observational research, the astronomers have almost joined up with those in ufology who believe that some UFOs may be currently active probes.

If it were not for the existence of the scientific rationale which has motivated some astronomers to search for probes, I would personally be ready to accept that all UFO reports result from a powerful modern mythology, delusions, mistakes and hoaxers, plus natural phenomena as yet not understood. But because the scientific rationale for SETI exists, I think that a very small proportion of reports – maybe only 1 per cent – deserve proper scientific investigation. This might have been undertaken long ago but for the fact that many people involved in the UFO societies are unfamiliar with science and do not yet fully appreciate the scientific rationale for SETI.

## OUR FUTURE IN ET'S PAST

We have only to look at our present technology and envisage what it may become, even in a hundred years, to see that ET visits during the past few hundred million years to explore the Solar System would have been possible. This does not mean that ET broadcasters do not exist. It could be, though it is unlikely, that interstellar space is uncrossable because it is pervaded by a vast quantity of as yet undetected matter. Even small automated probes travelling at high speeds relative to the speed of light might not survive impacts with pea-sized particles – though there appears to be a solution to this problem, at least in theory.

In the extreme case that interstellar space is uncrossable, and civilisations rare and widely separated, broadcasting would be the only means of making contact. But as we don't know what the situation is, we need all the approaches to SETI we can think of – which will not be many. If we consider the scientific rationale for

SETI in detail, then the probability of there being evidence of ET's explorations and presence in the Solar System is at least as great as the probability of detecting ET's broadcasts.

One conceivable source of evidence could be signs of mining in the Solar System, especially on the asteroids which offer a source of building materials to space travellers with the technology and motivation to build space habitats – not to mention a fleet of flying saucers.

The photographs of Miranda in 1986 showed this moon of Uranus to have unnatural-looking scars on its surface. I thought about possible mining at the time, though not too seriously, having then just dealt with the subject of space colonies, as envisaged by Professor Gerard O'Neill of Princeton University, New Jersey. His group had done persuasive work on ways to mine the Moon and the asteroids to build future space colonies. But I was satisfied by the NASA geologists who, after weeks studying the data, were convinced we were looking at natural phenomena. They came to the conclusion that Miranda had a crust of ice at least a few hundred miles thick – not a good place for ET to mine for building materials – and that the unnatural-looking scars on the moon's surface were created by the fusing of parts of the moon after it had been fragmented by the impact of another body. Gravitational attraction had then brought the parts together again.

## SCIENCE AND UFOs
In this situation we should perhaps listen to scientifically minded investigators of the UFO phenomena, even though they are almost an endangered species – endangered by a morass of UFO mythology and nonsense in the media. The difficult task is to find new ways to investigate the phenomena from the available data, of which there is a constant flow. But the apparently reliable data have to be rigorously separated from the nonsense that clutters ufology, and which has wasted so much time in the past. This could be worth doing because the most credible reports, as in the Rendlesham case, provide the kind of evidence that we might expect to exist and which should therefore be investigated with the best science and technology available. Otherwise we are not taking SETI and some UFOs seriously.

The trouble is that scientists in general become uncomfortable at any mention of UFOs because of the rubbish published on the subject and because of the many fantasy-prone people that it attracts. 'Getting your name in the popular press as Number One

UFO Hunter would be a nightmare – worse than being convicted for embezzling the laboratory funds,' said one scientist.

To be fair, interested scientists should read the UFO journals. If they could endure the initial cultural shock, which some provide, they would find reports ranging from fantasy, which makes *Star Trek* look like a documentary, to reports that begin to ring a few scientific bells. The problem for professional scientists hearing those bells and admitting an interest is that they risk being labelled undercover ufologists. It is a bit like being a cannibal in a vegetarian society. Yet if the scientific rationale for SETI is even roughly correct, and that is probably the best we can expect, then certain aspects of the UFO phenomena provide the vague kind of evidence that we might expect to encounter. The current problem is that *most rational people who think UFOs are a lot of nonsense are unaware of the scientific rationale for SETI*.

For several years I have read the UFO literature as many people read science fiction. Some of it is as good as *Star Trek* and has about the same number of alien humanoids, although in ufology the humanoids are visiting us instead of the other way round. I have waded through more fantasy than Captain Kirk, but I have also read accounts that seem sufficiently credible to justify scientific investigation. What surprised me was the large number of reports of UFOs from airline and air force pilots, from the police and the military – thousands during the past few decades, with consistency in the details reported. Can we conclude that all these accounts result from misidentifications, hoaxes and psychological factors in the witnesses who, in the normal course of life, we would regard as very reliable people?

The answer in many cases may be 'Yes' because the mythology of UFOs is so widespread. Psychologists tell us that people confronted with unusual phenomena see what they expect to see: if they have read about flying saucers they may see flying saucers. Yet the continuing stream of well-documented reports by reputable witnesses makes one wonder why no group of professional scientists anywhere is involved in on-going research to test the extraterrestrial hypothesis. What scientific expertise *is* at work is mainly undercover and self-confessed ufologists have no place in the science community at present, though those working for top-security government projects, if there are any, would not have to worry about that.

In the minds of most scientists, UFOs fall into the same category as ghosts and things that go bump in the night. But you cannot provide serious scientific reasons for the possible existence of ghosts and other paranormal phenomena, whereas you can provide scientific reasons for the consideration that some UFOs are extraterrestrial artifacts, although we must allow that some well-publicised UFOs are almost certainly atmospheric phenomena which we do not yet understand.

For too long acceptable research on UFOs has been left to academic psychologists and sociologists because, if nothing else, UFOs provide psychological and sociological phenomena, and in this respect are unquestionably a legitimate subject for science. Psychologists are better equipped than anyone else to study the witnesses and what they report. The conclusion by most investigators is that a small proportion of witnesses are reporting actual events, which lends some support for the ETH. But the ETH cannot be tested in this way, no matter how useful psychological research is in determining the relative reliability of reports.

## FOCUS ON LIFE

With all the difficulties faced by SETI it is as well that the subject provides a valuable bonus. For those interested in the ETH, the essential background to the subject, the science that makes the hypothesis tenable, happens to be about the most relevant science for anyone interested in the human situation in the light of current scientific knowledge. This alone makes the ETH worth pursuing, even if at the end of the day we have not confirmed the universality of life, discovered that flying saucers have a physical reality or received a message from Planet-X. 'It forces you to think of the human race from a cosmic perspective,' said Bob Arnold, formerly a member of NASA's SETI team.

SETI highlights a rich understanding of life at its most fundamental level. The revolutionary advances in cell biology, developmental biology, molecular biology and genetics have not explained everything about life, but they show us the scale of the problem of what there is to understand. And life increasingly looks like a universal phenomenon. We can see better what has taken place since the origin of life some four billion years ago. We could not see or begin to understand the awesome complexity within living cells before the electron microscope and the modern techniques of cell and molecular biology – which no one could have anticipated even a few decades ago. Today molecular biologists are determining the basis of life, studying the molecular cogs in the machine and how they operate within the cells of organisms.

For the first time we are in a position to see that the evolution which took place within independently living cells during the initial stage of life on this planet was comparable in its complexity to the evolution which followed in the Earth's many-celled organisms, which first appear in the fossil record of about 700 million years ago. We have gained some idea of what has been involved in the evolution of intelligent life – ourselves and other vertebrates – on this planet, and why it has taken four billion years. It is not as simple as spontaneous creation in a benign primordial sea of organic molecules and an inevitable evolutionary pathway to *Homo sapiens*.

We can only look back in awe at the continuous survival of life through four billion years of Earth history, at the durability and power of the phenomenon of life. Spreading from the first bacteria through great dynasties of organisms, continuously growing in complexity, transforming the planet. The apparent fragility of the physical basis of life took some terrible knocks from time to time from large meteorites and comets. Yet the catastrophes that befell Earth seem if anything to have boosted the evolutionary process. From space photography we can see the apparent precariousness of our position beneath the thin blue film of atmosphere covering our planet. But it is only an apparent precariousness. If life is so durable and versatile here with such a physical base, then it should be so on other worlds.

The space programs have provided a wealth of new data and insights into the nature of planetary origin and evolution. Astronomers think that planetary systems are by-products of star formation, and have therefore been developing techniques to try to detect the planets of neighbouring stars.

So, if you were an advanced ET interested in life on other worlds (and what self-respecting ET would not be!), and you had the necessary technology, you would first send your exploratory probes to planetary systems with blue planets. They would be your main targets because blue planets, like the Earth, with continuously flourishing biospheres, must be the most interesting places in the universe. Blue planets may be rare, judging from research on the origin and evolution of the Earth and its atmosphere, so we could well have been a favoured target for exploration.

Much depends on the nearness and distribution of blue planets, but if anyone proves the ETH to be correct we will know that other blue planets exist without actually finding them, and one wonders who will make it first: the astronomers or those testing the ETH in other ways. The implications of what science shows us should make us ready to investigate with both plenty of scepticism and scientific rigour any indications that come our way that our counterparts from elsewhere have discovered Earth at some time in the past.

## *ADVICE FROM THE SCIENTIFIC FRINGE*

I hope my reasons are clear for not ignoring the most credible information on the UFO phenomena. Most people in science have decided to do so, including many distinguished individuals who have contributed to the advances in SETI. Only a few entertain thoughts of UFOs entering their field of study. It is all right in the literature and at conferences to consider the possibility of extraterrestrial probes in orbit somewhere in the Solar System, but they have to be very ancient probes. This is not altogether unreasonable: the longer the period possible for visiting probes the more likely they are to be here. For most scientists, though, they must not be active probes because if they were, they might be active enough to be visiting us today, and there might be something in this UFO business.

Scientists would sooner look the other way and get on with their research. Yet UFO reports keep coming in from every part of the world. During the past forty years the whole subject has snowballed out of control, picking up rubbish all the time along with serious accounts, and, faced with a gigantic snowball, we ask, 'Is a profound reality hidden within?' There may be none. From a scientific viewpoint we must be ready to admit that. It may all be fraud and mythology and illusions and natural phenomena, in which case we have nothing to fear but the weakness of the human brain. This is, however, becoming increasingly difficult to square with the most credible UFO events.

We must keep in mind that, according to the best estimates from palaeontology and geology, the Earth has been a continuously observable life-supporting planet from about 350 million years ago because of its oxygen and ozone spectral lines. Any civilisation detecting those spectral lines and having advanced interstellar spacecraft would at least dispatch intelligent probes to explore, if the source were near enough. In theory, such probes could have entered the Solar System at any time in the last 350 million years, so that the Earth may have been known about for rather a long time. And this knowledge of Earth might have passed to other civilisations.

Many probes could have entered the Solar System – 350 million years is a long time. This is not to say they have done so, but it is a serious possibility. Whether or not the biological beings of other worlds will brave the light-years to explore the Earth and our neighbouring planets is an open question. If they are near immortal they may not risk it. I guess it depends on how hazardous, and boring, such journeys are. Highly intelligent robots fed on pure energy and simply switched into deep robotic sleep for most of the travel time would make much better explorers. The ideal astronaut would be a robot. It would not need food or air to breathe, and it could ignore the microbes and other biological dangers of alien biospheres. Conceivably, the species behind the probes and artificial intelligences might be created after arrival from their equivalent of DNA, which would be a lot easier to transport across interstellar space than fully grown biological beings.

My bet is on reliable robots and, perhaps, some natives (*Homo sapiens* in our case) to help with the work. But the bet is only on if interstellar space is crossable at speeds which are a significant fraction of the speed of light, or in some other way as yet unknown to us and impossible to speculate upon. The nearest civilisation capable of coming here also has to be no more than a few hundred light-years away. However, there are a lot of Sun-like stars within that distance, and many more have come that close during the past 350 million years, as the Sun and all the other stars have been orbiting the centre of the Galaxy.

This is dangerous ground to speculate upon and speculation can take us past a respectable hypothesis, if we get into elaboration that would be more at home in science fiction. To think up ways of testing the hypothesis – that is the important thing to do.

Ron Westrum, Professor of Sociology and Interdisciplinary Technology at Eastern Michigan University, said in the mid-1980s:

> While most UFO reports are the result of mistakes, the evidence in favour of some UFOs representing extraterrestrial spacecraft is strong. It is essential that these reports be investigated by properly trained technical personnel and not simply swept under the rug, as is currently the case.

We will now review what has been done since that time.

# CHAPTER 3
## Science and
## Strange Phenomena

Some years ago, Peter Sturrock, Professor of Space Sciences at Stanford University in California, summed up the problems of carrying out research on anomalous phenomena, such as UFOs, thereby stepping outside the circle which surrounds scientific orthodoxy. He said:

*Why you should not study anomalies*
Your friends may doubt your judgement.
You may lose the respect of some of your colleagues.
You will get no funding.
You will have difficulty publishing your work.
Your boss may think you are wasting your time.
And if you don't have tenure don't even consider it.

*Why you should study anomalies*
The grey area of science is the crucial area of science.
You will learn much about the scientific process.
You will learn much about scientists.
You may – perhaps without knowing it – start a scientific revolution.
You may, conceivably, discover something you can patent.
And, above all, you may be honoured – posthumously.[1]

The history of science is not short of hypotheses that in their time seemed preposterous. But, while most remained preposterous, some led to important developments in human understanding. Continental drift and black holes first came to our attention as hypotheses which were not taken seriously by geologists and physicists: they conflicted too much with the assumptions of the

31

time. Yet nowadays all geologists accept that the continents have been slowly moving over the Earth's surface during its geological history, and that about 200 million years ago most of the continents were part of one large land-mass, Gondwanaland, which broke up to form Australia, India, Africa, South America and Antarctica. As shapes on a map the continents can still be fitted together like pieces of a jigsaw. Also, most astronomers and physicists these days have been persuaded by observational data and theory that black holes pervade the universe.

This comparison with the ETH is not perfect. The two hypotheses above were well within science, not on the sidelines as the ETH, and numerous dedicated scientists investigated continental drift and black holes whereas hardly any long-term research within a university department or equivalent establishment has focused on UFOs, except for work on the psychological and sociological aspects of the subject.

Another problem for the ETH of ufology, which has not afflicted scientific hypotheses, is that the interesting data are mixed up with a mass of material written by well-meaning and enthusiastic people outside the science community who do not appreciate the level at which research must be carried out to be acceptable and published in the science journals. Some contributors to the UFO literature would be more at home in a new-age religion, as they are looking for a god substitute and even searching for their origins in the visitors in flying saucers. It would not take much to induce in them the belief that their own grandfather was an alien, since some harbour the equally absurd idea that *Homo sapiens* may be the result of a cross between the ape-like pre-humans and visiting extraterrestrials, which would be biologically impossible.

## GREAT BALLS OF LIGHT

Most reported UFOs do not have the classic flying-saucer shape. Some craft observed at high altitudes are cigar-shaped and large; other craft, reported to have landed, are small and conical. Another class of reported phenomena are balls of light, observed both in the sky and at ground level, and many UFOs which remain unexplained would seem to come into this category. They are not alien artifacts but natural physical phenomena, and we need to gain some understanding of them and see them for what they are, so that the clutter and muddle in ufology can be reduced.

There is also confusion in the scientific camp because we use labels, such as ball-lightning and balls of plasma – two apparently separate phenomena that go under the convenient name of BOLs [balls of light] – without understanding what we have attached the labels to. Physicists cannot explain the mechanisms of ball-lightning and the luminous spheres of atmospheric plasma, mainly because few physicists have worked on the subject.

Marsh gas is easy to deal with. Mystery lights over marshes have a long history and have led to lots of tall tales. The decomposition of organic matter releases hydrocarbon gases, especially methane, which are combustible, so that the lights from marsh gas are always associated with damp decaying land – in short, marshes. Not so the other two phenomena, the BOLs.

Although ball-lightning and plasma balls have not attracted much attention, their study is closer to the hearts of scientists than any consideration of some UFOs as possible extraterrestrial artifacts. Yet because the existence of BOLs has been indisputable, and some have behaved in strange and inexplicable ways, certain people in the UFO societies have suggested that these BOLs may be an advanced form of monitoring technology. We can say 'Nonsense!' – and we may be right – but that's not enough. We have no idea what the technology of an advanced monitoring system might be like and we need to be able to explain what, in terms of physics, these phenomena are.

Balls of light have been reported for centuries, but much more in recent years. There are places, such as Hessdalen in central Norway, where they hover in the snow-covered valleys in winter waiting for physicists to come and study them.

Some years ago, Hilary Evans, a scholarly writer on strange phenomena who lives in London, set up the 'Ball of Light International Data Exchange', but it received little support. He believed that individual accounts, although they made good stories, would tell us little about BOLs. But bring together hundreds of reports from different parts of the world and significant patterns might begin to emerge. In recent years the situation has improved scientifically. There have been two international conferences on the subject: at Salzburg, Austria, in 1993, and at Hessdalen, Norway, in 1994. And behind the scenes scientists have been at work setting up data banks. One established by Russian and Austrian scientists, including physicist Boris Smirnov, of the Russian Academy of Sciences, contains 1,500 cases of BOLs. The various species of BOLs have yet to be determined.

Smirnov shows how complicated the subject is in his comments about the Hessdalen phenomena:

There are three types of strange lights in Hessdalen. The first one is similar to a yellow ball: it exists during one to two hours and through five to ten minutes changes its place. The second type of light has a white-blue colour: it can flash sometimes and is observed above the valley and mountains. The third type relates to several tied lights [string of lights] of different colours. These lights move together.

It is not surprising therefore that Hessdalen has at last attracted a continuous scientific research program to try to solve these mysteries.

## CONFUSION IN SCIENCE

The many accounts of BOLs leave us with questions which few people in science have tried to answer. Because of the great differences in the behaviour of ball-lightning and plasma BOLs, it looks as if we may be dealing with two distinct classes of physical phenomena. Some physicists think the same basic mechanism may account for both, while other physicists think otherwise.

There are low-altitude BOLs, which manifest themselves on or near the ground, the kind which people have reported for centuries and which could include both ball-lightning and plasma BOLs. There are also high-altitude BOLs. Many were reported during the Second World War by American, British and German aircrews. The Allies used to called them foo fighters and claimed they stayed alongside their aircraft for various periods of time. One American bomber crew reported a large orange BOL alongside for forty minutes. Discs were also reported at the time, and this confuses the subject horribly because if they were discs and not spheres then no physics can explain them. Michel Bougard, a chemist and historian of UFO events, relates how in December 1944 a Major Leet of the United States Air Force observed an amber disc which tracked his B-17 bomber as he flew over Klagenfurt in Austria.

Air crews still see BOLs today on routine passenger flights. An airline engineer I know, plus his pilot and co-pilot, on a night flight across the Atlantic, saw three BOLs in front and to the side of their airliner. As they watched all three BOLs vanished in a flash. On landing in London they reported this event to British Airways and were told not to say anything about it. I guess British Airways didn't want to worry passengers. They may receive the occasional report from air crews which either indicates that air crews are seeing things or that something is out there which cannot be explained. Neither would be good for business, so staff are told to say nothing. And this, I gather, is what happens in all airlines.

Actually, plasma physics can partially explain high-altitude BOLs. Dr Robert Bingham, a plasma physicist at the Rutherford-Appleton Laboratory, Oxfordshire, suggests that enormous electrical discharges in the upper atmosphere should be capable of forming very large plasma BOLs. They would be composed of atomic particles, disassociated by electrical discharges and maintained in that state by the very high temperatures within the BOLs. The density and size of the BOL would depend on the energy input which formed it and on the atmospheric pressure where it was formed.

At low altitude, near ground level, pressures on BOLs are going to change with movements of the atmosphere. And this could explain why they are observed moving over the mountains and through the valleys at Hessdalen, although the reported variations in shape defy physical explanation so far. Could it be that the electromagnetic fields which contain the plasma change shape? Powerful fields must in some way contain the plasma for the BOLs to endure for the hours reported. Without such containment BOLs would fizzle out in an instant, as heat was lost to the atmosphere and all the atomic particles came together. There is here a lot of work for physicists: how, for example, do these powerful electromagnetic fields form when a sudden input of energy creates a BOL?

## BALL-LIGHTNING

Most reports of ball-lightning describe objects about the size of footballs. They can shrink, explode, fizzle out or just disappear round the corner. Ball-lightning is unstable. It is often described as moving with a sizzling sound, and can explode when it bumps into objects. Balls of ball-lightning enter houses through windows and chimneys, hover in rooms, go upstairs and downstairs and leave by windows and chimneys. Sometimes they do not leave – they explode, burning furniture and people. What ball-lightning balls are composed of no one knows – there is not even a working hypothesis. Strange stories date back centuries, but if we concentrate on these we will enter mythology – and no explanations can be found in that direction.

Science has been in very close contact with ball-lightning. Roger Jenison, a former professor of electronics at the University of Kent but now retired, was one night on a bumpy flight through a violent thunderstorm from New York to Washington when a ball of lightning drifted down the aisle and disappeared.

Suddenly, through the doorway of the pilots' compartment there emerged the most beautiful ball, slightly smaller than a football, glowing in the most ethereal blue. It passed me at roughly shoulder height as I was sitting, travelling at about walking pace down the aisle.

The object frightened a stewardess and Jenison explained that they had just witnessed ball-lightning.

Roger Jenison took an active interest in the subject after that experience:

All reports tend to agree that ball-lightning is roughly about the size of a football. And one wonders why ball-lightning is always that size. There must be a good reason for it.

Jenison believes that the size of ball-lightning is determined by the wavelength of the radio frequency associated with its formation, but how the phenomenon maintains its temporary integrity is a mystery. Jenison suggests the mechanism might be similar to that by which the electron maintains its integrity, but admits his thoughts about ball-lightning are rather heretical.

The reports gathered by Jenison include some which describe ball-lightning moving over the wings of aircraft during storms, clinging to them and not being blown off by the slipstream. He told me one story which provides a little evidence about the physics involved. A BOL entered a kitchen where a woman was working by her cooker. The ball came to her and climbed up her arm. When she brushed it aside it exploded, leaving a small burn on her work-top. She also found that her gold ring was warm yet her fingers suffered no burning. Jenison points out that because gold needs a lot of heat to warm it up as it has a very high thermal capacity, the only way by which the ring could have been warmed without burning the skin would have been by microwaves. Whatever the mechanism of ball-lightning is, it seems to radiate microwaves when it explodes.

The strangest characteristic of certain BOLs is their reported interaction with observers. They approach and retreat as the witness moves away or towards them, keeping at a constant distance. A BOL often does this till the end of the encounter, when it either vanishes or travels out of sight.

The following is not untypical of reported BOL behaviour:

We stopped and watched it for a while, then tried to walk

around it, but it would move over and head us off. When we walked forward it backed up, and when we backed up it came towards us. Then we stood there with that thing about a dozen feet in front of us as silent as death itself. It was transparent . . . It was just a ball of light, yet apparently this strange object could see us and it checked our every move.

There is no explanation for this sort of behaviour in physics. Either these BOLs are displaying some unknown physical phenomenon or the witnesses are displaying a well-known psychological phenomenon, though the movements of witnesses would displace air and BOLs, being very light, might be moved in this way.

## FOO FIGHTERS
The British Airways observation of BOLs at the altitude of a commercial airliner raises questions about BOLs at altitude and the mystery of the foo fighters of the Second World War. All sides in the war reported BOLs flying with them during missions, tracking aircraft for periods of up to about an hour in some cases, almost as if carrying out observations. Anyone reading UFO reports from pilots in the latter years of the war will find descriptions of spheres of light, discs of light and metallic-looking saucers. All the reported observations have been lumped together as UFOs. Certain people in ufology have fastened upon this phenomenon and speculated that BOLs may be the ultimate in surveillance technology from extra-terrestrial sources. Such speculation may be fanciful, but we are wide open to such conjecture if we cannot provide answers. Research on BOLs is therefore worthwhile, if only to put speculation to rest. Perhaps we might begin with a research project involving airline crews from the major carriers, with companies, such as British Airways, supporting the project for passenger peace of mind. I know university physicists who have said they would be pleased to carry out the research.

## A GIFT TO SCIENCE
The Hessdalen BOLs are a gift to science. UFO literature is often concerned with lights in the sky which do not linger long enough for scientific analysis, but the Hessdalen UFOs are the rare kind which do. They seem to have taken up residence in that region of Norway, conveniently available for study.

The Hessdalen Project takes its name from the district of Hessdalen, south-east of Trondheim in central Norway. In winter its bleak valleys and mountains are covered in deep snow, but the BOLs/

UFOs seem to like the conditions because they appear mainly in mid-winter, especially in early evening. However, the lights would be difficult to spot in daylight, and during summer in this part of Norway there is hardly any night.

Hessdalen began to attract outside interest in 1981 when the local population of about 150 who live in the district began to report lights in the sky. The lights, which continue to appear, behave in ways which call for an explanation, and teams of investigators visited Hessdalen from 1984 onwards, supported by the Norwegian Defence Research Establishment and the Universities of Oslo, Bergen and Trondheim. 'The support was mostly instrumentation and survival gear,' said Odd-Gunnar Roed, a leading member of the research teams. (See photographs 2, 3 and 4.)

The teams have used different recording and observational systems to study the UFOs and track them on radar. They have used a special camera system to try to record the spectra of the BOLs to determine the energy source. But they have lacked the very sophisticated technology needed to obtain good spectra of BOLs over three miles away, and it is even more difficult to obtain spectra of reflections of the laser beams they have fired at some of the BOLs. However, clear spectra should show the wavelength of the laser used and the frequency lines of the elements actually in the BOLs.

Plasma physicists agree that the dryness of central Norway in winter would favour the generation of high electromagnetic charges in the atmosphere and the creation of balls of plasma. Throughout investigations a seismograph was always in place to detect any tremors – to check if the lights might have been produced by escaping gases from minor quakes in the bedrock. No local tremors have been recorded.

Sometimes the lights hovered motionless over the landscape for an hour or more. Sometimes they moved slowly at low altitude through the valleys, or raced away at an astonishing speed. On one occasion the Norwegians reported: 'A light was tracked by both radar and visually and was calculated to be travelling at approximately 8,500 metres a second.' That works out at 30,600 kilometres an hour (19,003 miles an hour).

Erling Strand, who was a leading member of that research team, maintains that this surprising observation was not due to a 'bug' in the equipment.

It was a light travelling from south to north. The witnesses standing outside the Project Hessdalen headquarters could not tell the distance to the light. They could only tell the direction and movement. They were in direct communication with the radar operator inside the headquarters who reported a recording on the radar exactly in the same direction as the witnesses saw the light. The light moved fast. The witnesses followed the light visually and talked with the radar operator, who saw it on the radar in the same direction as the witnesses reported. The light moved so fast that it was captured on radar only twice. But in both of those recordings, it was in exactly the same direction as the outside witnesses reported. I therefore conclude that it was the same light that the witnesses saw.

There is no mechanism in physics which could account for this observation.

The BOLs shone with an intensity that prevented the investigators seeing or photographing any structure associated with them. They therefore assume that only intense light is present. Local people have reported seeing structures within the lights, but it is not difficult to see structures in an intense light. Good photographic evidence would be needed from the teams before the reality of structures could be accepted. With current image enhancement techniques, the details reported might be captured photographically, if such details exist. The structures reported are egg shapes, cigar shapes and some that look like an inverted Christmas tree, which seems strange – upside-down Christmas trees are not readily imagined.

A radar expert from the Norwegian Defence Research Establishment, Dr Magne Eggstad, after analysing radar photographs, concluded that if the reflections did not come from solid objects, then the gas [plasma] had to be thoroughly ionised to produce such strong reflections. Plasma physicists say that a plasma will reflect like a metal, reflectivity depending on the density of the plasma and the wavelength of the laser used. The denser the plasma the better it will reflect.

Roed explained:

The lights appeared to have several different specific shapes. This was something that became quite apparent when the lights were photographed. The main shapes were: bullet shape with the sharp end pointing downwards; a round football shape; and an upside-down Christmas-tree shape. The colours of the lights were mostly white or yellow/white. Sometimes a small red light

39

could be seen among the white. On a few occasions the lights were made up of every colour in the rainbow.

If the balls of plasma are contained by a magnetic field, the different shapes observed are difficult to explain. The different colours of the BOLs, according to plasma physics, would be determined by their temperature – the amount of energy they contain for their size. This does not apply to ball-lightning which, according to the many cases studied by Professor Jenison, are either yellow-orange or blueish. Jenison suggests that the physical mechanism for ball-lightning is different from that of the plasma BOLs, but this is in no way certain.

The Norwegian researchers reported that the lights are of three kinds, as Professor Smirnov did in his review paper.

One: Small and strong white or blue flashes which could show up anywhere in the sky.

Two: Yellow or yellow/white lights usually observed in the valley and below the horizon. (To be able to estimate size and distance it is necessary to observe a light against a solid background.) Sometimes they were just above rooftops and even down near the ground. They could be stationary for more than an hour before moving off slowly around the valley. Sometimes they accelerated to very fast speeds. They were also observed high in the sky.

Three: Several lights together at fixed distances from each other. Mostly these were yellow or white lights with a red light in front. These lights moved slowly around the mountain tops.

It is interesting that the Hessdalen phenomena are relatively recent. Roed said:

We do have a few recordings from before 1981, but nothing like the wave of reports between 1981 and 1986. They became less frequent in 1985, but sightings continue to be reported in the area.

One characteristic of the BOLs which, according to their reports, fascinated the teams in Norway, was their capacity to react to the stimulation of a laser beam. Roed's report states:

A laser was pointed at the lights a total of nine times, and on eight of these occasions we managed to obtain a reaction from the lights. There was a regular flashing light, slowly moving toward the north. On 12 January 1984, at 19.35 hours, the light flashed very regularly all of the time until we pointed the laser at it. At this point, the flashing sequence of the light changed to a more urgent double-flashing sequence. After about ten seconds we stopped the laser and the light immediately changed back to its former sequence. The exercise was repeated four times, each time with the same result.

Erling Strand was also understandably bemused by this strange and unexpected response.

The results from the laser test are very surprising. Even though we heard that one person had done a light test before and succeeded, I personally thought that result was only a co-incidence. But we did also get the same result: eight out of nine times. We could have done this test more times and I think we will another time – maybe with a stronger laser.

How can we explain these responses to a laser beam transmitted across several miles to the BOL? As the plasma physicists assure us, dense plasmas can be as reflective as metal. A partial explanation, therefore, is that the physical vibration of the plasma is temporarily interrupted by the arrival of a laser beam. But nothing much beyond that can be said.

This characteristic of plasma to reflect radiation has led to a lot of typically rash speculation in the UFO literature. The true believers in ufology, without first exploring a possible physical explanation, proclaimed that this was evidence of intelligence in the Hessdalen phenomena. Some unknown intelligence within the BOLs was responding to the laser beams. It is an episode in UFO history which shows how easy it is to be bemused and misled.

Yet Hessdalen harbours phenomena worthy of top scientific attention, although few atmospheric and plasma physicists I have talked to in Britain have even heard of Hessdalen. In 1994 Roed said optimistically:

The new Project Hessdalen with a scientific workshop has changed all that. This spring we had there more than twenty scientists from Japan, Russia, America, England, Italy, Austria, Sweden and Norway.

Most of these scientists work on ball-lightning and plasma physics, and most thought the Hessdalen phenomena had nothing to do with ball-lightning. David Fryberger, a physicist from the Stanford Linear Accelerator Center, has said that 'the explanation of these phenomena lies outside the scope of already known physics'. Plasma physicists I have talked to doubt this. Their view is that we know enough to explain the BOLs if the research is done. I have asked plasma physicists why they haven't worked on BOLs. The reply is always the same: there is no commercial value in understanding how BOLs work, so it is not possible to get grants to study them. It may indeed be uncommercial, but it is nevertheless surprising that physicists have not studied BOLs, since they relate directly to one important aspect of today's technology – radar.

BOLs, as balls of high-density plasma, reflect light and other forms of electromagnetic radiation, including radar frequencies. This fact would seem to be relevant to all radar defence systems everywhere. Radar operators say they often find strange objects on their screens and do not know what they are. Could these sometimes be BOLs? We might reasonably assume that those in charge of radar systems also have no knowledge of plasma BOLs, since no plasma physicist can explain how they are formed and how they manage to stay intact in the atmosphere for periods of time long enough to produce images on radar screens.

Our understanding of what is going on may improve with the establishment of the research centre at Hessdalen. It is called CRULP [Center for Research into Unidentified Light Phenomena] and was established by Erling Strand and his colleagues in 1993 at the Østfold College of Engineering. 'We stand in front of something unknown, and we must collect everything that might lead us to an answer of what this is,' said Erling Strand. The current guess is that Strand and his colleagues are dealing with balls of plasma, created by the very high electromagnetic energy discharges in the dry conditions of central Norway in winter. But how the plasma is held together and how it manages to persist for hours in several different forms are questions that should keep the scientists in Hessdalen occupied for years.

## *PROJECT IDENTIFICATION*
Project Identification was a similar research project in which BOLs were routinely observed. Harley Rutledge, then professor of physics at Cape Girardeau, Missouri, started the study in 1973 because his students asked him to explain the lights often seen in the hills near Piedmont in Missouri.

Rutledge assembled a team which took scientific equipment into the hills to study the lights. He expected to provide an explanation within a few months. Investigations continued until 1981 when he published his book *Project Identification* – but there was no final explanation. During that time his teams observed 178 BOLs on 157 separate occasions. And in thirty-two observations, the BOLs seemed to respond to stimuli from the observers, such as a transmitted light or radio signal, in a similar way to the BOLs at Hessdalen.

The investigators observed BOLs from widely separated points so they could use triangulation to measure distances, directions, sizes and speeds of movement. These observations conclusively ruled out any conventional objects, such as aircraft, balloons, lights from motor vehicles and so on. Rutledge did not solve the problem, but the last time I heard of him he was seeking support to pursue this research.

# CHAPTER 4
## A Universal Phenomenon?

Most people instinctively believe in the universality of life. My local vicar once said, 'The uniqueness of life to Earth was only a tenable proposition while we believed that the Earth was the centre of the universe.' But this feeling is firmly rooted in the realm of belief, which in science is not enough. A *feeling* for truth is not in itself enough, it has to be testable – but it is not easy to find ways of testing the ETH.

The main way so far, the search for broadcasts and radiation from the activities of other civilisations, fits in more or less comfortably with established science. Success in astronomical SETI would confirm, in a very acceptable way, the universality of life and intelligence. Acceptable because that life and intelligence would be light-years away, safely remote yet revolutionary in the impact of its discovery. Not even the most naive would then fear ET's imminent arrival to take over our world. But confirmation that the ETH of ufology is correct would be uncomfortably different. It would mean that ET is on our doorstep! While the response to successful radio astronomers would be 'Well done lads, take a Nobel Prize', the response to proof that ET is here in flying saucers would be 'Good God, what sort of predicament are we in?'

Yet when we examine the background to SETI we realise that in such a situation nobody would need to worry – not even the Minister of Defence. If ET or his artifacts are in the Solar System, they have been here since before human history, perhaps for millions of years. No other conclusion is statistically tenable. So why worry? If ET is here and has not taken us over yet, he is not here for that purpose.

### ANCIENT PROBES
A few scientists in astronomical SETI moved very close to testing

45

the ETH of ufology. Professor Ronald Bracewell and other scientists in the 1960s suggested that alien probes may have been waiting in Earth orbit for many millions of years, ready to pick up broadcasts as soon as some lifeform woke up and invented radio. This idea of listening probes, however, did not seem a likely scenario then and it does not today. If our extraterrestrial neighbours detected oxygen and ozone lines in the spectra of light coming from the Solar System, they might have sent probes to explore – but surely not to search for radio broadcasts.

In the 1980s, several astronomers in the United States and the Soviet Union looked for the relics of exploratory probes in orbit, which seemed more likely to exist than probes waiting to respond to broadcasts. They scanned the Lagrangian points which are gravitational sinks of the Earth–Moon and Earth–Sun gravitational systems, and therefore possible parking places where probes might remain more or less indefinitely. No probes were observed – a not unexpected result – but we have to keep in mind that 99.9 per cent of the Solar System remains unknown to us in the detail required to detect probes. There could be thousands of probes stationed within the Solar System and we would know nothing of them. But that is not to say that there are probes out there.

Michael Papagiannis, Professor of Astronomy at Boston University, looked at about 2,000 spectra of asteroids which were obtained by the Infra-Red Astronomical Satellite [IRAS] in 1984. Papagiannis wanted to see if any looked suspiciously unlike the infra-red spectra one would expect from normal asteroids. In other words, could ET have placed a probe or two in our asteroid belt during the past few hundred million years?

Papagiannis later pursued another search, using the 140-foot radio telescope at the National Radio Astronomy Observatory at Green Bank, West Virginia, to look for evidence of probes orbiting the Sun. This involved searching for a spectral line of tritium, an unstable element which is a by-product of nuclear fusion. The idea of looking for evidence of tritium originated after some probe searching in 1979 and the early 1980s, when Robert Freitas and Francisco Valdez used large optical telescopes in California and Arizona to scan the Earth–Moon and Earth–Sun Lagrangian points. On their photographic plates Freitas and Valdez could have detected any probe larger than ten metres.

Freitas later had the attractive idea of looking for radiation from tritium. Anyone using fusion technology in other planetary systems, Freitas speculated, would probably be releasing tritium into space during their production of energy. If so, this could be detected because tritium radiates at a known frequency (1516.701 MHz). It also has the very short half-life of twelve and a half years. This is very convenient for SETI searchers because it means that it cannot be present in nature in detectable quantities, so any detectable tritium must come from artificial sources.

This idea motivated the search by Papagiannis. He said:

> If they [our counterparts] are not rare, our nearest stellar civilisation must have detected the presence of oxygen in our atmosphere, which is a strong indication of the presence of life. Automated observing stations would then follow to keep an eye on developments here. Such space stations would need energy, and if it came from nuclear fusion it would probably produce detectable levels of tritium.

Michael Papagiannis searched for evidence of tritium in the plane of the Earth's orbit. He did not find it. Although I admire such determination to search for a remote possibility – and such research, as a by-product, does attract public interest into new areas of thought about life and the universe – it seems very unlikely that any advanced neighbour, thousands of years ahead of us technologically, would still be using such a source of energy as nuclear fusion. One would hope that Nature offers a better source of energy to propel explorers across interstellar space because if Nature does not, then ET's probes are probably not here.

## THE TIME PROBLEM: WHY VISITS NOW?
Most people at some time have thought about the possibility of ETs in flying saucers visiting the Earth. And in some countries the majority think it more than a possibility, according to polls taken. Acceptance of this, however, presents us with a problem – the time problem. The time problem has to be explained away if we speculate that extraterrestrial spacecraft are behind some of the most credible UFO reports. It is virtually impossible for statistical reasons that spacecraft from other worlds are visiting us for the first time now when they could have come at any time during the past few billion years. This is an awkward but inescapable conclusion for those who favour the ETH, although there is little or no indication in the literature of ufology that this problem is recognised.

There are scholarly studies by people outside ufology which claim that visiting spacecraft have been in evidence since biblical times, but the whole period of human history is almost insignificant compared to the geological timescale which we have to allow for.

We are considering several thousand years of human history compared to four billion years since the first life formed on Earth.

We have to acknowledge that people today are spaceship conscious, which has allowed the media to establish the myth of flying saucers and saucernauts. The credible reports have made people interpret strange observations in terms of flying saucers and have stimulated the fantasy-prone to see them and report their own encounters. UFOs may be no more abundant today than in past ages, but the coverage they now receive in the media encourages people to see them, which in turn means more reports in the media and more people seeing UFOs.

Yet even the pre-media historical reports of what could be flying saucers cannot solve the time problem. We need to think about past visits at least in terms of millions of years ago, because the Galaxy contains Sun-like stars twice the age of the Earth – and some may have Earth-like planets. If the Earth was discovered many millions of years ago and has been monitored since then, the problem of 'why now' lessens, although an uncomfortable time problem remains of millions of years compared with a few billion years. Can we reduce it further?

We have to refer back to astronomy here and the plans for orbiting telescopes which could detect the tell-tale spectral lines of oxygen and ozone coming from Sun-like stars where planetary systems may exist. Such telescopes would detect the presence of Earth-like planets with biospheres by searching for oxygen and ozone lines in the spectra observed. Like all elements and molecules, oxygen and ozone radiate and absorb energy at certain specific wavelengths. Thus life-bearing planets with the equivalent of plant life, which over a couple of billion years produce oxygen atmospheres, could be detectable at great distances, judging by our present plans for astronomical technology. The oxygen and ozone 'signatures' would signal the presence of a life-bearing planet, and those with the appropriate space technology could send probes to explore.

## A FASCINATING HOBBY

Exploring Earth-like planets might be a fascinating hobby for beings with long lifespans and the appropriate technology. And they would want to send their probes to the most interesting places, even though robots manufactured the probes by the thousand, as we make cars today. Within a hundred light-years of Earth there are some fifty Sun-like stars. If you have the astronomical techniques to be selective, it is the Sun-like stars with oxygen and ozone signatures that you would target. If planets with flourishing biospheres exist in only one in fifty planetary systems, it is to those systems rather than to any others that the probes would go. Signs of an oxygen atmosphere should attract ETs like wasps to a honey pot.

Given that situation, the Earth could have been a target for the past 350 million years, since the beginning of the Carboniferous Period when something like our present atmosphere was in place. Evidence from the Earth sciences supports this because for more than the past 350 million years an abundance of life has existed on land. Without enough oxygen in the atmosphere to form the protection of the ozone layer this would not have been possible.

However, if ET detected our oxygen and homed in there is still a time problem, though a smaller one than the four billion years with which we started. Can we reduce this period of 350 million years further? Well, the oxygen and ozone lines which the Earth's atmosphere added to the spectrum from the Solar System have not disappeared. They have been continuously radiated into space throughout the millennia. Any intelligent lifeform which evolved near enough and then invented the necessary astronomical technology could have detected those lines any time during the past 350 million years. That is a long time in which to be discovered. And once discovered we could speculate that the presence of the Earth was recorded in some way.

So what has happened to make Earth in recent ages a more interesting place to visit? The emergence of technological intelligence in the bipedal apes could have raised the equivalent of extraterrestrial eyebrows, but there would have had to be some very observant probes around at the time for that news to have been transmitted to Planet-X. Super civilisations might have highly intelligent probes in many planetary systems which support life, and the growing populations of early humans, *Homo habilis*, *Homo erectus* and so on, might have been enough to induce Planet-X to send more probes. But what was more likely to have attracted ET's attention would have been the rapid growth of civilisations on the Earth's surface, a growth rate that has been quite astonishingly rapid during the past ten thousand years.

## ZOO HYPOTHESIS

At this point we are approaching the 'Zoo Hypothesis' proposed some years ago by Professor John Ball in a classic SETI paper. If we are in a sort of planetary nature reserve we may not be aware of our situation any more than the intelligent animals in our national parks, even though our species is unique in its degree of awareness of events. I do not think the zoo analogy is a good one because we must be, for statistical reasons, the latest world civilisation in the Galaxy. It has taken four billion years from the origin of life for civilisation to develop. And then, within only ten thousand years it has virtually covered the planet – a four-hundred-thousandth part of life's span here. In a Galaxy teaming with inhabited planets, ET may therefore have come to study this very rare event.

Because our civilisation must be the latest to evolve in the Galaxy, it could make us a prime target for study by far older civilisations. There may not have been a new technological species evolve for a million years or more. We would be cosmic news. And if our neighbouring ETs had our planet in their records, maybe recorded in the distant past, or they had monitoring systems permanently in place, then it is during the birth of our world civilisation that they would come. We might even expect their observations to become more comprehensive with our increasing activity. It all sounds like science fiction and maybe it is, but some reported phenomena do provide vague support for such a scenario.

Another attracting factor often suggested in the literature of SETI by folk who should know better is the leakage of radio waves into space since broadcasting started some seventy years ago, a leakage which has greatly increased due to television and powerful radar defensive systems. But seventy years is an insignificant period of time compared with the possible emergence of technological civilisations in the Galaxy. Anyway, reports of flying saucers, or what could be interpreted as flying saucers, are far older than broadcasting. So leakage from broadcasting is not going to be a main attractant, though the detection of radio frequencies might motivate new surveys, if ET was already studying us.

But would ETs make contact with us? My guess is that this would be the last thing they would want to do. It would destroy the situation they had come to study. Contact avoidance would be a basic principle, as it would if we were in their position. The behaviour of flying saucers and saucernauts, as reported, is what we should expect. This is another reason for doubting the contactee and abductee reports, in addition to the fact that the people contacted or abducted never have anything to say that could not have come out of their own heads after decades of viewing *Star Trek* and *Dr Who*.

At this point we may be wandering into science fiction, but it is fun to invent scenarios, and those who think that flying saucers are extraterrestrial artifacts do need a scenario to explain the 'time problem'. I would be interested to read another that explains the time problem differently because this has frequently been a major theoretical objection to the ETH of ufology – quite apart from the awkward fact that there is no firm physical evidence like bits of saucer technology!

## EXPLANATIONS: PROBABLE, POSSIBLE, IMPROBABLE, IMPOSSIBLE

We can accept that natural phenomena, misidentifications, delusions and hoaxes account for the majority of UFO reports, and consider only that small proportion that cannot be explained. Alan Hendry, who was once chief investigator at the Center for UFO Studies in Chicago, found that only 11.4 per cent of reports he received could not be explained. But with many thousands of reports every year this leaves a very large number of unexplained cases.

Let us look at some of the explanations provided by the Center for UFO Studies for the unexplained reports – and at some other explanations.

1.   Partially understood physical phenomena such as ball-lightning, marsh gas and luminous atmospheric plasma. It is certain that many witnesses have reported these phenomena as UFOs – which of course they are. All are open to conventional scientific investigation, but little research has been carried out and the physical characteristics of these phenomena, which are often bizarre, remain a mystery.

2.   Misidentification of conventional things such as aircraft, clouds, astronomical objects and balloons of various kinds, for example the highly luminous balloons used by the military to illuminate territory, which could be inexplicable to witnesses. Unusual light and conditions can make the conventional look strange and lead witnesses to interpret what they see with reference to what they know about UFOs.

3.   Aircraft of various kinds, especially automatically controlled target craft. Mike Ashworth, who was a pilot in the RAF and later made a study of such craft, wrote to me on this subject:

These craft are known in military parlance as *remotely piloted vehicles*, or *unmanned aerial vehicles* in the United States. So far I have catalogued about sixty types. These vehicles are either parts of, or in some cases complete, weapons systems

51

and can carry a very wide range of such things as sensors, cameras, warheads and laser target designators.

He went on to emphasise that these craft can bear little or no resemblance to what most people think of as an aircraft, so that they could easily be seen and reported as UFOs. As an example he mentioned the Sprite, a grey Kevlar reconnaissance and target-designation drone:

> This vehicle is just less than a metre across with the classic flying-saucer shape. It flies by having two contra-rotating rotors mounted on a short mast on its upper surface, and is said to be virtually inaudible above everyday background noise. And because of its small size, it is rapidly lost to the naked eye, thus giving the impression of very high speed flight.

The problem here is that manifestations of our recent technology cannot explain those reports of UFOs in past centuries which are sometimes impossible to explain away as natural phenomena. If the reports of our ancestors were accurate, they fit in well with the ETH.

4.   The re-entry of satellite debris. Thousands of satellites orbit the Earth, and orbits frequently decay to a point where satellites break up as they begin to enter the atmosphere.

5.   Psychological explanations. Some witnesses genuinely believe they have seen a flying saucer. Some give accounts of conversations with the occupants of saucers, and of being captured by ETs. When the ETs speak they are often perfectly fluent in the language of the witnesses, which is no mean feat for beings who allegedly land among practically every nation on Earth. Scientific studies show that these cases are examples of a modern equivalent of folklore and mythology, or due to psychological factors. When analysed, the stories reported by UFO contactees and abductees show striking similarities with the folklore of non-scientific times. But folklore may not be entirely responsible. The 'Homo sapiens with knobs on' syndrome is common among close-encounter witnesses, and con-tactees and abductees, when they describe the aliens, but more often they report humanoids about three feet tall, slim, with large heads and eyes, greyish skin, tiny noses, a short slit for a mouth and no visible ears. Are advanced beings from other worlds actively engaged in producing primates to explore our world? Are witnesses of close alien contacts suffering from too much close contact with

alien contacts reported in the media, or with science fiction on television, whose producers, not knowing about Darwin and having to work with the actors' union, give all ETs a basic primate form? Psychological research shows that our brains have become so soaked in science fiction films and television that even those who have never met an alien of any kind have unconsciously absorbed enough to produce detailed abduction stories, involving alien humanoids, if given appropriate psychological encouragement under hypnosis.

6. Hoaxes are common in ufology. In a study of 355 landing events, the Spanish data analyst Ballester Olmos, found that 31.2 per cent were hoaxes. UFO investigators need a talent for spotting fraud, delusions and misidentifications.

7. Our distant descendants are using time travel, which a few theoretical physicists say may be possible, coming back through time to pay us a visit in flying saucers. This would explain the reports of human and humanoid occupants of saucers which, if from another world, defy by their form most of what we know about biological evolution. Future historians would find backward time travel irresistible, if it were possible. We may go forward in time by relativistic spaceflight [at near the speed of light], according to Einstein, although even relativistic spaceflight may not be possible. But according to most theoretical physicists, time travel backwards offends against the logic of the universe, threatening the sequence of cause and effect. Even so, theories have been devised to find a way out of this quandary, to try to avoid chaos in the present if time travellers were constantly changing the past and thereby restructuring the present. Nevertheless this possibility is best left to science fiction because we cannot devise a scientific test for it.

8. A physical phenomenon and/or intelligent visitors from a parallel universe. It, or they, somehow break through into our universe, into our reality. This suggestion does not look in line with the reports, since UFOs/flying saucers do not usually vanish into another universe, but fly away into another part of our universe. A few do vanish according to some witnesses, but that does not imply a parallel universe. Investigating parallel universes at the moment anyway looks a lot more difficult than testing the ETH. Abnormal brain chemistry or a blocked artery in the brain, just a temporary block in one of the temporal lobes, would be equally valid explanations, except where there is more than one witness.

9.   A psychical phenomenon. Something created by mind but having a physical reality, at least a temporary one. The mind responsible could be that of a supreme intelligence in this universe, or outside it (God) – or the lesser minds of witnesses. That is to say, the UFO is created outside the witness by the power of his mind, which seems one of the least sensible suggestions in the literature of ufology.

10.   Visitors from other worlds studying the Earth. Maybe the extraterrestrials themselves are not here but have built the phenomenon which has been exploring the Earth and the Solar System. The presence of more people on the Earth and modern communications have combined to make us aware of phenomena that may have existed for millions of years. This hypothesis is better than the others because it can be tested. It is also consistent with what we know of astronomy and biology and the ways in which our technologies are developing.

# CHAPTER 5
## *Our Counterparts on Other Worlds*

Susan Salaman, a thoughtful observer of things ufological, once said that some ufologists have an ache in the soul and a deep longing to make contact with ET. On one occasion a member of a UFO conference told her that if he met an extraterrestrial he would weep with joy and relief. My guess is that if he ever did meet an extraterrestrial, he would recoil with surprise and horror. His reactions might not be justified, but they would be human.

What would our counterparts on other planets be like? The examination of this question about the possible nature, especially the psychological nature, of our counterparts on other worlds has provided essential background for SETI. We know there are billions of stars like our Sun in the universe. Our Galaxy alone has more than a hundred billion stars with several billion like the Sun, and most astronomers think that planets form as part of the formation of many stars. Discs of gas and dust and rubble remain orbiting stars after their formation. Matter within a disc clumps together to form larger bodies and the larger a body grows, the more gas and matter and smaller bodies its gravitational attraction will accumulate. Eventually planet-sized bodies are formed. Astronomers calculate that it took half a billion years for our planetary system to form. Therefore, as Sun-like stars are so abundant, an enormous number of planetary systems should exist with Earth-like planets. That is the accepted astronomical theory.

Earth-sized planets orbiting Sun-sized stars within the right distance range, what is called the 'habitable zone', should provide the physical and chemical conditions for the origin of life, which appears to be inherent in the nature of organic molecules and the forces acting upon them. And with the origin of life (that is, the formation of self-reproducing entities which initially could have been no more than functional assemblies of molecules) organic evolution automatically takes place. But we only know where evolution has taken life on this planet. Because of the large number of possible Earth-like planets, the assumption is that evolution on a high proportion of Earth-like planets will produce lifeforms with high intelligence like cats and dogs and monkeys – and technological intelligences like ourselves. Our counterparts on other worlds may be very different biologically and even more different culturally from us, but the same in that they use a technological intelligence.

An important question we may ask without getting much of an answer is: what limits are there on lifeforms on other worlds? We have to ask that question to see the reported occupants of saucers against a background of biological reality. Biologists classify all species of animals with the same basic body plan into what they call a phylum. Today up to thirty-two animal phyla exist, depending on the classification one accepts, while about twenty phyla have become extinct since the beginning of the Cambrian Period, 600 million years ago. Once established, animal phyla have proved very durable in the history of life. We cannot know how many basic systems, or body plans, would be viable on Earth-like planets, but it would seem that there cannot be a limitless number of viable lifeforms in the universe.

Some biologists estimate there are tens of millions of animal species alive today, though only about a million have been classified. Go back through the history of life and there have been thousands of millions of species. Through the ages, some species have converged in their evolution, so that similar-looking animals have evolved from different points within the same phylum, though their evolution may be separated by many millions of years. The most striking examples are seen in the dolphin (mammal), shark (fish) and ichthyosaurus (reptile). But these animals are, and were, all vertebrates and all related within one phylum. This phenomenon of evolution has been offered to explain why UFO occupants have so often been reported as humanoids, but such evolutionary convergence in lifeforms from completely independent biospheres would seem unlikely.

Any technological species visiting us from a far-away biosphere would not look like us. We are vertebrates, and vertebrates have a long history of evolution going back to a certain group of fishes. The bones which form the human skeleton can be traced back through that evolutionary history and are not going to be duplicated in another planetary biology. Statistically it would be impossible. Beings with four limbs, a backbone of sorts, with a large skull and manipulative hands and digits may evolve on other worlds, but you would certainly notice the differences if they turned up here in flying saucers.

I prefer to accept that the observations and experimental findings of thousands of anatomists, evolutionary biologists, molecular biologists, geneticists and biochemists, who have arrived at the same general conclusions from different starting points, are on the right track, and that those who suggest the probable universality of humanoids that are very like us in their anatomy are on the wrong track.

## RULES OF LIFE

The label exobiology was attached to some important science in the 1960s and 1970s. But, though even university and government departments were giving themselves this label, what the scientists were up to was mainstream science. It was not exobiology because no such discipline can exist until we find some exobiology to study. What the exobiologists were into was origin of life research, and it would have been better to have described their work as such. Flying the flag of exobiology only attracted flack from the scientific community, and it is a label best stored away for the future.

The research that was carried out did, however, lead many of us to think about the rules that life in general might follow on other worlds. We may not yet know enough to make guesses about alien life at a fundamental level, about its molecular structures and processes, but through our knowledge of organic evolution we can make guesses about what may be the more visible aspects of life on other Earth-like planets.

If we look at the history of life on Earth from the first bacteria of three and a half billion years ago right up to the present, we can see two kinds of evolved attributes. There are those that must be unique to Earth, such as our human anatomy with its 1,830 features in the vertebrate backbone alone, and those that may be universal such as the process of photosynthesis without which there would be no oxygen in the atmosphere and no food for anyone. The biochemists and molecular biologists who work on the structural chemistry of the photosynthesising machinery in plants and bacteria will tell you that there is plenty of room chemically, in the molecular structures of photosynthesis, for different systems to have evolved.

Our system of photosynthesis is a very complicated chemical one, involving hundreds of molecular sub-units. Dr Bob Ford of Manchester University, a specialist in this field, once told me that he considered the machinery of photosynthesis one of the most complicated systems to have evolved in Nature. This fundamental process, which contributes almost all of the energy used in living organisms, could evolve elsewhere, but the precise chemical structures of the machinery of photosynthesis would vary from planet to planet. Photosynthesis anywhere in the universe would capture radiant energy from a planet's sun and transform it into chemical energy, trapping the energy in energy-rich molecules for use by plants and animals (or their equivalents elsewhere). The energy-rich molecules would be used by the photosynthesising organisms (plants and some bacteria) or by the organisms which consume them, as animals either eat plants or eat animals that eat plants.

There are exceptions: some bacteria are independent of the Sun's energy, meeting their energy needs by chemically reacting directly with their environment. Some bacteria lead chemically supported lives deep within the Earth's crust. But organisms with that system of nourishment have remained stagnant in their evolution for the past few billion years. It is not a system to be recommended for the evolution of interesting biospheres. Hence the need for the evolution of systems of photosynthesis.

## LIFE'S ESSENTIAL ELEMENT

So we breathe oxygen and consume food without much thought about how oxygen and food are intimately connected, or how they are here for our convenience. We depend absolutely on the intricate and elaborate chemical mechanism of photosynthesis, and we don't realise how complicated the whole business is. And our counterparts on other worlds, unless they have become computers nourished by electricity, will probably have the same attitude. Not long ago, palaeontologists discovered fossils of bacteria in Australia which look remarkably like today's photosynthesising bacteria called cyanobacteria. The rocks in which the fossils were enclosed are three and a half billion years old which makes these ancient bacteria the oldest known fossils of any complete organisms. Photosynthesis has a long history.

A few years ago I questioned Dr Bob Ford about this fossil evidence for the antiquity of photosynthesis. He told me:

Those bacteria may look the same on the outside, but the photochemical assemblies of molecules operating in today's bacteria must have evolved since that distant time, although the basic chemistry may not have changed much in three and a half billion years.

58

The molecular machinery of photosynthesis is in two parts: Photosystem I and Photosystem II. A few years ago, biochemists and molecular biologists at the Universities of Manchester and Leeds jointly discovered the molecular structure of Photosystem II. Bob Ford said: 'It is about the most complex assembly of molecules to have evolved in nature.' Photosystem II consists of half the molecular machinery which provides almost all the energy in the biosphere and all the oxygen in the atmosphere. The molecular complexity of Photosystem II is built of fifteen different protein molecules, 300 molecules of chlorophyll (the green substance in every plant cell in which photosynthesis takes place) and forty carotenoid molecules (yellow and orange pigment molecules).

We should look at what happens here to see how life on other worlds would have to grasp the energy available to it, and transform it for its purposes. Plants and photosynthesising bacteria use the energy of light to raise the energy level of electrons in their chlorophyll. Thereafter the chemical machinery takes over and stores this energy in molecules of ATP [adenosine triphosphate] and other energy-rich compounds of phosphorus.

ATP is the main energy-rich molecule formed in photosynthesis – it's the common energy currency of all life on this planet. And the question we would like answered is: would life on other worlds also evolve to use this molecule as its energy storehouse? There are hundreds of similar questions that could be asked about the foundations of life on other worlds. That's why even a single cell from another planet would lead to a revolution in our understanding of life.

Plants use the chemically stored energy to split compounds of nitrogen and carbon dioxide molecules. They then recombine the atoms of these molecules to form carbohydrates and other organic molecules which animals eat. Photosystem II performs the first phase in photosynthesis; the other half of this fundamental mechanism is Photosystem I. It also is a complex assembly of protein molecules, and both systems function in all organisms which carry out photosynthesis, from bacteria to the most advanced plants. Certain groups of bacteria, however, have only one system or the other – not both. And some of those groups of bacteria have probably lived for the past three and a half billion years in that condition, and are still here. There are therefore likely to be vast numbers of young Earth-like planets with abundant life, but all of it bacterial life or something similar. In fact this could be the state of the majority of planets supporting life at any given time in galactic history, because the fossil record tells us that nothing more advanced than bacteria lived on Earth for the first two and a half billion years.

Scientists have studied slightly different versions of photosynthesis in widely different organisms and have found that all have similarities which indicate a common point of origin in Earth history. And it is thought that because the basic chemistry of photosynthesis is so complex it probably evolved here only once. The fact that it appeared in bacteria so soon after the origin of life may lead us to speculate that such a system of trapping radiant energy was more or less inevitable once life got started. Without it life could have remained in a permanent bacterial condition.

A scientific review of photosynthesis may make us wonder at the remarkable convenience of this system. It is hard to believe that while the potential for its evolution exists in the chemistry of the universe, it has developed on just one planet – the Earth. It looks like a universal phenomenon. Besides packing the Sun's energy into molecules that living organisms can use to meet their energy needs, photosynthesis very conveniently frees oxygen from the water molecule, so giving life a breathable atmosphere. The whole set-up looks prearranged. My guess is that any extra-terrestrial visitors to land on Earth would find the oxygen to their liking and at about the right level. But they would not like the micro-organisms floating around in our atmosphere. Something microscopic would get them before they could say 'Take me to your leader.'

## HUMANS ARE UNIQUE

We can see that human anatomy is a terrestrial attribute while photosynthesis could be a universal attribute. The universal attributes would be universal biological solutions to basic problems. Lifeforms, of whatever kind, have to maintain their viability and follow some activity. For this they need energy and materials for growth. This means taking matter and energy from the environment in some way. Lifeforms from bacteria to trees have done this by photosynthesis while animals as mobile lifeforms can get their energy and materials by eating the photosynthesisers and other animals or both. This looks like a probable universal arrangement. And it is only the animal way of life, so it would seem, that can provide enough energy to fuel nerve cells, if nerve cells evolve on other worlds.

We can see evidence in fossils that nerve cells must have evolved by 650 million years ago, though they probably did so long before that time. The fossils are of many-celled organisms, many like today's jellyfish, though much smaller. So it is obvious that such creatures would have needed quite complex nervous systems to control their bodies.

Once nerve cells evolve to control the functions of organisms, then better systems with more nerve cells would give improved survival to at least some groups of animals. This is the way in which increasingly intelligent animals evolved. But does this trend generally continue, given the opportunity, to the level of technological intelligence? This is the question that SETI could answer if it discovered evidence of extraterrestrial artifacts.

Within the vertebrates, and only in this dominant group, there are many lines in evolution which have led to a rat and cat level of intelligence, yet only one line which has led to technologists. So technology could be universal though not exactly abundant, given that the evolution of nerve cells is a universal phenomenon. One problem is that the energy requirements of big brains are very high, a fact which mitigates against their evolution. Big brains have got to provide survival value despite the high levels of energy needed to maintain them. They would not evolve otherwise. The energy needed to run them would be better spent in other ways.

Animals need the means to catch and break up their food for consumption, so the equivalent of teeth and claws would be universal. Animals would need means of locomotion which would probably include limbs of some kind. Could there be a planet where animals move on organic wheels rather than legs? The fact that wheels have never evolved in any of the millions of lines of evolution on this planet would seem to indicate that there has been no demand for biological wheels. Maybe an organic basis for wheels cannot exist. Here fishes have evolved fins to swim and fins evolved into the legs of all four-legged animals. The ancestors of other animals, such as insects, had their legs for walking on the sea bed – before coming ashore.

Given oceans and lakes, organisms are going to swim. And given habitable dry land they are going to exploit that environment as soon as they can. A world completely and permanently covered by ocean would be fine for life, though technological beings might never evolve. Yet a world without plenty of water for a few billion years could not provide the cradle which life seems to need for the evolution of land life. The life on Earth had evolved in water for three and a half billion years before it came ashore.

## LEGS AND BRAINS
That large intelligent land animals have four legs or limbs could be a

universal characteristic. The brain does not want any more limbs to control than is strictly necessary, and four limbs are the minimum needed. The octopus, with eight legs, is the most intelligent invertebrate, and the most intelligent animal to have evolved entirely in water. (Dolphins and whales evolved their mammalian brains on dry land and went back into the sea where their brains became larger, partly to incorporate their echo-location systems. The processing of sound waves needs a lot of brain cells.)

The oldest known fossil of an octopus is about 125 million years old. One therefore wonders why the octopus, living for so long in a benign environment with opportunities to better itself, has not evolved into a primitive technological creature. (H. G. Wells, who was a biologist, may have wondered about this when he wrote his famous *War of the Worlds*, because he made his Martians octopoids.) The advantages of intelligence to the octopuses, in an environment where no one except the marine mammals was very bright, would seem to be considerable. The answer may be that octopus evolution got stuck with the equivalent of eight limbs, or rather tentacles. Eight limbs need twice as much processing power in the brain as four limbs, so that if a brain is being used for limb control there is less processing capacity for other functions. Anyway, research has shown that no octopus can learn a maze, although other biologists have discovered that the octopus can learn to differentiate between different shapes.

There are of course all the arthropods to consider – all those tiny creatures with jointed limbs and bodies. The insects with six legs and the spiders and their relatives with eight have been highly successful in colonising the land. But their evolution was based on marine creatures with even more pairs of legs, such as centipedes, legs that were needed to move such creatures along the sea or lake bed. With so many legs to control, the arthropods could only evolve as pre-programmed automata with little or no scope for intelligent adaptation to unusual events. Remember the story about the centipede that tried to be intelligent? It tried to work out how it was moving its legs and got so confused it could not walk any more.

Flying could be a universal attribute, given a dense enough atmosphere to fly in. And without a dense enough atmosphere the atmospheric pressure would probably be too low to keep water permanently on a planet's surface. Wings should be abundant on Earth-like planets. Here they have evolved in all the major groups of land animals except the amphibians. Insects, reptiles, birds and mammals such as bats have all evolved wings, in that order. Even some fishes have evolved wings, though when in Earth's history we cannot say.

Wings may be universal, but it looks as if four limbs will be universal for all candidates for technological status. And all ETs should be moving mainly on two limbs, having the need in their evolution to free two limbs from the function of locomotion to manipulate their environment. This line of thinking leads us to the conclusion that creatures with some kind of primate form, though not like us, might emerge from flying saucers, should flying saucers have a physical reality with biological beings inside them. But no ET could be like the beautiful people reported by many contactees and abductees, unless they were specially bred from human stock.

Thus, in one speculative way, hundred per cent *Homo sapiens* are more credible than *Homo sapiens* with pointed ears, four digits per hand instead of five, grey hairless skin, pink eyes, and all the other superficial features stuck on to humans to make them look extra-terrestrial in the space sagas on television (*Star Trek* has a lot to answer for). The *Homo sapiens* who are saucernauts, as long as they are not beautiful blondes who say they are 250 years old, are more credible because they could come from Earthly stock.

A range of humanoids have been reported and there is some consistency in the different types, but the mythology of the subject could explain such consistency. Many claims have been made by people in ufology – especially about dead bodies from flying saucers – but no one has yet been able to provide one item of biologically significant information.

## LIMITATIONS ON LIFE

We know that the laws of physics and chemistry are universal. We know that life began by the application of those laws of physics and chemistry. We now have to ask about the laws of biology: how limiting and deterministic are they? We know that lifeforms through the mechanism of differential rates of reproduction respond to environmental forces, but to what extent do the laws of biology limit and govern those responses? Biology at its molecular and developmental levels may limit and determine the possible forms and functions of organisms. And it could be that life on Earth has already tried all those forms out, or nearly. We could accept that as a possibility, although we do not have any certain answers in this field yet. We cannot say, for example, that the laws of chemistry have determined precisely the twenty amino acid molecules used by life in the synthesis of proteins. We cannot say that those laws have determined precisely the chemical structures of DNA and RNA and

63

the mechanism of the genetic code. We do not yet know how far the laws of physics and chemistry penetrate into biology but advanced research is in progress to try and find some answers. If the laws of physics and chemistry are not overwhelming in their influence, then natural selection in the first self-reproducing molecular complexes may have determined, partly by chance, the twenty amino acids used in Earthly life, as well as the molecular structures and functions of RNA (and later DNA) and the mechanism of the genetic code. With a specimen from another biosphere, biologists could begin to answer these fundamental questions. The sophistication of experimental biology today could give us a vast amount of information to expand our knowledge and appreciation of life as a universal phenomenon. Biologists who had access to such a specimen would never be able to keep quiet about it. The stories that the United States government has dead extraterrestrials locked away in cold storage can only be entertained by those unfamiliar with biology and the revolutionary importance such material would have for science.

## COUNTER ARGUMENT

Maybe, in the future, we will find that no Earth-like planets orbit our neighbouring stars, though there might be plenty of sterile planets or orbiting debris. Perhaps the development of such planets is far less likely than we now assume. Astronomical theory in recent years has shown that a rather demanding set of conditions must exist for an Earth to form, and it is estimated that only one in a hundred suitable planetary systems may have such a planet. But the truth is we just do not know – and we do not need to know. We can get on and test the ETH without knowing.

Maybe future biologists will find that the probability of life forming is so remote that it could not occur often in the whole history of time and space – though judging from what has happened here this does seem unlikely. And even if life is a relatively common phenomenon, it may be that the evolution of technologically intelligent creatures, our counterparts, is very rare. We already know that a unique and unpredictable chain of events led to our evolution. But then unique chains of events have led to each of the several million other species currently on this planet. Certainly other technological species, if they exist, will each be the result of a unique evolutionary history – the history of a planet and its biosphere will always be unique.

Biologists studying the rain forests before they disappear reckon that the number of unclassified species living there could increase the total known number of species on Earth by several million. Go back through time to the first monkeys, which evolved in the Eocene Period of fifty-four to thirty-eight million years ago, and hundreds of millions of species have evolved and disappeared. Yet only one small group of species, *Homo sapiens* and our direct ancestors, such as *Homo erectus* and *Homo habilis*, have emerged with the level of technological intelligence that could develop and ultimately create a civilisation.

This line of thinking, which indicates the low probability of the emergence of technological species, is partially countered by one important fact. It is that the Earth is only middle-aged. Hundreds of millions of years of evolution would have remained for the mammals, the only current candidates on this planet for technological intelligence, to give rise to a different technological creature, if our species had not taken over most of their habitats. When you look at certain mammalian species apart from the primates, such as the racoons, the meerkats and the marsupial possums, the potential appears to be there, given another fifty million years or so of evolution. Having considered all this, we still have to admit that we cannot know what the answer is. Advanced technological intelligences in any galaxy could be very rare, or abundant.

## WAYS TO TECHNOLOGICAL INTELLIGENCE

Professor William Calvin of the University of Washington says that our large brains, and the ability to plan and simulate actions in our heads, may have evolved from the need to throw stones accurately at prey, and to be able to hammer things well with sticks, stones and bones. Anyone watching films of chimps in the wild trying to perform these actions can see that they are not very good at it. The reason is that these actions demand a lot of brain processing power, and our nearest primate relative does not have enough nerve cells for the processing required.

We know from the fossil record that the apes who were our ancestors stood upright long before bigger brains began to evolve. It could be that not until our ancestral apes began to walk upright did throwing and hitting become important activities in life, that an upright stance was necessary before higher brain functions would evolve. Also, abilities in throwing and hitting probably continued to evolve until relatively recent times. I doubt if *Homo erectus* of a million and a half years ago would have been much good at cricket or baseball or football.

Like other major advances in life's history, the right level in evolution was in place for the development of bigger brains when unspecialised and adaptable animals like the apes evolved. Their

65

large brains had their evolutionary origin in monkeys, whose sharp eyes, quick wits and great agility had been prime survival factors in the forests. Fossil evidence shows that some apes evolved a more or less upright stance around five million years ago. The evolutionary pressure for this may have been too many apes and too few trees, but one cannot imagine our ancestors easily giving up the protection gained through climbing into trees.

It seems that for between one and two million years the australopithecines (apes with an upright posture) had brains not much different from the brain of today's chimp. But Calvin suggests that the evolution of the necessary neural equipment to support effective throwing and beating, which had considerable survival value for the upright apes, provided spare neuronal capacity. And that this spare capacity was eventually used to simulate actions in the mind before committing them in reality. This ability in its turn had survival value which forced the evolution of cleverer and more detailed simulations. In this way the growth in consciousness of self began and continued.

Nervous tissue, containing neural networks of great complexity, is necessary to generate the mental simulation needed to become even a primitive technologist. What, therefore, were the factors which caused these neural networks to evolve in our ancestors? There are over eighty different muscles which have to be activated by neural impulses in appropriate sequences and intensities for us to throw accurately or hammer with precision. Throwing and hammering, as we can now perform such actions, demand an enormous amount of brain power. Think of the incredible accuracy with which some of us can throw cricket balls and baseballs, or hit (hammer) with a tennis racket with amazing timing and control – not all of us, but it is possible for a human being. Playing the piano is another precision hammering example.

So where did the first technologist, sitting in the dust of an African savannah some three million years ago, get his neural equipment to imagine a better tool or weapon? He inherited it from a long line of ancestors who learnt to throw stones with increasing precision at small prey, and to beat prey with sticks and bones, and probably beat his neighbouring apemen on occasions. The best throwers and hitters had an edge on survival and passed on the neural networks needed for those useful activities. Good throwers and hitters ate more frequently and were better at warding off predators and competitors.

Like other biologists, William Calvin sees no great obstacle to the evolution of clever animals. But very clever animals, technological animals, are another matter. He gave his views to a SETI conference in France in 1991:

> So far as I can see, there is nothing inevitable about higher intelligence evolving from mere cleverness of the sort evolved by the ancestors of rat, raven and octopus. Smarter may be better, everything else being equal, but everything else is seldom equal – and so species often settle into dead-end stabilities. I suspect that our uniquely human abilities, such as plan-ahead consciousness, language, music, dance, accurate throwing and kicking, are mostly due to a fortuitous consequence of getting better and better at projectile predation. Such styles of hunting are hardly inevitable; getting through the winter would seem to accelerate it, and the many climatic changes would seem to spread these advantages around the world.

Calvin does not support Professor Frank Tipler's argument (which we will meet later) that intelligence like ours is absent from the rest of the universe:

> I can imagine various other ways to evolve neural-like machinery that could be secondarily used ... Fortuitous does not equate with improbable.

Fortuitous here refers in part to the succession of ice ages which coincided with the latter stages of human evolution. These must have put great evolutionary pressure on human populations which later spread their favourable genes into the general human population with constant migrations, south before the ice sheets and north again in the warm inter-glacial periods.

## ALL IN THE MIND
Our capacity to simulate in the mind is an essential attribute in humans. Our nearest relative, the chimp, and some other mammals show this ability, but only in a rudimentary form. No other animal is much good at it. We would not make things and make them work without being able to simulate a range of possible actions before deciding on the most appropriate. So we need to be able to place ourselves in our simulations which requires self-consciousness, something which only a few mammals have been shown to possess. No science and technology would be possible without mental simulation and self-consciousness; there would be no civilisation

without them. Without these characteristics of the human mind, we would never form testable hypotheses or spend years developing new technologies. Consider the theoretical physicists who hit the high notes in mental simulation, constantly constructing universes in their heads as a way of life, and then getting experimentalists to see if outside reality matches up with their inner simulations of it. We can therefore say that there will be no extraterrestrial technologists without an advanced capacity for mental simulation, the evolution of which also brings self-consciousness.

For this reason our assessment of the abundance or otherwise of ETIs who may broadcast to us or visit us depends on our assessment of how likely the evolution of mental simulation and self-consciousness was on this planet. This evolutionary step was the latest major one in a vast number of major steps leading from the origin of life to the human race, and like many major steps it looks a difficult one to take.

Unlike some of the other essential evolutionary events leading to *Homo sapiens*, such as the evolution of cells, of many-celled lifeforms, the first nerve cells and so on, we can see more or less how we became the world's first technologists once an unspecialised mammal like a monkey had evolved. Things came together in the right order and at the right time for the evolution of the human race. The same series of events is unlikely to occur elsewhere in the way it did here. Therefore, to speculate on the abundance of ETIs or otherwise we have to review the evolutionary factors which turned an upright ape into *Homo sapiens*, and then to think of other evolutionary ways of achieving the evolution of technologists.

Upright apes and apemen and primitive humans had been improving their mental equipment by throwing and hitting for some two and a half million years. Then the ice ages arrived, by which time they had evolved an advanced capacity for mental simulation. The abrupt environmental changes which the periodic ice ages brought rapidly boosted genetic improvement and the secondary uses of the extra brain power in communications, planning and social life.

Calvin says:

My argument is that our kind of intelligence arises from a secondary use of neural machinery evolved for its usefulness at the mundane task of throwing accurately and hammering skilfully. And that, as we have gotten better and better at them, there has been something of a jump in language and intelligence . . .

Calvin's argument ties in precisely with what we know about how the evolution of major advances takes place. Four legs for the first land animals did not evolve directly. They evolved from four sturdy fins that were used by a group of fishes some 400 million years ago to stabilise themselves on the beds of inland lakes. The lungs of the first land animals did not evolve to enable animals to live on dry land. They evolved to help certain groups of freshwater fishes obtain their oxygen from the atmosphere and thus survive conditions of drought. Lungs first evolved to enable fishes to remain fishes. Wings did not evolve for flying but to enable early reptiles to run faster. There is a very long list of such secondary uses by Nature. So did we throw and hit our way to technology and civilisation? It is the most likely hypothesis.

## WHAT NEWS FROM ET?

We can see from looking at our own origins that there may be too much optimism about what we may be able to understand from any contact with ETs. They could not tell us how to cure cancer or solve our social and moral problems, as some fanciful people have suggested. Our medical needs are specific to the biology of this planet, as are our cultures and societies. Such ideas result from a poor appreciation of the scale of organic evolution and, by comparison, the astonishing speed in the development of civilisation and technology. The differences between technological civilisations are potentially enormous and unbridgeable because of the sheer pace at which scientific development advances. And the biologies and cultures of different worlds would be even more dissimilar than their respective technologies. As technology is based on the way the universe works, and this is the same everywhere, it seems possible that the development of technologies on different planets could converge. An optical telescope or a radio receiver on Planet-X may be similar to the same technology here, but we would not expect to be able to understand an ETI civilisation as we understand the ancient civilisations of Earth. And anyone who claims to have had a cosy chat in their own local lingo with beings from other planets is either lying or in need of psychotherapy.

## NO FOOD FOR MARTIANS

The octopoid Martians of H. G. Wells' *War of the Worlds*, published in 1898, were soon defeated in their invasion of Earth by bacterial infections which rapidly killed them all. Nothing else could have stopped their vastly superior weapons technology. An odd situation for such highly intelligent creatures, being wiped out through ignorance of basic biology. But Mr Wells had to stop them somehow. So the Martians had mastered the physical sciences and technology beyond anything we could achieve, yet remained naive in matters biological. Not a believable scenario, but it enabled the story to come to a happy end – although not for the Martians.

Actually there was more on Earth to stop them than bacteria in the air, resulting from the reckless way they consumed people. A diet of human beings, full of microbes as we are, would kill any alien. And some of the amino acids of which our bodily proteins are composed might have played havoc with a Martian metabolism. The point is that all life on Earth depends upon proteins which are formed from various complex combinations of the same twenty amino acids. The number of different proteins that can be formed is virtually limitless although the number of components is restricted to twenty. And we cannot expect that any extraterrestrial life that is made of proteins, as we are, uses exactly the same amino acids to make them.

There are many other amino acids not used by life on Earth, as well as right-handed versions of each of the twenty kinds that are used by life on this planet which are all left-handed. All life is geared to use these and not the other kind.

The Martians which H. G. Wells brought to Earth would have had their tissues and organs built of proteins made from the amino acids used by all life on Mars. And those used by life here could have been different. This would have meant big trouble for their synthesis of proteins, many of which would have been different from our proteins. Also, the chemistry of life depends on enzymes, which are all proteins and keep that chemistry going in all organisms. If we could not get a regular supply of those twenty amino acids to make our proteins, our life would soon come to a halt. And the combination of those twenty amino acids available in the right quantities in the food we eat may only be available in our particular biosphere. Go to any other planet that is full of life and you would not find food to sustain you. The invading Martians would have come to a sticky end anyway – even without the severe bacterial infections they sustained through eating too many people. And, to bring us up to date, the hospitality of food lavished on Captain Kirk and his *Star Trek* crew by friendly aliens can never be a reality.

So it is a grim outlook for interstellar tourists. Go to another planet like ours and you would not even be able to replace your proteins with a good meal. But even before you wasted away from this problem, your metabolism would seize up and go into terminal decline. The reason: your body could not make the large number of enzymes, the chemical machinery, that carry out the metabolic processes of your life. If the alien proteins containing alien amino acids did not poison you, the lack of your natural amino acids would soon lead to functional collapse.

There are therefore good reasons why no biological being should go to live on another life-bearing planet, and why an ET colonisation of Earth is not at all likely – *ever*. Frank Tipler and his supporters are wrong in saying that if any ETs are out there in the Galaxy they would by now have taken up residence on Earth. The micro-organisms might be filtered out through whatever breathing apparatus was used, but the main problem would be nothing to eat. The alternative? Synthesise all your food from scratch. With advanced chemistry this might be possible, but the job looks horribly difficult as a permanent way of life on a strange new world – and you wouldn't want to move far from the chemical factory. When you add this problem to that of the time needed to cross interstellar space, one can see that the exploration of alien worlds is not compatible with being a biological creature.

Why put yourself in that position in the first place, if it is not necessary? Why not stay at home, comfortable in your own biosphere where you do not have to worry about your proteins and enzymes, or lethal microbes and threatening monsters. Just send bright young robots off to other planetary systems to do the exploring for you.

# CHAPTER 6
## ET's Landing Sites

I was once at a conference in London surrounded by dozens of analytical chemists when the subject of UFOs cropped up. 'Would a heavy space vehicle, the conventional flying saucer, landing on our planet leave detectable chemical traces?' I asked.

'Yes,' they replied, 'depending on the nature of the surface and the weight and composition of the saucer.'

I pushed my query further: 'So if we carried out proper chemical analyses of landing sites, just the credible sites out of the hundreds reported, we might find a consistent chemical pattern?'

'Yes, we might,' they agreed, showing some signs of unease, wondering what they might be dragged into next. But they all looked interested and a few might have been ready for analytical action, if given the opportunity.

That was twenty years ago and the analytical chemists have never been called in, except for rare isolated cases, to look for unusual chemical traces at landing sites. There has been no co-ordinated research program to take effective advantage of the technical expertise available. There is one established exception: the work of SEPRA which is part of the French space agency.

The consistent study of a large number of credible landing sites might raise the study of this strange phenomenon of reported landings to a repeatable experimental level. It might become possible for scientists to predict that certain chemical traces and biological effects would be found at genuine landing sites. On the other hand, they might be able to show that there are no genuine landing sites, although what little scientific evidence there is seems to indicate that something *is* landing. We cannot get to grips with this problem until more research is carried out at the appropriate level. If our world is being studied by technology beyond anything we could envisage, we cannot expect to detect its presence easily. Thus that instinctive reaction, that 'gut feeling', that as no evidence has been detected no evidence exists, is not a rational argument against the ET hypothesis. There are more powerful arguments against the hypothesis, if one wanted to use them.

## ARTIFACTS FROM SAUCER LANDINGS

The most acceptable evidence – and the most surprising – would be artifacts that one could handle, rather than chemical residues and radiation damage to plants at and near the landing site. Many such artifacts have been presented, but not one has stood up to close scrutiny. After watching strange primates in overalls repair their spacecraft, witnesses occasionally report finding fragments of saucer technology. Apparently our visitors can be careless about their extraterrestrial cables because the discovery of cable cuttings is sometimes reported. In a few accounts, the saucernauts actually present objects, such as metal tablets with strange inscriptions, to astonished peasants, usually somewhere in South America, who just happen to be labouring in the fields when the UFO lands. What happens to such extraterrestrial gifts no one knows. No UFO society has ever been able to locate even one of the many reported. Artifacts are handed over to local authorities, as one might expect, but there are apparently no reports of ufologists investigating the local authorities and the missing artifacts. The loss of alien artifacts, such as the metal fragment in the Meier case which was lost by a laboratory, is a real occupational hazard in ufology. Eduard Meier was a Swiss caretaker who claimed to have frequent meetings with extraterrestrials of the perfect human kind.

The trouble is that inscribed metal plates and cable cuttings are too obvious to be credible – they bear the trademark of the hoaxer. But just one minor item of technology could confirm the ETH. Any time traveller from the present going back just a hundred years with a few selected items of today's technology, say a pocket calculator and a quartz watch, both carried in a plastic bag, could convince scientists of the time that he or she was indeed from the future. Items of technology from civilisations thousands of years ahead of us should therefore be even more surprising and convincing. Yet no such items have been left behind by flying saucers. Is it that no advanced monitoring system, in which contacts are rigorously avoided, will leave behind any bits and pieces? Or is it that all the reported flying saucers are natural physical entities of an, as yet, unknown kind? In this case there *would* be physical evidence to gather and analyse.

## OBVIOUS HOAXERS

There are many hoaxes – some obvious and some not. Hoaxers report a version of the current image popularised by the media. The craft will be disc-shaped, leaving a circular impression on the soil and vegetation. Such reports could be checked but few are. There may be depressions within the circle, three or four, where landing legs of some kind supported the craft. And evidence of burning may be present because the hoaxer assumes that ET will still be using a primitive rocket system of propulsion.

But witnesses are not all hoaxers and some report physical traces which they genuinely believe were associated with the UFO. Psychologists say this may be done unintentionally to add extra credence to their reports. Even where the reported UFO remains unexplained, the traces are not necessarily connected with it. But where traces are shown to be associated with a UFO event (and this has been done) it follows that something physical, but not necessarily a flying saucer, must have produced those traces.

## MICROSCOPIC EVIDENCE OF UFOs

It is the not easily seen evidence which really deserves our scientific attention. For example, there have been several reported struggles with what, in the more colourful pages of the UFO literature, are called 'bellicose hairy dwarfs'. These are one of several kinds of primate-like saucer occupants described by witnesses in different parts of the world, but unlike other saucer visitors who appear serene, wise or just plain indifferent to humankind, the hairy dwarfs habitually attack anyone on sight. They appear intent on dragging any stray *Homo sapiens* to their saucer and an unknown extra-terrestrial fate. Whether they have yet succeeded or not is an open question, but according to reports they do seem to pick on the wrong sort of prey, such as large long-distance lorry drivers who put up a vigorous fight, having a strong disinclination to being dragged away to another planet, no matter how technologically advanced and intelligent its inhabitants.

The result is that the 'bellicose hairy dwarfs', after a struggle, give up and retreat to their saucer. But they don't give up easily and fierce fights have been reported. One might expect that in such struggles the hairy dwarfs would lose a few hairs. It may be that this category of extraterrestrial visitor has a very high quality coat, but the reports have said nothing about anyone ever looking for the odd fallen hair, when the bemused local police come along to investigate. Just one extraterrestrial hair for microscopic examination and analysis would be worth a thousand detailed reports of UFO encounters, no matter how clear the visibility at the time and how reputable the witnesses, which are aspects of UFO reports so frequently emphasised. But if you don't believe in the 'hairy dwarfs' you are, of course, not going to look for their hairs.

Serious investigators don't expect to find pieces of incredible technology, or even the odd extraterrestrial hair, when they visit the next reported landing site. They are spare-timers, a few professional scientists included, who do the best they can to see that any physical evidence is analysed and studied, and they catalogue reports and any associated traces. Vincente-Juan Ballester Olmos, for example, a leading figure in ufology who lives in Valencia, Spain, has made a special study of UFO landing reports on the Iberian Peninsula and has produced a comprehensive catalogue of these events.

Olmos found that 60 per cent of the reports could be explained satisfactorily – definitely no saucers involved! He then went on to catalogue 355 of these false reports. He found that

31.2 per cent were fictitious (hoaxes, frauds); 25.1 per cent meteorological (whirlwinds, ionisation, lightning effects); 31.5 per cent miscellaneous (vehicles, fires, lights); 10.7 per cent mental (hallucinations, illusions, psychological, psychopathological visions); 8.2 per cent astronomical (planets, moon, stars, meteoroids); 7.1 per cent aeronautical (balloons, aircraft, rockets, re-entries of spacecraft debris); 4.2 per cent biological (misinterpreted people).

After years studying the techniques of investigation, Olmos has said:

We must proceed on the assumption that the human being is a fallible recorder, particularly when faced with unexpected and unknown events. No witness testimony can be taken at face value because facts will be inevitably and systematically distorted or misrepresented.

His advice to investigators is simple:

An elementary principle in any UFO interrogation is that it must start with a request to the witness to tell what happened, in depth, fully and without interruption by the investigator. Only when the story has been told in full should the witness be subjected to a long battery of questions – some of them standard, others specific to the particular event. To take a report at face value is intellectual suicide.[1]

## WORLDWIDE PHENOMENON

Other investigators have done similar work in other parts of the world. But it is certainly true to state that not one of the few thousand catalogued landings has received the level of scientific investigation that is currently possible. Any reader who doubts the correctness of this statement should check the libraries for scientific papers on the investigation of UFO landing sites.

Bill Chalker, an industrial chemist living in New South Wales, Australia, has investigated UFO landing sites in his spare time for more than twenty years. He is one of the most prominent researchers and is mainly interested in cases where physical traces have been found. He sees the investigation of such traces as the main scientific approach because if flying saucers have a physical reality and are actually landing on Earth, then the landing sites may offer interesting information. As Chalker says:

The physical trace phenomenon is an enduring aspect of the UFO mystery, having manifested for the entire duration of the modern era of the UFO controversy. And like the UFO phenomenon itself, it is global in its extent.

Chalker has mentioned some of the problems he has encountered in Australia:

We have had camp-fires, wind-vortices, and even a lump cut up by a council lawnmower, all appearing at first sight as proof that a UFO had landed nearby. It only requires a typically zealous investigator or witness.

To establish in a scientifically acceptable way that objects with certain characteristics are landing on this planet would only be a first step towards testing the ETH. Chemical and biological evidence, such as the effects of heat and intense electromagnetic radiation on chemistry and vegetation, has been found at a few sites. But it does not follow from such evidence that what has landed has an extra-terrestrial origin. Additional evidence would be needed to draw that conclusion. We cannot expect a careless ET to leave an extra-terrestrial spanner behind one day at take-off, but we might get a photographic record to back up the physical evidence from landing sites. The increasing use of camcorders offers a possible way of obtaining evidence as there is much more information in a moving image, and video tapes are more difficult to fake than still photographs.

## MICROBES AND UFOs

It is the physical traces and biological effects that we cannot see which are important for scientific consideration, rather than evidence that we can see. We need to measure effects of weight on a landing site, patterns of radioactivity and electromagnetic phenomena, the effects on vegetation and microscopic life in the soil.

Temperatures at landing sites might be estimated by studies of the death of micro-organisms in the surface soil, but investigation would have to be carried out within a few days of the reported landing. If there was no evidence of microscopic death, then we would have to assume that saucer landings are either very benign or the witnesses are very imaginative. To my knowledge, no one has applied microbiology to the investigation of landing sites. Even the work on the Trans-en-Provence landing in France didn't study the effects of the impact on the microbiology of the surface soil. But good research papers were published which is essential in any field of research. If one can judge the health of any area of research by the quality of its research papers, UFO research should be in intensive care, while astronomical SETI is bubbling over with good health.

## SAUCERS AND CHEMISTRY

The idea of chemists analysing samples from landing sites to detect 'scrapings' from nuts-and-bolts saucers is a bit dated. Consistent chemical effects may be produced by the flight mechanism, by the intense electromagnetic fields created. Hundreds of reports do indicate that intense electromagnetic fields are associated with some UFOs. It seems that if nuts-and-bolts saucers exist, they fly by technology based on physics as yet undiscovered by us.

Physicist Valeriy Buerakov has suggested in a paper, published by the Research Institute on Anomalous Phenomena in Kharkov, that the propulsion system used may involve generating electromagnetic fields outside the atom which are as strong as those within the atom. (The electromagnetic forces operating within the atom are relatively much greater than any that can be generated outside the atom.) How this might be done is any physicist's guess, but that does not matter to us at present. What we would have to show is that reports of UFO landings are associated with such fields. That is a big enough task for the present. Any success in this line of investigation may encourage the belief that funding particle physics is not just pouring vast sums of money into pure scientific research, which will never make discoveries with which to create new technologies. The technological pay-off may be some time in coming, but when it comes it could be revolutionary. A quantum leap in the technology of our systems of propulsion could be one of the spin-offs.

## THE MYSTERY OF FIELDS

We think of space as completely empty. Except for the odd particle, the vast void of the universe exists with the galaxies of stars within it – plus clouds of gas and other, smaller astronomical objects and oddities. But although space is a void it has the capacity to carry electromagnetic fields. Light and radio waves and all other sections of the electromagnetic spectrum would not travel across the universe if electromagnetic fields could not exist in space. And radio and television transmissions would not go anywhere. But how do we confirm the reality of those electromagnetic fields?

Most people will be familiar with the simple experiment of scattering iron filings on a sheet of paper and passing a magnet underneath. The iron filings move to show the lines of force of the magnet's field. We cannot, however, use iron filings to show the presence of UFO fields which may be billions of times more powerful than our magnet. If such intense electromagnetic fields *are* associated with UFOs, they could produce chemical reactions in our environment in the same way as intense heat would.

The atmosphere contains some of the elements for the chemistry we would have to consider, to which we can add the chemical and biochemical effects of intense electromagnetic fields on soil and plants. But the fields would have to be really intense. The level of fields we might encounter in daily life, such as those produced by high-voltage power lines, would not produce much instant chemistry.

## UFO RESEARCH IN PERSPECTIVE

Professor Allen Hynek, an astronomer in the United States who led the scientific approach in ufology for many years and died in 1986, has explained the lack of scientific progress:

After years of frustration without the funds to pay for adequate laboratory and other professional work, I bristle at the lack of understanding on the part of the scientific sceptics, who wouldn't get to first base without well-funded research projects with

79

staff, travel and laboratory facilities . . . It is my contention that *hard* data may well have been present in many UFO cases but their discovery and definitive establishment have repeatedly gone by default for lack of professional [funded] treatment.

The very visible physical traces, such as oily deposits, powdery chemicals and crystals, burnt areas and damaged vegetation, are sometimes analysed by local scientists who occasionally find something unusual, such as magnesium of exceptional purity or an unknown compound. A lot has been made of such findings in the UFO journals, but that sort of chemical investigation of odd samples can lead nowhere. The American Chemical Society has about four million chemical substances listed in its catalogue, which demonstrates the magnitude of the problem of trying to show that any one substance at a landing site might have an unearthly origin. If a UFO lands, the impact site and surrounding area need a lot more attention than the gathering of a few samples weeks after the event.

Intense heat and radiation from a landing could kill micro-organisms on the surface soil, but, as soil is a good insulator, micro-organisms will be unaffected just beneath the surface. So what should we look for at reported landing sites where high levels of radiation and heat may have been present? Dr Peter Harris is a microbiologist at the University of Reading with no connection with UFOs, plasma BOLs or whatever. For years he has studied the effects of various disturbances on soil micro-organisms, for instance when straw stubble is burnt in fields. He was kind enough to offer his advice when I asked how one might investigate the impact on micro-organisms at a site subjected to high heat and radiation.

Stubble-burning is a guide to answering this question because it can produce surface temperatures up to 600 degrees Centigrade for ten to fifteen minutes as the fire moves across a field. Although micro-organisms on the surface are killed, the burning does not affect the soil ecology because micro-organisms a few centimetres below the surface are unaffected. Peter Harris explained that when microbes are killed they release a lot of nitrogen which produces ammonium, and this excess of ammonium will be present in the top soil (no deeper than four centimetres) for two to three days. Single samples would provide no information because soil is so variable in its content, but a thorough sampling which showed above-average amounts of ammonium would indicate that the site had been subjected to high temperatures or high levels of radiation.

## FRANCE SHOWS THE WAY

In 1977, the French government established GEPAN [Groupement d'Etudes des Phénomènes Aérospatiaux Non-identifiés] in response to the many unexplained UFO reports. GEPAN was made part of the Centre National d'Etudes Spatiales, the French equivalent of NASA, and could call on laboratories throughout France, at universities and other institutions, to do research. GEPAN received information from the French Air Force, the police and military – all had an official obligation to report UFO events and collaborate with GEPAN. It was the first research program of its kind.

In January 1981, GEPAN began the best investigation to date of a landing site. Compared to other UFO events it was very brief – the landing of a small UFO in a garden near the village of Trans-en-Provence in the south of France. Numerous scientists were involved in very thorough research and the final report, which was published three years later, established that something unknown and unexplainable had landed. Nothing more, but it was a start in the right direction.

## THE UFO ARRIVES

A Monsieur Renato Nicolai was fifty-five at the time and retired due to ill health. He had lived with his wife at their house for fourteen years, an unusual residence in that the garden is on four levels or terraces. He was on one of the garden terraces building a little shed for a water pump when a small UFO landed at about five o'clock in the afternoon of 8 January 1981. The next day the event was reported to the police who arrived to investigate – the police in France being obliged to investigate all UFO incidents. The following extracts from Nicolai's interview with the police outline what happened:

> My attention was drawn to a small noise, a kind of little whistling. I turned around and I saw in the air a ship [he called it a *ship* throughout] which was just about at the height of a pine tree at the edge of my property. This ship was not turning but was descending toward the ground. I only heard a slight whistling. I saw no flames, neither underneath or around the ship.

Having seen the UFO descending, Nicolai hurried towards a cabin on the topmost garden terrace from where he could see the UFO on the ground.

At that moment, the ship began to emit another whistling, a constant, consistent whistling. Then it took off and once it was at the height of the trees, it took off rapidly in the direction of the forest of Trans-en-Provence ... As the ship began to lift off, I saw beneath it four openings from which neither smoke nor flames were emitting. The ship kicked up a little dust when it left the ground. I was at that time about thirty metres from the landing site. I thereafter walked toward the spot and noticed a circle about two metres in diameter. At certain spots on the curve of the circle there were tracks ...

The ship was in the form of two saucers upside down, one against the other. It must have been just about one and a half metres high. It was the colour of lead.

The police carried out the first investigation the day after the event.

We observed the presence of two concentric circles, one 2.20 metres in diameter and the other 2.40 metres in diameter. The two circles form a sort of corona ten centimetres thick ... There are two parts clearly visible, and they also show black striations. [See Figure 1.] Nicolai thought he saw two kinds of *round pieces which could have been landing gear or feet* as the UFO took off. He felt no heat, no vibration, no illness, neither during the observation or after. He was simply very impressed by the inexplicable spectacle.

The police took some samples that day, and some more on 23 January, of vegetation up to twenty metres from the impact. GEPAN requested these for analysis at a biochemical laboratory.

A GEPAN interview with Nicolai on 17 February stated that

As a result of several points furnished by Nicolai, we can guess that the entire length of the observation would be several dozen seconds ... The brutal shock at the point of impact he pointed out and the sound that resulted from the point of impact is compared to that, in his words, of *a rock falling on the ground.*

Although Nicolai's wife had not returned from work when the UFO arrived, she said she believed her husband, although she later asked the GEPAN investigators if they 'thought her husband was crazy'.

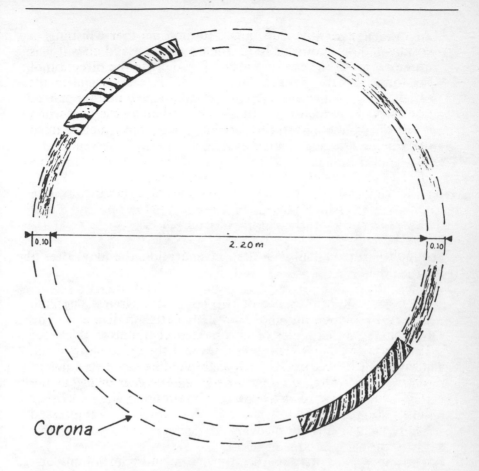

Figure 1: Drawing made by the police of the landing site at Trans-en-Provence.

They didn't think him at all crazy and the scientific investigation continued. GEPAN had already checked with the air traffic authorities and the military for a terrestrial explanation of the UFO – Camp Jouvan, a major area for army manoeuvres, is suspiciously close, just south of Trans-en-Provence – and ruled it out.

On 17 February, GEPAN's investigators took samples of various wild plants at precise distances from the impact These were to prove important in subsequent research.

A study of the impact site showed that the soil was highly compacted compared to outside areas. And microscopic examination of the surface showed that it had been 'subjected to a rubbing which had had the same effect as sandpapering'. The fracturing of flints indicated that they had either been smashed into the ground or had cracked through being subjected to a high temperature.

The laboratory which did GEPAN's preliminary analyses found blackish particles, which were thought to have been produced by some sort of combustion. But no organic compounds were present, so the particles did not come from characteristic motor combustion. There was also more iron in the site samples than in the control samples.

At the University of Metz analysis of the soil taken from the corona revealed a high concentration of negatively charged ions and the presence of carbon polymers in other samples from the site.

Scientists at the University of Rangueill tried without success to reproduce the crystallisation found in compounds in the site soil.

Analytical chemistry is a formidably technical area of science beyond the scope of this book, but for those interested the original research reports are available.[2]

GEPAN stated that:

The methods of analysis and microscopic observation brought out elements that indicate that the terrain or soil where Nicolai claims to have observed the phenomenon underwent certain specific modifications.

There was a strong mechanical pressure forced on the surface, probably the result of a heavy weight.

The appearance of a superficial structural modification of the soil, with both striations and erosion.

A thermatic heating of the soil, perhaps consecutive to or immediately following the shock, the value of which did not exceed 600 degrees Centigrade.

An eventual residue of material in the form of detectable traces on the samples analysed, such as a weak quantity of oxidous iron on grains of calcium and minute quantities of phosphate and zinc.

## STRANGE BIOLOGICAL EFFECTS

Professor Michel Bounias, a biochemist at the National Institute of Agronomy Research in Avignon, worked with GEPAN and published a paper on the biochemical effects of the landing. He explained that 'plants of a wild strain of alfalfa, *Medicago minima*, were found inside [the site], on the trace [corona], and throughout the surrounding area' and that 'this species was thus chosen as the biological model'. He focused on the physical stress on a specific organism caused by the landing event.

In reporting his research, he said that:

The aim of this paper is to give an example of how to study the effects of a phenomenon of unknown origin [of the UFO-type] on the biochemistry of living non-human organisms – on facts that cannot be suspected of lacking objectivity.

Bounias said that it was not the purpose of his research to try to identify the nature of the UFO which landed on 8 January 1981. 'But it can reasonably be concluded that something unusual did occur that might be consistent, for instance, with an electromagnetic source of stress.'

Summing up his conclusions in another report, he has said:

In most cases, the amount of mutilation or transformation in them [the plants] is a function of distance from the centre ... None the less, the actual results and the knowledge that we gained from the actual deformations that the plants underwent, still remain too scattered to form a whole picture, so that as of this moment, we cannot give a precise and unique interpretation to this remarkable combination of results.

According to GEPAN and Bounias, we may therefore conclude that something landed. That is progress. But the question remains: 'What landed?' Currently we have no clue, but the only way to pick up clues is by carrying out more research like that made possible by GEPAN.

Professor Bounias explained his findings in an interview with Jean-Yves Casgha of the Paris newspaper *France-Soir*:

We worked on very young leaves. They all had the anatomic and physiologic characteristics of their age. However, they had the biochemical characteristics of advanced senescence, of old age! And this does not resemble anything known to exist ...

We have found differences sufficiently important that the statistical significance of the results is irrefutable ... All we can say is that something certainly happened. We have observed the effects of a phenomenon. We don't know its precise nature or, above all, its cause.

## GEPAN TO SEPRA

From an experimental phase, GEPAN became more operational in the early 1980s. In 1988, it became SEPRA [Service d'Expertise des Phénomènes de Rentrées Atmosphériques] and nowadays SEPRA is officially responsible for monitoring the re-entry of all satellites and their debris into French airspace. SEPRA continues to receive reports of all unidentified aerial phenomena from the *gendarmerie*, civil aviation and the military and to pursue investigations of anything that cannot be explained.

Since GEPAN was established, over two thousand cases have been investigated. Only 4 per cent of all these cases remain unexplained.

There have been some very thorough investigations which have made some very conventional discoveries. In May 1990, the *gendarmerie* of Pleine Fougère was puzzled by a ring of yellowish, almost burnt, grass in a local pasture. It was some seven metres across with the ring about twenty centimetres in width. The *gendarmerie* reported to SEPRA which called in the experts in soil biology and plant pathology at the agriculture college in Rennes.

SEPRA considered several possible causes. A hoax: someone had produced the circle with a herbicide; the vestige of some ancient construction just beneath the grass; a fungal fairy-ring. The experts drilled and dug a deep trench and took away many samples for analysis, which showed conclusively that a fungus of the type *fusarium* had produced an almost perfect circle – a rare and exceptional phenomenon had been discovered.

On the morning of 7 July 1990, a farmer came upon a slightly different phenomenon. A large shallow crater some fourteen metres across had appeared in the middle of one of his fields. The local *gendarmerie* investigated the same day and informed SEPRA, after ruling out the possibility of a hoax or an act of vandalism. SEPRA thought the crater might have been produced by a meteorite and began its investigation with the help of an expert from the Natural History Museum. The police guarded the site and the work commenced.

The investigators found large lumps of broken chalk, some of it blackened, and fractured flints. Was it a metallic meteorite impact or had something exploded? Then, with the help of a magnetometer they found two pieces of metal a couple of metres down. As the investigators dug deep – down to six metres – they found thirty more fragments of metal, plus fractured flints and traces of soot. Experts at an armaments establishment then confirmed the conclusion that a bomb from the last war had exploded forty-five years late. A study

7. Guadalzhare: 15 March 1992, 4.00 p.m. Julio Orozio Cejz.

8. Tulancingo, Hidalgo: 15 June 1992, 5.00 p.m. Hector Carranza.

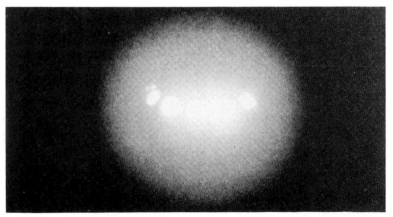

9. By El Mirador Heights near Atlixco, 7 July 1991, 8.00 p.m. Four Judicial Police officers were travelling by car towards Atlixco when this UFO approached them. There was no sound. Photographs were taken before the object moved away towards the mountains near Popocatepetl. The object was about 50 yards away and the lens of the camera has distorted the image. (*Quest Publications*)

Video tape material showing UFOs over Mexico since the solar eclipse at Mexico City in 1991 provides extensive evidence that extraterrestrial craft may be in our environment. A comprehensive scientific analysis of the evidence from the Mexican wave of UFOs has yet to be carried out.

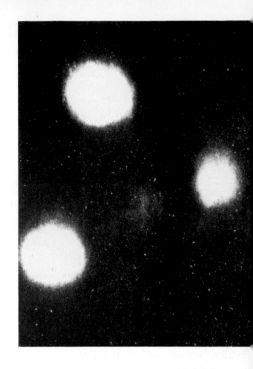

10. A frame from an amateur video, taken on 31 March 1990, showing the three powerful lights at the points of what could be one of the triangular-shaped UFOs frequently observed during the Belgian wave. This frame does not show the triangular shape, but the accompanying photograph, below (11), also taken in March 1990 but at Zagresk in the former Soviet Union, does show what could be an object with the outline of an equilateral triangle. (*Quest Publications*)

12. One of four photographs taken from the Brazilian Navy's *Almirante Saldanha* as it was moored off Trindade Island in the South Atlantic on 16 January 1958. Many members of the crew of about fifty, plus professional photographer Almiro Barauna, were on deck to witness the UFO as it circled the peak of Trindade Island and flew out to sea. Like the Trent photographs (17 and 18), those taken by Barauna provide some of the most credible evidence for the extraterrestrial hypothesis of the UFO phenomena. The enlargement below (13) shows a frequently reported type of saucer-shaped UFO. (*Fortean Picture Library*)

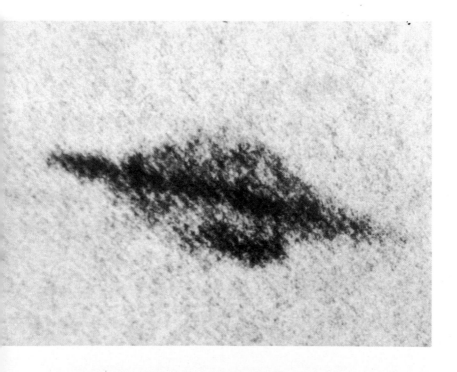

14.  A UFO over Lake Bariloche in southern Argentina – an interesting
photograph taken about 1978 and initially studied by a UFO group in Mendoza.
(© *Dr Richard F. Haines*)

of the fragments later revealed that the bomb had been made in England.

## THE PRIZE-WINNING UFO

The Delphos UFO was literally a prize-winner and received genuine but fragmentary scientific attention over a number of years. From among some thousand reported UFOs, the Delphos UFO won the 1973 $5,000 prize given each year by the newspaper *The National Enquirer* to the UFO case which provides the most baffling scientific mystery. The judging panel were 'completely satisfied that the sighting was real', but unlike the Trans-en-Provence case none of the scientists involved was able to confirm this. It remains a fascinating episode that eventually led nowhere.

The story began on the evening of 2 November 1971, when a highly luminous UFO visited the farm of Durel Johnson, near the Kansas town of Delphos. Mr and Mrs Johnson had just finished supper when their sixteen-year-old son rushed in to say that he had seen a mushroom-like object hovering just above the ground some twenty-five metres away among some trees. The object was about nine feet across and glowed intensely, 'like the light of a welder's arc'. The lad found himself partially blinded and paralysed by the object, but after several minutes the object became brighter at its base and began to move away. He rushed indoors to get his parents. When they arrived they saw the object departing through some trees several hundred yards away. They went to the area above which the object had hovered and found a greyish-white circle about eight feet across marked in the soil. The circle varied from about one to two feet wide and glowed in the evening darkness. They touched the glowing material and it numbed their fingers. Mrs Johnson fetched her Polaroid camera from the house and photographed the luminous circle, and Mr Johnson drove into Delphos to report the event to the local paper. He tried unsuccessfully to get someone to come and look at what the UFO had left behind.

The next day Mr Johnson again went into town. He met Mrs Lester Smith, a local journalist he knew, and she and her husband visited the site. She took soil samples and bits of branches apparently broken by the departing UFO. She noticed that while recent rain had muddied the surrounding soil – and also the soil inside the circle – the circle itself remained completely dry. At the time this physical evidence cried out for professional scientific analysis, but such attention was not provided till much later.

Three policemen, including Sheriff Ralph Enlow, arrived from Delphos the same day – called in by Mrs Smith. They took samples and photographs and found that the greyish-white 'soil' of the circle was present to a depth of fourteen inches. They also noted the dryness of the grey-white soil and found it could not be wetted.

The Primary Investigator from CUFOS (Center for UFO Studies), in Chicago, did not arrive till a month later, by which time the circle was covered in snow. He took samples, interviewed the witnesses and talked with local people. Five weeks later he returned to take more samples and continue his investigations.

In the months which followed, many other ufologists arrived at the farm. Things became so busy that a fence was erected around the circle to protect it. And in May 1973 the Johnsons won the $5,000 from *The National Enquirer*. But it was not until 1989, some eighteen years after the event, that a comprehensive chemical study was published on the soil samples which had been stored in refrigeration.

Several important research establishments and universities had analysed samples from the site and the controls, but none carried out a full-scale program of research which might have produced useful information. Differences were shown to exist between samples from the circle and the controls. But these findings did not point to any one possible cause.

The Oak Ridge National Laboratory found that affected soil contained 5 per cent calcium whereas the controls contained only 1.8 per cent, and 3.8 per cent copper against the maximum copper content of the controls of 1.7 per cent. Other laboratories obtained similar results – and relative differences in other elements Some tests showed the same relative abundance of elements in the circle and in the controls. The scientists pointed out that soil is very variable in its composition, and that this fact had to be taken into account when considering the results of the analyses.

Scientists at the Texas A & M University said that intense microwaves could cause trees and branches to break by rapidly changing the water within them to steam. But no one, apparently, had examined the broken branches at the site for that possibility. (Broken branches have been reported at other prominent UFO events, for example by the United States Air Force patrols in Rendlesham Forest. It has always been assumed that this resulted from the UFO colliding with the branches, but in future it might be worth while checking whether it is freshly dried out wood. Broken branches from living trees normally contain about 50 per cent of their weight as sap.)

All the publicity pleased the Johnsons – they had become

celebrities. Then other reports of sensational UFOs in the early 1970s stole their limelight as interest in the Delphos case declined. This may or may not have affected the Johnsons, but in 1974 the UFO returned to their farm. And to make matters worse, Mr Johnson claimed that his son had not only acquired psychic abilities and was predicting future events but had also met a wolf-girl with wild blond hair in the forest.

No one can claim to have met wolf-girls with blond hair and keep their credibility, although when ufologists initially interviewed the witnesses and examined the reported UFO deposit, there were few people among those involved who did not accept the reality of the visiting UFO. So is this another case of UFO investigators being misled by fantasy-prone people with a strong urge for publicity? The great public interest in UFO phenomena does provide certain psychological types with an on-going opportunity to gain attention and excitement. Given enough time, though, they do tend to gild the lily. For them temporary attention is not enough. They are ready to reinforce the original tale, apparently unaware they are undermining their credibility with each step along this path.

I remember a lady who claimed to be plagued by poltergeists. Things flew from her mantelpiece and chipped the paintwork in her sitting-room. Neighbours took her seriously at first. She then acquired the gift of bending spoons better than Uri Geller, and by laying her hands on invalids began to cure a range of ailments. One old fellow told me he had not danced for seven years because of bad legs, but after a few sessions of hands-on experience he was back in the ballroom. There was some good in all this, of course. Who minds a little lunacy if it does some good? But the next report I had of her was in a national newspaper and on television, where she was giving a long account of how she had met the occupant of a flying saucer. According to her description he was a modern member of the species *Homo sapiens*, from his stylish haircut to his space-age boots. Did she really con the news editor and the television producer, or did they think 'Here's some light relief for the public – no one will take her seriously'? I don't know, but the media allowed a lot of their viewers and readers to be deceived. Even some leading ufologists picked up on the reported details and have included them in their otherwise serious speculations about the nature of the UFO phenomena.

This is not the only case of its kind; it often looks as if the UFO literature is riddled with such nonsense. The only way to avoid this damaging kind of involvement is to concentrate on the evidence.

This is not to say that the apparent quality of the witnesses should he ignored, but that it is only the evidence and the scientific conclusions to be drawn from that evidence that matter. To believe something to be factual because of the apparent genuineness or trustworthiness of witnesses is simply asking for trouble and ridicule. Yet claims for the truth of UFO events are constantly made by leading figures in ufology on the grounds that witnesses are genuine and sincere.

Anyone who cares to read the UFO literature can see how much time and effort ufologists use up in trying to detect hoaxes. Weeks, months, sometimes years of effort go into the task. A rigorous scientific concentration on the evidence and only the evidence would have saved much of that time.

But I suppose we must accept that the occasional dubious witness may be genuine after all. Dr Erol Faruk, who has published the main research paper on the Delphos evidence,[3] takes this view of the Johnsons.

It is pointless to make any judgement on the Delphos case without considering the soil chemistry, which people are still apt to do, unfortunately. My view – coming as it does from an analysis of the ring soil chemistry – is that a simple hoax interpretation is not tenable.

He maintains that if the reports about the Johnsons' later claims are true, then they probably stemmed from an irresistible desire to reproduce the fame and public awareness that their original sighting had created.

The real crux of the matter is *what* caused the ring! The instability of the chemical substance in the ring and its very unusual characteristics make it inconceivable that something was simply poured on the soil, whether by the Johnson family or by anyone else! The alternative explanation that the ring was a fungal fairy-ring is also not acceptable, for the reasons I've already discussed in my original paper. If we start from the position that the Johnson family might conceivably have reported a real event, and then we investigate the soil chemistry to check whether what they described had been possible, we can arrive at a rational view – as I did in my original report. Yes, it could have been possible.

By what he has said, Faruk has expressed precisely what the

scientific approach should be in the investigation of UFO cases. If you accept the witnesses' report, then you should apply the best knowledge and technology that science can provide to search for any evidence that may be present. But there needs to be some organisation in place, as in France, with the necessary resources and time available, so that good cases are investigated immediately and that research is carried out over as short a period as possible. To carry on detective work for years and to publish innumerable arguments about why or why not something happened in the way it happened is a terrible waste of time for both the UFO detectives and those who get caught up in reading their reports.

The mistakes in the Delphos case were made at the beginning, and have led to a vast amount of consideration and speculation that cannot reach any acceptable conclusion. The primary CUFOS investigator arrived a month after the event when snow covered the evidence – not the best conditions for a thorough investigation. He returned later to continue his work, but apparently failed to eliminate the obvious possibility that the circle was a well-established fairy-ring. Had he called in a couple of mycologists at the beginning, they could have established if that were so or not. All future investigations would then have been better based – or not needed at all. And the further army of investigators, scientists and UFO enthusiasts would have been saved countless and pointless speculations on this particular matter. But as things turned out there is nothing conclusive to report after a vast amount of work, including considerable professional scientific analyses of the samples. We cannot even say definitely that something unknown landed on the Johnsons' farm. At least that can be said from SEPRA's scientific analyses of the landing site in Trans-en-Provence. The Delphos UFO looks like another good opportunity wasted.

## FOSSILS AND UFOs
Working on reported landing sites could be a bit like field work in palaeontology. Fossils of a new species are discovered and all the available information is extracted from the site and its fossils. A picture of the species begins to emerge. Then more sites and fossils are found and studied and a more complete picture is built up. Palaeontologists have thus gained an understanding of many vanished species, their ecosystems and ways of life, simply by the scientific study of numerous sites over the years. Future progress is assumed but no one can say when or where the next site will be discovered. Likewise, no one can say when the next credible UFO landing will he reported. But one does need experts ready to go and

investigate the next site. One cannot hope to build up a picture of the phenomenon of UFO landings from a few incomplete investigations. Adequately supported scientists need to see each new landing site as another opportunity to gain a better understanding of the 'species UFO'.

Teams of five might do the work: a physicist, an analytical chemist, a biochemist, a microbiologist and a co-ordinator who could call on outside help when necessary – like the French system. It might not take long to gather samples and make measurements, but the laboratory work and report writing would be time-consuming. Even so, the people involved need only be part-timers.

Filters would be needed in the form of skilled interviewers and psychologists to evaluate reports. Few would justify calling out a scientific team. With this kind of set-up, with teams in different parts of the world collaborating with each other, we might, after several years, make progress at a scientific level. Such a wide-ranging research program would cost no more than astronomical SETI, which itself is a very low-cost enterprise. And it would definitely produce information that would be more valuable than its cost. The least we could expect would be an improvement in our psychological and sociological understanding, plus greater insights into some currently unexplored and unknown areas of physics. The Hessdalen Project clearly confirms this point. On the other hand, we might discover far more than most scientists would anticipate.

# CHAPTER 7
## *The Aliens Who Fell to Earth*

The Majestic-12 document was supposed to be a top secret briefing of eight pages prepared for President-elect Eisenhower in November 1952. It reports two saucer crashes in the United States, in 1947 and 1950, and the recovery of wreckage and the bodies of four alien beings from 'a remote region of New Mexico located approximately seventy-five miles northwest of Roswell Army Air Base [now Walker Field]'. The four aliens, judging from where their bodies were found, had ejected from the saucer two miles before the crash.
  The document states:

All four were dead and badly decomposed due to action by predators and exposure to the elements during the approximately one-week time period which had elapsed before their discovery. A special scientific team took charge of removing these bodies for study.

The document also reports that the remains of another crashed saucer was recovered:

On 6 December 1950, a second object probably of similar origin, impacted the earth at high speed in the El Indio Guerrero area of the Texas–Mexican border after following a long trajectory through the atmosphere. By the time a search team arrived, what remained of the object had been almost totally incinerated. Such material as could be recovered was transported to the A.E.C. facility at Sandia, New Mexico, for study.

No alien bodies associated with this saucer crash were reported.

93

The events near Roswell had already been reported and investigated long before the Majestic-12 document made its appearance. The story began on 2 July 1947, when a rancher named William Brazel discovered pieces of wreckage scattered over his land. He assumed it was from a plane and didn't contact the authorities until 6 July when he went into town and rang the sheriff who in turn phoned the Air Force. This brought Major Jesse Marcel from the Roswell Army Air Force Base about seventy-five miles from the Brazel ranch. Some years after retiring as a lieutenant-colonel, Marcel described what he found:

> There was all kinds of stuff – small beams about three-eighths or a half-inch square with some sort of hieroglyphics on them that nobody could decipher. They looked something like balsa wood, and were of about the same weight, except they were not wood at all. They were very hard, although flexible, and would not burn.

His son, now a surgeon, is able to confirm the strange nature of the wreckage because Major Marcel, after loading his vehicle with some of the wreckage, drove to his home where he kept it overnight, it being too late to return to base.

The next morning Marcel reported to his base to find that a press statement had been issued:

> The many rumors regarding the flying discs became a reality yesterday when the intelligence office of the 509th Bomb Group of the Eighth Air Force was fortunate enough to gain possession of a disc...

All the wreckage was collected and sent by air to what is now the Wright Patterson Air Force Base, Ohio, where the Foreign Technology Division was established. (The Roswell Army Air Force Base was part of the Strategic Air Command and not an establishment where technical research could have been carried out.)

The press statement was soon contradicted by another from the base commander, Colonel William H. Blanchard, who later became a four-star general. It stated that the wreckage came from a weather balloon. A press conference was called and pieces of a balloon produced for examination. But Marcel said later that he was sufficiently familiar with weather balloons to know that the wreckage definitely did not come from one. Over the years ufologists have investigated the Roswell incident and have found many witnesses, both inside and outside the military, who have confirmed the unearthly nature of the wreckage. Some witnesses have also confirmed the existence of the four dead aliens, though no one has been able to provide any biologically interesting details.

But on 8 September 1994, after UFO investigators had been working on the case for almost five decades, it was officially announced that the statement about the weather balloon was a cover story. What had really crashed was a top-secret spy balloon, a Project Mogul balloon, which carried electronic equipment to detect the testing of nuclear weapons in the then Soviet Union. This seems a likely explanation: a weather balloon story instead of the truth about a crashed spy balloon, an easy substitution – one balloon for another, so to speak. Bearing in mind the political climate of the time, one can appreciate the military's measures to keep the truth secret and to gather up every scrap of this then new military technology. The extent of these measures to ensure secrecy has been used by UFO investigators to support their belief that the government had collected and hidden away all the remains of a crashed saucer. However, according to a study and report by the Fund for UFO Research, a crashed Mogul balloon could not account for the evidence recorded.

## MJ-12 DOCUMENT
The MJ-12 briefing document came to the public's attention after two copies were received in the post in December 1984 by Bill Moore and Jaime Shandera, two prominent American investigators of the Roswell incident. The copies were on an unprocessed 35mm film and there was no return address on the package. Stanton Friedman, a nuclear physicist who had been investigating the Roswell incident for some years and was a colleague of Moore and Shandera, was called in. An investigation then began to check the authenticity of the MJ-12 briefing. Friedman went on to carry out a five-year investigation of the Roswell incident, supported by the Fund for UFO Research in the United States and published in 1991.

## FRIEDMAN'S REPORT
Friedman admits to the possibility that the MJ-12 papers may be a hoax, but says that

> Almost certainly there was a recovery of a crashed flying saucer
> ... recovered with alien bodies outside Roswell, New Mexico,
> in July 1947. By the time of the publication of *The Roswell*

*Incident* [a book published in 1980], Bill Moore and I had located sixty persons connected to the event. By the time of publication of Bill's update, our total had risen to ninety-two. As of 1 May 1990, the grand total of persons contacted in one way or another about Roswell is well over 160.

One can admire the persistence of the investigators, but one would want to know how many of the 160 persons interviewed were scientists who had worked on the recovered saucer and alien bodies? The answer to that question is apparently none. Talking to local inhabitants anywhere will produce strange stories – my village has its own 'well-documented' ghost – because a local mythology can easily be created. The only people who could confirm anything in a reliable way would be some of the hundreds of scientists who would have studied the recovered materials and bodies, if such were ever recovered. But no one has discovered any evidence that such people and their research reports exist, which seems odd considering how many scientists, technologists and administrators would have been involved. How could one keep such activity a secret? It would be like trying to hide the Apollo Moon Program.

## WHAT'S THE ANSWER?
It seems odd that the investigations have been left to curious journalists or interested amateurs and that no one apparently has considered the science implied in the MJ-12 document to see if it rings true.

A very small point first, which may not be significant. I hesitate to mention it, but I will do so. In the MJ-12 document *Homo sapiens* is written *homo sapiens*. Biologists would not write it like that because *Homo* is the generic name in the Linnaean system of classification and has to have a capital letter, followed by the specific name, *sapiens*, with a lower-case letter. It looks as if no biologist checked the papers after they were typed and before they were sent to President Eisenhower, yet biologists would have been intimately involved and two biologists were on the MJ-12 Committee, according to the MJ-12 document.

There is a far more important consideration. After comments on the study of the craft itself the document goes on to say:

A similar analysis of the four dead occupants was arranged by Dr Bronk. It was the tentative conclusion of this group [30 November 1947] that although these creatures are human-like in appearance, the biological and evolutionary processes

96

responsible for their development have apparently been quite different from those observed or postulated in *homo sapiens*.

This is the kind of thing which clever hoaxers unfamiliar with evolutionary biology might say. Although there are plenty of examples of convergent evolution in land vertebrates during, say, the past 200 million years, there is not one that shows the level of convergence implied by the description of the humanoid aliens in the MJ-12 document. And what is more, the examples of convergence that we know about took place here within one biology in organisms that had a large part of their genetic endowment in common.

Even if we disregard the improbability of convergent evolution on two separate planets producing similar humanoids at any time in their planetary histories, there is also the time factor to consider. Vertebrate evolution has progressed on Earth for about 450 million years, though, according to the SETI rationale, advanced life has been possible in the Galaxy for the past eight billion years. By comparison, the earliest intelligent humanoids (primitive pre-humans) appeared only about three million years ago. One can therefore see that two planetary biologies producing similar humanoids at about the same time in the long history of the Galaxy is extremely remote. There are reasons, when we consider the evolution of structures and functions, for thinking that technological creatures might have a form roughly similar to our own, but they would not be 'human-like in appearance', as the document states, and their evolution would be very unlikely to coincide with our own.

The MJ-12 document raises another biological objection. The document states that during the recovery operation

> aerial reconnaissance discovered that four small human-like beings had apparently ejected from the craft at some point before it exploded. These had fallen to earth about two miles east of the wreckage site. All four were dead and badly decomposed due to action by predators and exposure to the elements during the approximately one-week time period which had elapsed before their discovery. A special scientific team took charge of removing these bodies for study. (See Attachment 'C'.)

This 'attachment' would be the most interesting document in the history of science, if it existed.

A scientific report on an alien biology would be formidable in its detail, bringing in as it would all the highly technical disciplines of today's life sciences. With all the undreamt-of possibilities for research that this rarest of materials would offer, Attachment 'C' would have blossomed into a vast library of biological reports. The same can be said for the other attachments mentioned on the physical sciences and technology.

The physical scientists and technologists might have a problem coming to grips with a technology that was thousands of years in advance of our own and based on science that we are still hundreds of years from discovering. But the biologists would have had their best time in science. They would have written volumes on the anatomy, physiology, histology, biochemistry, molecular biology and genetics of the four ufonauts. Those alien bodies would have been even more valuable in recent years than they were in 1952 when the MJ-12 document was supposed to have been written. Today the equipment and techniques of biology could provide fine detailed information down to a molecular level, if given access to an alien biology. And the research papers that would have come from all sources could not be faked – and they could not be hidden. Too many enthusiastic scientists would be involved. The biologists would have been sitting on the greatest discoveries ever in the life sciences. Some of them would have been certain to have disclosed information to their colleagues.

## NEVER EAT AN ALIEN
Another statement in the document that does not ring true is that predators had partially eaten the alien bodies. This seems unlikely but is something someone with little knowledge of biology might have put in, thinking it would happen, as it would of course with any terrestrial pilots who died on baling out in sufficiently wild country.

The science-fiction subject of alien lifeforms eating us on Earth, or of those space voyagers who land on an alien planet and proceed to eat a hearty meal provided by the inhabitants, is central to the whole subject of interstellar travel and visitors from other worlds. It has apparently never crossed the minds of film directors that this sort of activity would be impossible in alien-human contact. Carbon and water-based life could be universal and the only 'life' phenomenon. But there are going to be chemical differences substantial enough to make an alien a very unsuitable meal for predators on this planet, and vice versa. Predators are unlikely to eat unsuitable food produced on this planet, and are even less likely to eat an alien.

And just imagine the billions of alien microbes being freed into our environment as those alien bodies decayed – probably by the

98

activity of microbes inside them rather than from the microbes in our atmosphere. Those alien bodies, if they had existed, might have posed the greatest threat to our health in medical history.

## LIBRARY OF SECRETS

One cannot imagine that government scientists and academic scientists associated with government, would let the greatest opportunity in the history of science pass without pursuing major research programs. Their research reports would have filled one of the most important libraries of all time.

Though numerous people familiar with government documents could have forged the eight pages of the MJ-12 document, no one – not even our best scientists – could have forged the research attachments mentioned, but conveniently absent. No one could dream up the sort of biological surprises that we would surely encounter in any scientific examination of extraterrestrial corpses. No one would have the imagination to make such a report convincing. The same could be said for the reports from the physical scientists and the engineers.

So the clever and time-consuming detective work on the form of the document, on the history and personal relationships of the people mentioned, on the government language and the official stamps used, on signatures, and on the typewriters used has been expended on a very superficial document, though the investigations have been far from superficial. One wonders about the wisdom of long arguments, with no agreements, about a document which seems rather naïve when considered against the relevant scientific background.

One other fact indicates a hoax. When the document was received by the ufologists, all twelve members of the committee were dead. The last one had died a few months earlier. That looks too convenient to be a coincidence, although Stanton Friedman does say that

> It is of considerable interest that the last survivor of MJ-12 was Dr Jerome Hunsaker, who died on 10 September 1984, just three months before the document was received. If anybody was paying attention to when these people would no longer be available for questioning, he would have been waiting for Hunsaker's death.

Yet would the most important controlling committee in human history be allowed to die out? Surely its deceased members would have been replaced, since research would have to go on? Stanton Friedman himself points to the need for long-term research: 'Clearly the determination of the means of propulsion for the crashed saucer was a project that might require decades or centuries.' That would undoubtedly be so. Therefore a controlling committee would continue to exist and hundreds of scientists and administrators would be involved. The problems of how the saucer worked could not have been discovered otherwise.

## FILMING THE ALIENS

In March 1995, broadcasting stations around the world announced that the British UFO Research Association [BUFORA] had access to a film, reportedly taken in 1947, of autopsies being performed on the dead aliens from the Roswell incident. The aliens might be dead but the media was alive to a good story. The Director of Investigations for BUFORA, Philip Mantle, became quite hoarse after a few days of interviews. One satellite television company sent his interview around the world. But BUFORA was not going to accept the film as genuine without indisputable proof.

The story behind the film seemed somewhat vague. Ray Santilli, a businessman who runs a publishing and video company in London, was in America when he was contacted by a retired cameraman living in Ohio. The cameraman explained that he wished to raise some money by selling a film he had taken at Roswell in 1947 while working for the American government. He had filmed scientists carrying out detailed autopsies on the alien bodies. Santilli bought the film and brought it back to London where he contacted BUFORA.

Some people began to think that the film, if genuine, could provide acceptable evidence that aliens did crash at Roswell in 1947. With a sample of the film in their hands, the first step for BUFORA and Philip Mantle was to establish whether it was 1947 stock. That would not make it genuine, but it would be progress. The first question to be asked was whether the film could be dated by the manufacturer's batch number. Also, the contrast range of black and white film has changed since 1947, so some idea of a film's age might be reached from that. And a microscopic examination of the layers within the film might provide information with which to date it. But so far the film has not been dated.

About forty minutes of the film was shown to an invited audience, though Santilli said he had more footage in about fourteen canisters. It was obvious before the film was shown that the scientists doing the work on the alien bodies would not be 'dressed for the period'.

Working on an alien biology would be about as potentially dangerous for the individual as handling plutonium. Scientists, even in
1947, would have been fully aware that alien bodies could be a
biological minefield of disasters and would therefore have been
suitably protected. But hoaxers and film makers might not appreciate this, especially if the film had been made some years ago. They
might have put their 'actors' in neat white laboratory coats.

As it turned out, those in the film doing the autopsies were
dressed as if they were handling plutonium in a nuclear power plant.
Only the people viewing the autopsies from behind a window were
not completely protected. And on the wall the sign 'Danger' was
prominently displayed.

The dead aliens were of the classic type: small, slimly-built
humanoids with no hair, large eyes, tiny noses and mouth. And they
had six slender digits on hands and feet. The skull of one alien was
opened and a protective membrane over the brain removed. The
brain was a surprise. 'It looked smooth, more like a liver than a
brain,' said Mantle. 'It was not highly convoluted like our brain.'
There was no evidence of genitals and the large eyes were covered
by a black membrane.

So the film seems to be more interesting than one would have
expected. What makes one doubt its authenticity more than anything is that the aliens are so close in their bodily proportions to
ourselves. That two such similar creatures could have evolved at
about the same time in the billions of years of galactic history seems
very unlikely.

It is not impossible, I suppose, but even if the film is genuine
(which seems very unlikely) it is not going to provide conclusive
proof of the extraterrestrial hypothesis. A film would not be the
appropriate medium through which to document an alien biology. It
could not contain the necessary information to convince the science
community that the United States government had extraterrestrial
bodies in its possession. One would need high-definition photography and micro-photography, not a film, to record the scientific
aspects of an alien biology.

It cannot be emphasised enough that it would be impossible to
fake the details of an alien biology. An anatomist might manage to
fool us with the bones of the skeleton, but other anatomists would
probably come along and show that the skeleton was not credible
for various reasons. But it would be the biological data, especially
the microscopic details and those revealed by modern laboratory
techniques, that would be overwhelmingly important in any evidence: the cell types and range of structures within cells, the

101

structures of protein molecules, the range of amino acids from which the proteins were formed, the genetic mechanisms at a molecular level, and so on. All this information would have to fit together biologically. And there would almost certainly be biological surprises that no one could invent. If an alien body was ever studied, we would in time be able to see how the functions of all its parts would produce a viable creature. And through such research we would probably get an idea about how it evolved on its home planet.

# CHAPTER 8
## What's Wrong with Flying Saucery?

Allen Hynek, a professional astronomer who, until his death at the age of seventy-six in 1986, was considered the leading authority on UFOs, wrote in *The Hynek UFO Report*, published in 1977:

> It is very important to remember that the *raw material* for the study of the UFO phenomenon are not the UFOs themselves but the *reports* [his italics] of UFOs. These reports include the total circumstances surrounding each case and the calibre and reputations of the witnesses – information that will allow us to make a logical and rational judgement about the nature of the UFO phenomenon, if such judgement is at all possible.

This approach to a possible solution to the UFO problem has predominated with competent UFO investigators. The problem is that this is the method used by detectives and investigative journalists trying to analyse and explain a mystery. In science the status of witnesses is not enough. What they have witnessed has to be backed up by analyses of physical evidence. We can see that this is so from the Rendlesham case where some of the most reliable people one can imagine were involved. Given detailed scientific analyses of the physical evidence and video recordings of the events witnessed, it would be very difficult to deny that ET had landed in Rendlesham Forest. (The scientific and photographic evidence may exist, of course, but the public has no access to it yet.)

Most ufologists are spare-time investigators without enough spare time and hardly any resources, trying to do a job that would tax the best brains in science. Good intentions and sincerity, however, are not enough – in fact they have been counterproductive in ufology. In about four decades the subject has been brought into disrepute because of reports and conclusions that should never have been published.

## IN PRAISE OF SCEPTICS

One often meets the word 'sceptics' in UFO literature. It is almost used as a term of abuse, a sort of defence reaction against any attack upon an almost religiously held set of beliefs. That is not the scientific approach. Science is marked by a high level of scepticism. That is its strength. It will not take anything on board unless it passes all the available tests. Thus a data base in any scientific discipline is reliable, one can work with it. Ufologists, if they want serious scientific attention, should therefore welcome a high level of scepticism and intellectual rigour. Some already do, but many do not.

No reasonable person wants to attack scepticism. The more scepticism we have in this world the better. But sceptics have to be adequately informed for their scepticism to be of any value. Mike Hutchinson, a British representative of the *Skeptical Inquirer*, a trans-atlantic journal, once said to me: 'Those people who claim that certain aspects of the UFO phenomena could indicate an extra-terrestrial presence have not been able to provide any proof.' That is true. It is a point frequently repeated. Yet no one can expect to obtain proof without an appropriate research effort and this has not been made. The scientists involved in astronomical SETI have yet to provide any proof, although they have been engaged in numerous research projects for more than three decades. The scientists in astronomical SETI will tell you that they have barely begun to make a comprehensive search. If a comparable scientific effort had gone into testing the ETH of ufology and had failed to find some confirmation of the hypothesis, then it might be reasonable to say that they have failed to provide proof. But with almost no professional scientific effort to find evidence it is not surprising that none has been discovered.

What sort of evidence would convince the scientific community that the ETH had to be taken seriously? It would include any biology or technology which could have an extraterrestrial origin. For instance, evidence which forms significant patterns: consistent chemical traces or physical or biological effects associated with sites of reported landings, provided they were indisputably linked to the landing events. Or photographs which could be shown without a doubt to be genuine. This may not be possible with still photography, but video tapes provide a moving image which is more easily verified. Several tapes of the same UFO taken by different witnesses would provide good evidence. Mere lights without structures could be natural phenomena or a man-made artifact, such as a balloon. Spectra from UFO lights that stay around long enough, such as those at Hessdalen, should also carry useful information.

Detailed reports from the biological analyses of dead aliens, which are claimed to exist, could not be made up. Data from anatomical examinations, cellular details and structures at the molecular level, biological information which could fill a small library, would convince biologists. But we don't want the '4 fingers instead of 5 digits' nonsense which could be imagined by most directors of science fiction films.

So far, all claims of alien artifacts have failed to deliver the goods. Odd bits and pieces that witnesses said fell from flying saucers have always had an Earthly origin. And ET apparently only takes perfectly honest people on board his flying saucers because nobody ever steals anything. The fact that no one can produce just one extraterrestrial artifact looks bad for the credibility of hundreds of folk who claim to have been aboard saucers. The normal temptation to take some evidence of time spent in a flying saucer would be irresistible. Personally, given access to a saucer, *I* would have no hesitation in pinching ET's family silver!

## MISLEADING CASES

Ufologists complain that certain cases, which have been discredited, are still being published because at one time they were interesting. That they existed at all was often due to the over-enthusiastic field investigators and the readiness of the press to pounce on a good story.

One case which was initially considered exemplary and figured prominently in the literature of ufology began in January 1970 at Imjarvi in southern Finland. Two men in their thirties, Aarno Heinonen and Esko Viljo, were skiing. It was sunset, the stars were beginning to come out and it was very cold. As they paused for a moment they saw a brilliant light heading across the sky. They watched it make a wide sweep and descend in their direction. They could hear a buzzing and see a red-grey mist surrounding something. At a height of about fifteen metres it showed itself as a metallic craft, something like an inverted basin, flat at the bottom and about three metres across.

Heinonen reported: 'The round craft hovered a while completely motionless above us while the buzzing could still be heard.' It began to descend until it was so close they could almost touch it. It stopped about four metres above the snow. From a large tube at the centre of the craft a brilliant beam of light hit the snow. Heinonen continued:

I think I took a step backwards, and in the same second I caught sight of the creature. It was standing in the middle of the light beam with a black box in its hands. Out of a round opening in the box there came a yellow light, pulsating. The creature was about ninety centimetres tall with very thin arms and legs. Its face was pale like wax. I didn't notice the eyes, but the nose was very strange. It was a hook rather than a nose. The ears were very small and narrowed towards the head. The creature wore some kind of overall in a light green material. On its feet were boots of a darker green colour, which stretched above the knees. There were also white gauntlets going up to the elbows, and the fingers were bent like claws around the black box.

(Note that the creature has the characteristics of a humanoid, plus human-like clothing.)
Viljo said:

The creature stood in the middle of the bright light and was luminous like phosphorus, but its face was very pale. Its shoulders were very thin and slanting, with thin arms like a child's. I did not think of the clothes, only noticing that they were greenish in colour. On its head was a conical helmet shining like metal. The creature was less than a metre tall.

Heinonen was then hit by a pulsating beam from the black box in the creature's hands. He said:

The pulsating light was very bright, almost blinding. It was very quiet in the forest. Suddenly a red-grey mist came flowing down from the object and large sparks started to fly from the illuminated circle of snow. The sparks were like tapers about ten centimetres long, red, green and violet. They floated out in long curves, rather slowly; many of them hit me, but although I expected them to burn me, I did not feel anything.

Viljo confirmed this scene:

The sparks were shining in several colours. It was very beautiful. At the same time the red mist became thicker and hid the creature. Suddenly it was so dense that I could not see Aarno even though I knew he was standing only a few metres away from me ... The beam melted, it flew up like a flickering flame and was sucked into the gap in the craft. After that it was as if the fog curtain was torn to pieces. The air above us was empty.

At that point Heinonen realised he couldn't use his right leg which was 'stiff and aching'. But Viljo helped him home, a journey of some three kilometres. Heinonen became ill, as if, according to the doctor, he was suffering radiation sickness. 'Unfortunately I had no instrument to measure that,' said the doctor.

Professor Matti Tuuri, a physicist at Helsinki University, became interested in the report. He said: 'If the radiation penetrated Heinonen's clothing, it must have been a short-wave radiation such as X-rays; and overdoses of these would cause symptoms such as those he reported.' But soil, snow and vegetation from the reported site were tested for radiation and found to radiate no more than normal background levels.

The fine detail described by the witnesses led a lot of people to accept the report as genuine, but some time later the case fell apart when Heinonen claimed to have seen a UFO on twenty-three other occasions. He also began to have meetings with a beautiful saucer-naut with long golden hair and blue eyes. She spoke fluent Finnish and admitted to being 180 years old, but looked twenty. Yet despite her age, and having crossed interstellar space, she had nothing new or important to say. Or, if she did, she did not say it to Heinonen, which may show that one cannot trust a woman of 180 who looks twenty. Or is it that you cannot trust someone who sees too many flying saucers?

This pattern of events is not untypical. Some of the major UFO cases have ended when the witnesses showed themselves addicted to fairyland. The initial detail reported, and the apparent initial sincerity of the witnesses, attract serious interest. The cases are superficially investigated by a few scientists – usually nothing very thorough because they are just called in once or twice to carry out tests and state their findings – enough to give a case an unjustified scientific stamp of approval which is then widely publicised. A few unguarded remarks by scientists during a coffee break get reported as 'scientists conclude that . . .'. Readers begin to think that ET's arrival has received official confirmation. Then, later, the witness, or witnesses, have further UFO experiences which discredit the earlier reports that appeared credible. In one well-known instance, publicised worldwide in books and magazines and accepted as a classic case by ufology, the main witness later began seeing saucers most times when she left her house. Such cases remain interesting for psychologists and sociologists, but need to be given a wide berth by anyone looking for data to test the ETH.

Ufologists have only themselves to blame for this mess. They should follow the practice of good scientists and not rush into print before they are sure of their facts. If they do (and they do much of the time) and are later proved wrong (as they are much of the time), they should not complain when people, especially scientists, do not take them seriously.

## TOO MANY REPORTS

Allen Hynek once complained about the sheer quantity of UFO reports:

A few good sightings a year, over the world, would bolster the extraterrestrial hypothesis – but many thousands every year? From remote regions of space? And to what purpose? To scare us by stopping cars and disturbing animals, and puzzling us with their seemingly pointless antics? It really becomes embarrassing when we try to present this aspect of our riches to the public, to science, and if we are really honest, to ourselves also.

Hynek has not been the only leading ufologist to express unease at the large number of UFO reports. But should the 'riches' cause unease? First, the vast majority of reports offer no physical reality which can be investigated. Thus to support the extraterrestrial hypothesis we do need a large number of reports, if we accept that only 1 per cent of them may describe extraterrestrial artifacts. The world is a large place to study and there could be numerous saucers at work at any one time; and a large number of reports gives us plenty of choice about what should be studied.

And extraterrestrial antics? Could they be more informative than embarrassing to those supporting the ETH? If powerful electro-magnetic fields are associated with the saucer propulsion system, the cars that they study are stopped incidentally. What happens results as much from our system of propulsion as theirs. (According to reports, UFOs don't stop diesels.) And could the uncanny manoeu-vrings of saucers in flight be a demonstration of superior technology or just putting on a show for the natives, rather like entertaining our cat or dog with a piece of human technology? Such behaviour might explain a proportion of those puzzling corn circles which are not formed by hoaxers or atmospheric vortices, if they are formed by rotating beams of energy directed at our cornfields, as some investigators suggest. Fields of ripe corn would provide a lovely environment for such extraterrestrial entertainment.

# CHAPTER 9

## *Contactee Communications and Biological Reality*

$M$any grand messages for humankind have come from UFO contactees and abductees. The stories they tell seem suspiciously facile, as if limited to what they themselves might know. Yet their fantasies (and we assume they are fantasies in the absence of acceptable proof to the contrary) raise questions about brains and intelligence in different species which are directly relevant to any contemplation of possible contact with extraterrestrials. This line of thinking calls into question our intellectual standing in the universe, which may be why it has been rather neglected. What space-age adventurer of fiction has ever doubted his intellectual status when socialising with the inhabitants of other worlds?

Biologists and psychologists have been trying to communicate with the chimpanzee and the bottle-nosed dolphin for years. Some communication takes place, but these most intelligent of our fellow mammals cannot bridge the gap between us, even though the brain of a chimpanzee is the closest in anatomy to our brain and the chimps are our nearest relatives (primates) not some unearthly creature with a totally different anatomy both inside and out.

According to modern genetics applied to evolution, the lines of human and chimp evolution go back only six or seven million years to a common ancestral group which would have possessed nothing better than chimp-sized brains. That is a very short time in evolutionary terms for such a great advance in brain development to have taken place. But although it is a great advance, outward appearances do magnify it. At a genetic level we have not changed that much from our ancestors of seven million years ago. Of the 1,500 genetic features now visible on the chromosomes of chimps and ourselves, fewer than a dozen show any differences.

Unlike the chimp's brain, dolphin brains (and the big brains of all the whale group) owe a lot to having evolved in the sea where their ancestors, which as land animals were rather like primitive bears, evolved extra brain capacity to 'see' by sound waves. But this development does show that the potential for big-brain evolution exists in very different animals. We would have to go back to the days of the dinosaurs to look for a common ancestor for chimps and dolphins. At that time none of the mammals was larger than a domestic cat.

Dolphins and whales have beautiful brains, showing an impressively convoluted cortex, the brain's top layer and most advanced component. And in the case of the bottle-nosed dolphin the brain is 25 per cent more massive than our own, though the body weight which the brain must control is greater. Dissected from its skull, the dolphin brain looks more advanced than a human brain, yet we have been unable to communicate with that brain at any higher level than we are able to communicate with an intelligent dog. We may imagine there is more intelligence in the dolphin than in any dog, but we are barred from any meaningful communication by the different nature of its brain and sensory system. We do not have this problem with the chimp and more progress has been made. But the researchers are dealing with a lower order of capacity than that possessed by us, and chimps are never going to share our understanding of the universe. We can only communicate at a simple level and this is generally only done with rewards of food.

It is a sad fact that the two most intelligent animals on the planet, after humans, have to be given food to persuade them to interact with us: in artificial set-ups, chimps and dolphins co-operate with us in order to eat. Though they are intelligent mammals and we are intelligent mammals, all of the same evolutionary group, we have not learnt anything about their inner thoughts and they can know nothing of ours.

Whether or not in future we will be able to improve our relations with the brightest of our fellow mammals remains to be seen. The point is that this situation puts communications with ETs into perspective. The gaps between ourselves and other intelligent mammals may be small compared to those which could exist between ourselves and any ETs, whether they might be broadcasting across the light-years or here studying us from flying saucers. We have to allow for the nature of evolution and the great periods of time involved in its processes, which may mean that our nearest ETs could be millions of years ahead of us and less able to communicate with us than we are with a chimp or dolphin. This shows up the reported conversations with the occupants of UFOs, who claim to have come from distant stellar systems, for the fantasies that they are.

Looking at the problem statistically, it is almost impossible for other technological species postulated by the ETH to be anything but considerably more advanced than ourselves, especially if they have crossed interstellar space to visit the Solar System. They would have been in the interstellar spaceflight business for millennia, at least. And they would probably have improved themselves biologically as well. We are already beginning to see what intellectual improvements future biological techniques could make to our species.

This prompts a sobering thought for all those who have accepted contactee stories as genuine. At best we may be able to detect an ETI presence, if there is one. And this should be the target for SETI. Communication, as we communicate with each other, seems a very unlikely possibility, unless humans were somehow incorporated long ago as assistants into an 'Earth monitoring program'. Humans are easily brainwashed, as we know to our cost. It might therefore be easy to train them for that purpose. This idea is bordering on science fiction, if not already in its mainstream, but it is more acceptable, biologically speaking, than that the humanoid occupants of flying saucers are biological aliens with a commanding grasp of modern languages.

## *ALIEN ACCENTS*

One unacceptable aspect of UFO literature is found in reports of ETIs having cosy conversations with witnesses in which the ETIs explain that they have come from another planetary system, sometimes even another galaxy – which seems a long way to come to tell us what we already know. In one abduction case, which has provoked a library of books, the captain of the spacecraft told the abductee that he had come from a planet orbiting a star some fifty light-years away, yet he was described as being a *Homo sapiens* with a good command of English. This is utter nonsense, yet thousands of people have taken the case seriously.

The evolution of the anatomical structures that make human speech possible was part of the general evolution of humankind, which depended on a fortunate series of events happening at the right time. It is unlikely that that series of events is going to be duplicated elsewhere, so that nothing identical to human speech and conversation is going to be produced by any extraterrestrial. You

111

may at this point think about parrots and a wide range of other birds which can convincingly mimic a variety of sounds in their environments. Starlings, for example, mimic seagulls and even the sound of telephone wires in the wind. Numerous species mimic the calls of birds of other species. And some birds are able to mimic the human voice. These birds possess a 'voice' mechanism which enables them to mimic, and they use this ability for various biological purposes, depending on the way of life of the particular species. Some of these birds can mimic complete sentences – but they cannot carry on a conversation.

I do not therefore envisage future dialogues with the 'parrot people' from Planet-X. There may be lifeforms on other worlds with a great capacity for mimicry, but it does not seem likely that they would be able to carry on a fluent conversation in a human language.

Other beings with civilisations and technologies would have to have language, but the sounds they made would depend on their biologies, like the sounds of a dolphin depend on dolphin biology.

Professional psychologists have shown that the people who report contacts and abductions are not Mr and Mrs Average, psychologically speaking. Something like 4 per cent of the population in the United States appear to have 'encounter-prone personalities'. Some psychologists have suggested that anomalous experiences in adulthood may result from psychologically conditioning experiences during childhood. Even in the best UFO journals one finds emotionally charged arguments for and against the validity of abductions and close encounters of the fourth kind with chatty ETs. Those who believe that more than psychological factors are involved in this relatively recent phenomenon have the onus upon them to provide proof, since if they cannot do so then psychological causes provide a scientifically acceptable explanation, at least provisionally.

## ILLUSIONS AND HOAXES

Are all contactee and abductee reports psychological illusions or hoaxes? Apart from the reasons we have for not expecting any alien to possess the ability to speak a human language with natural fluency, the most surprising fact is that no contactee or abductee ever receives data of scientific interest – facts we don't already possess. One would assume that an intelligent human, finding himself or herself inside a flying saucer or space colony, would collect at least one small item of alien technology which could convince the world. But no one has. Their reports could have been produced from what they already know, including those items of information which can have a scientific interpretation. The point to be emphasised is that information as such, no matter how strange it may be, does not prove anything. What contactees and abductees need to tell us to confirm their stories is something new. If any of us went back in time, just a couple of hundred years, we could provide simple information about life and the universe which the people of that time would not know but which they could confirm as correct. Beings from other worlds would be in the same position, although they would certainly be more than a couple of hundred years ahead of us. Has any contactee or abductee provided such testable information? The answer is 'no', although I would be more than interested to be proved wrong.

## ALIEN SEDUCTIONS

The impossibility of human beings coming here from other worlds, or even creatures who could be mistaken for human beings, needs to be considered by those authors of UFO books who repeat the so-called classic cases with no scientific comment. One of these involved Antonio Villas Boas, a Brazilian farmer, in his early twenties in 1957 when he was captured by aliens. This is an old chestnut that needs roasting.

It was October and Antonio was catching up on farm work by ploughing the family's fields at night. Suddenly a bright ball of light entered the field he was ploughing. He chased it around for a while before it departed. The following night, as he ploughed, he was visited by a far more brilliant light which turned out to be an egg-shaped spacecraft which landed near him. Figures emerged from the craft. Antonio started to run. He was grabbed by a small creature but pushed it aside. Then three of them overpowered him and pulled him struggling up a ladder and into the spacecraft.

He was dragged into a room where the aliens inspected him. All five wore tightly fitting grey suits and helmets and tubes ran from their helmets into their clothing. All Antonio could see were their small blue eyes. They forcibly pulled off his clothes and smeared a clear liquid over his skin. Then they put him into a smaller room where he was left alone. As he sat on a sort of couch, puffs of smoke came from small pipes in the room. The smoke made him feel sick and he vomited in a corner.

Half an hour later a naked woman entered. According to Antonio she had all the attributes of a beautiful *Homo sapiens*, although he seemed to think she was an alien. He believed that the smoke which made him sick enabled her to breathe without a helmet. He described her as having blond hair and fair skin, blue eyes and high

113

cheekbones, small mouth, ears and nose. She also had freckles on her arms (which one would not expect to see on an extraterrestrial).

She hugged him. He hugged her. She became amorous. He became amorous – even though a prisoner who had just been sick in an alien spaceship. They mated a couple of times which says a lot for the Latin libido. A man then entered and took the woman away. As she left she pointed to her stomach and to the sky, indicating to Antonio that his offspring would have a secure celestial future. The aliens returned Antonio's clothes and gave him a tour of the spacecraft, which was the least they could do in the circumstances, before putting him back in his field to continue ploughing.

The craft began to rise. Its shining light became more intense. It hovered for a moment. The light changed to red and the craft rotated with increasing speed before departing like a bullet. Antonio said he had spent four and a quarter hours in the craft.

The case was investigated by numerous ufologists, including Dr Olavo Fontes of Rio de Janeiro. Antonio did show physical symptoms, including possible radiation damage. These injuries and Antonio's apparent honesty convinced many ufologists. Antonio, who went on to become a lawyer in Brazil, still sticks to the accuracy of his account. However, experts on folklore who have analysed the story in the context of its regional and social environment conclude that it stemmed from Antonio's imagination, stimulated by too much night work and too much ploughing. For Antonio it was a real event. Only one thing is certain: if the story is true the lady was no alien.

Commenting on Antonio's case, Carl Sagan, a leading American space scientist, said that there was more chance of an elephant mating with a petunia than a human mating with an extraterrestrial. This is a nice analogy. Because all life on Earth uses the same genetic system, one might in theory combine the genetic sequences of an elephant with those of a petunia. But although the cells of both species 'speak' the same genetic language, they would not fuse and produce elephant–petunia cells in the laboratory. Cells from animals of different species can be fused and cells from different plant species can be fused, and if the species are in the same phylum they will reproduce. But plants are geared to getting their energy from photosynthesis and animals get their energy from the oxydisation of food. Such a sharp metabolic difference prevents any fusion that would lead to reproduction. Also, the chromosomes of plants are large compared to those of animals, making them mechanically unsuitable for reproduction with animal cells.

So reproduction with extraterrestrials is just not on, although cell biologists have fused cells from very different animals and from different plants. It is a technique used by biologists to study the processes of life at a cellular level. Cell fusions have included human cells with those of mice, rabbits and chickens – all vertebrates and therefore all in the same phylum. But only the cultured cells of these organisms reproduce in the laboratory. Nothing more than cells, not giant petunias or flowery-eared elephants.

So although only cells from species which are relatively closely related will fuse and reproduce at a cellular level, there is unity of all life on Earth. From microbes to elephants, all species have the same genetic machinery, the same genetic code, the same ways of producing proteins for growth and metabolism. Nowhere else in the universe could there be lifeforms which are part of that unity. Thus the 'mating with aliens' stories (and a few ufologists seem fixated on the unpromising combination of sex and extraterrestrials) can only survive in the absence of an understanding of biology.

## DINNER WITH ET
In parts of the literature of astronomical SETI, and most of the literature of ufology, you will find a lack of appreciation of how unlike us the ETIs could be. All sorts of fanciful suggestions are made by otherwise sensible and able people. There is a high-powered American attorney who wants to create a basis of law to govern future relations and transactions between us and the ETIs. Another writer is worrying about how our leaders would entertain extraterrestrial visitors. This state of mind may be induced by watching too many space sagas in which relations and communications are carried on in ways similar to those between different nations on Earth.

Biology tells us that it could not be like that, but does life on Earth give us any idea of what our counterparts on other worlds may be like? Not long ago, strolling around a coastal town, I stopped to look into a fishmonger's shop where live lobsters were waiting for someone to select them for dinner. One lobster was still alert, staring out into an alien world so far removed from its own. There might be ETIs that would look much stranger to us. And how would we deal with such creatures from Planet-X? Would our leaders invite them to dinner? Perhaps we shouldn't be puzzled by the reluctance of flying saucer manufacturers, if they exist, to show themselves on planet Earth.

## TALKING TO OCTOPOIDS
Scientists in SETI have published scholarly papers that try to

imagine the unimaginable: the differences which may exist between the technological species of the universe. Technological differences might be overcome, but biological differences could be unbridgeable. Maybe we could communicate with beings of our kind and level of intelligence who were thousands of years ahead of us technologically. But would we be able to do so with beings at that same technological level if they were several orders of magnitude greater in intelligence? Levels of mental capacity and unimaginable biological differences could be the insurmountable barriers to understanding and communications. Some ETs might have senses we do not possess and thus a drastically different view of the universe.

Let us speculate that most ETs ahead of us scientifically by only thousands of years have an intellectual capacity far greater than our own. Our sense of being, of existing in this world, comes from our mental capacity. It would therefore make sense for advanced beings to improve this, thus gaining greater abilities, a more intelligent insight into things and, in general, a greater satisfaction with life.

With the majority of technological species in the Galaxy being far more advanced than ourselves, I begin to wonder about our making the first move and detecting them. Faced with a chubby octopoid with four times our brain power who communicates in highly sophisticated whistles and squeaks, we might think again about the anticipated pleasures of communicating with our celestial neighbours. As we have not yet learnt the language of the dolphins, I cannot imagine that we would master the language of the octopoids from Planet-X. Perhaps the octopoid, with its high intelligence, could learn to write an Earthly language. But visiting ETs are not going to say 'Take me to your leader!' Clever ETs with the technology would be better served by generalised robots who might adapt their structures to those of the most intelligent creatures on the planet under study. Biological beings are not going to be able to do that, but we can imagine sophisticated robots building themselves in the required form to match the intelligent species of the planet. Nevertheless, we could benefit from scientific confirmation that we are being monitored by a superior technology. As Frank Drake, the first scientist to attempt astronomical SETI, has said:

An implicit goal of interstellar communication is to draw together the residents of Earth, to make us recognise how intimately related we are compared to lifeforms elsewhere.[1]

116

But the confirmed presence of ET in the Solar System would draw together the residents of Earth rather quicker than a radio signal of the kind that Drake has in mind, coming from many light-years away. The fact that ET is out there a thousand light-years away is not going to worry the world's population nearly as much as confirmation that ET is busy in the Solar System, monitoring our activities – and sometimes even having the audacity to land on our planet.

## UNDERSTANDING ET

We need to think more about communications with ET. In order to communicate with other *Homo sapiens* we have to share the same intellectual concepts. This is why scientists have a problem when they try to explain their works to non-scientists, a problem that is greatest where the intellectual concepts are highly developed and abstract, as in mathematics and theoretical physics. All *Homo sapiens* can communicate, to some extent, because many of their intellectual concepts are shared – they have all grown up in human societies. But ETs will have matured in their respective ET societies which are going to be vastly different from anything we can envisage – maybe horribly different from our human viewpoint. Intellectual and cultural differences could be insurmountable. Imagine a mathematical physicist trying to explain the Big Bang to an early member of the species *Homo sapiens* just emerging from his cave. For this encounter we need go back only 30,000 years. Both the physicist and the caveman would be in for a difficult time – especially the physicist – and not only because the caveman would lack the intellectual concepts of the physicist. Our position at the receiving end of ET's attempts to communicate with us could be even more difficult. The differences between our respective intellectual concepts could be far greater. But even though we may not be able to understand ET's message, we would get our most fundamental question answered. We would have confirmed that life and intelligence are universal phenomena.

# CHAPTER 10
## *The Search for ET's Broadcasts*

To appreciate the extraterrestrial implications of UFO phenomena, we have to consider the work and thinking of astronomical SETI. We have to view SETI as one subject. Given one set of conditions out there, those in astronomical SETI could be on the right track; given an alternative set of conditions, those investigating the ETH of ufology could be on the right track. But the same scientific background justifies both lines of research.

If Planet-X beams in with a message within the next couple of decades, astronomical SETI would become the hottest topic both inside and outside science. One can imagine most nations setting up their own SETI observatories to see what the extraterrestrials have to offer. Radio astronomers would be the most sought-after professionals and their present funding problems would vanish.

But those in astronomical SETI are in a precarious position. If Planet-X does not beam in, there would be a decline in interest even though extraterrestrial broadcasters could still be out there. Their signals may not have been picked up because we do not yet know enough or have adequate technology. However, if some UFOs were shown to have an extraterrestrial origin, the reactions of the scientists in astronomical SETI would be intriguing. Meanwhile, the power of astronomical SETI is increasing because it is geared to developments in computer technology. Everything depends on the new computer-receivers which are plugged into old radio telescopes. SETI receivers these days scan millions of channels simultaneously: up to 240 million channels with the latest technology, which would have been inconceivable a few decades ago.

NASA's SETI Program had been hailed as the most powerful yet, but was taken over by the SETI Institute, in California, in 1993. It became the privately funded Phoenix Program because politicians in Washington decided that looking for evidence that life is universal was not worth the cost of a few million dollars a year. The SETI Institute plans to continue the Phoenix Program into the next century, the financial support coming from private sources and major companies with a spirit of scientific adventure.

## BIG EAR

Bob Dixon of the Ohio State University Radio Observatory has been using the 110 by 21 metre radio telescope in the longest-running search for ET. He started the Big Ear Listening Project in 1973, and the Ohio team have received some interesting signals since then, including the famous 'Wow' signal, when the person on duty was so impressed he wrote 'Wow!' on the recording chart.

Astronomical SETI is a low-cost high adventure. You can use old available radio telescopes, or small new radio telescopes as some SETI amateurs are doing, provided advanced computer technology is plugged in to process the observational data. The operator programs the computer-receiver to save only 'interesting' signals, which amount, at most, to a few per cent of what the telescope collects. The rest is recognised as natural radiation from stars and gas and galaxies or interference and is mostly rejected. Automation makes SETI possible, and the periodic checks on what the computer has saved can usually be traced to such un-alien artifacts as motorbikes and hairdriers. Yet some signals do remain unexplained. SETI scientists have suffered numerous frustrating experiences because they have always failed to rediscover those interesting signals on taking a second look.

Bob Dixon's team, for example, has never been able to rediscover 'candidate' signals when they have returned to the relevant co-ordinates. Those signals have remained unexplained, despite the sophistication of the Ohio observatory. This problem has persisted for a long time because SETI has had to be carried out automatically, with only periodic checking by the astronomers. The automatic systems record candidate signals and pass on. Resources have not extended to having someone continuously checking on the observations. But this situation is being rectified. To avoid the frustration of lost signals, the Ohio observatory was upgraded from September 1993 with a control system which continues to track interesting signals. The 3,000 channels it receives are analysed simultaneously in real time, twenty-four hours a day, and any 'Wow' signals are re-observed until the system is satisfied they have not come from ET.

## SERENDIP III

Stuart Bowyer, a professor at the University of California, Berkeley, devised the Serendip System as a way of overcoming the shortage of time on radio telescopes. It can be plugged into any radio telescope engaged in conventional astronomy and receives everything observed. There is no control therefore on what is observed, but the system, which is a sophisticated computer-receiver, scans all incoming signals and saves any which could possibly come from ET. There have been Serendips I, II and III. Since 1992, Serendip III has scanned about 5,000 hours of observations, piggybacking on the Arecibo Dish in Puerto Rico, the largest radio dish in the world, with a diameter of a thousand feet.

## FROM META TO BETA

Paul Horowitz, Professor of Physics at Harvard University, and his colleagues run the continuous SETI program at Harvard University, and like Dixon's team they also have suffered from lost signals. The META [Mega-channel ExtraTerrestrial Assay] system of Harvard has been scanning eight million channels simultaneously since 1985 and has scanned the northern sky five times. In 1990 a copy of the META system was made at Harvard and began observations, as META II, in Argentina, where astronomers at the Argentinian Institute of Radio Astronomy use a ninety-eight-foot radio dish to observe the Southern Hemisphere. It was the first time the whole sky was being scanned continuously for evidence of ET. Previously, all major searches had taken place in the north, although broadcasting extraterrestrials could just as well be in the southern skies.

Horowitz and an assistant checked up on the co-ordinates of thirty-seven old signals which looked like possible interstellar beacons, selected from about a million which META had saved during five years of observations. For example, signals lasting longer than two minutes were eliminated because no signal from space can be in META's beam for more than 2 minutes because of the Earth's rotation.

Horowitz has explained how META checks on interesting signals:

If a large signal is detected, META returns to the frequency band and reference frame in which it was first seen, approximately forty seconds after initial detection, and continues for three minutes (after which the source will have drifted out of the antenna's beam). Also, we often leave the antenna's declination (the north-south position of its search beam) unchanged for a second day, if we notice a suspicious event.

121

But these strategies have not been enough to keep track of possible signals from ET. 'It is a weakness of the META system that it is unable to track the position of a candidate signal immediately (hence the residue of the 37 unrepeatable candidates).'

The next advance at Harvard, in 1994, was Paul Horowitz's BETA system, which simultaneously analyses 240 million channels and covers a thousand times the frequency range of the META system. It also has two antenna beams to aid detection of candidate signals. Horowitz has said that 'its two beams, oriented east and west of each other, force a real source to run the gauntlet at a rate determined precisely by the Earth's rotation'.

A call-signal in the form of a beam which sweeps the Galaxy from a civilisation thousands of light-years away might only be observable for a moment, but it would return. Interesting signals have often remained in the antenna's beam for only twenty to one hundred seconds, so there has never been an opportunity to get another observatory to check on them. Horowitz has now modified his system to make further observations of such interesting signals. Carl Sagan and Horowitz, in a major paper in *The Astrophysical Journal* in 1993, wrote:

> It is most important that future SETI systems are able to follow up candidate signal detections immediately, in order to resolve this kind of ambiguity.

It could be that unintentional leaks, rather than directed broadcasts, will be detected. Frank Drake, who was Director of the Arecibo Observatory and is now President of the SETI Institute, has often convinced us of the detectability of radiation leaks from technology. He has pointed out that the radar system used to study the planets with the giant Arecibo telescope emits a signal detectable across the whole Milky Way by telescopes similar to the Arecibo dish. To an extraterrestrial observer, the band of frequencies used would be something like ten million times brighter than that same band of frequencies from the Sun.

## A WIDE CHOICE FOR ET

What frequencies would interstellar broadcasters use? This has been a major question for scientists in SETI. For scientific reasons most searchers have restricted their observations to a quiet section of the microwave spectrum between 1,000 and 10,000 megahertz, which is relatively free from natural interference from the universe. It also contains some interesting frequencies, including the universal hydrogen frequency and that of the hydroxyl radical – which consists of one oxygen atom and one hydrogen atom. The section of the spectrum between these two frequencies is known as the water-hole because if we bring hydrogen and OH together we have the symbol for water [$H_2O$]. But this is only symbolic chemistry. Oxygen and the hydrogen radical (OH) do not naturally combine chemically to produce water.

All life on Earth is water-based – and this could be a universal situation – but would extraterrestrial broadcasters send their messages on frequencies within the water-hole section of the spectrum? One may question this, but for ET broadcasters this band of frequencies would be the least demanding on energy for their transmissions. However, a troublesome fact for astronomers is that two-thirds of this quiet band of frequencies is absorbed by the atmosphere, and it is in that two-thirds of the band that, according to Frank Drake, the right frequency might reside.

Scientists in most astronomical searches have assumed that at least some civilisations will be transmitting omnidirectional signals. That is, they will be transmitting equally in all directions. This means that, while their coverage of the universe will be vast, their signals would not be detectable at great distances, unless they were putting enormous amounts of energy into their transmissions. Omnidirectional signals seem appropriate if you are trying to reach worlds a few tens of light-years away, but if listening civilisations are separated by thousands of light-years, this way of continuously transmitting information does not appear practical.

## THE RUSSIAN APPROACH

The former Soviet Union gave generously to astronomical SETI, and numerous searches were carried out during the 1970s and 1980s. The government seemed to think that all advanced civilisations would necessarily be based on communism, and that attempts should be made to contact their brothers and sisters among the stars. The scientists didn't think that way, but who argues when money is on offer for your pet research program? The basic approach was different from that used by the scientists in America. The Soviet scientists did not think it feasible to try to guess ET's transmitting frequencies. They assumed that ETs would appreciate the problem and send their signals in the form of broadband pulses or bursts of energy, whereas SETI searches in America and Europe have generally looked for evidence of ET on a very narrow band of frequencies. The theory behind this is that a very narrow band

123

concentrates the transmitting energy used, so that the signal would stand out sharply when received.

## THE GUESSING GAME

The frequency most favoured by searchers ever since Drake's pioneering work in 1960 has been the universal twenty-one-centimetre line (frequency 1.4 GHz) of neutral hydrogen. This is the radio astronomers' most important frequency. As it can provide a great deal of information about the universe, we might expect extraterrestrial astronomers to be continuously observing this frequency.

The universal hydrogen frequency is also within the water-hole band which has so interested SETI observers because it is the quietest band on which to transmit and receive. The problem is that the frequencies within this broad band are going to be affected by the electron clouds in interstellar space.

According to Frank Drake:

Very high frequencies would fare much better over interstellar distances. This is an observable fact. Extraterrestrials would not have to come up with theories to figure it out. They would see it, as we do, when pursuing ordinary research in radio astronomy.

The extraterrestrials would observe, as has Drake, that the best way to keep a signal from being spread out by the electron clouds is to transmit on high frequencies. As Drake has said, 'Many times higher than the frequencies of the water-hole.'

From this factual position, Drake went on to suggest what he thought might be the optimum frequency, one that would still lie within the quietest section of the electromagnetic spectrum, while being high enough not to be affected by the electron clouds. 'When you do that,' said Drake, 'you arrive at an optimum frequency of about seventy gigahertz. Here is where the most detectable signal can be created using the least power.'

There's just one snag about this. That frequency does not penetrate the Earth's atmosphere. It could only be observed from space. But civilisations thousands of years in our future might reasonably assume that anyone worth talking to would practise their astronomy in space and not beneath an obscuring atmosphere.

The scientists who supported astronomical SETI came to the conclusion from the start that ET would probably be broadcasting on microwaves, and most searches have tuned into them. The classic paper by Giuseppe Cocconi and Philip Morrison, both Professors of Physics at Cornell University, published in 1959 in the science journal *Nature*, proposed neutral hydrogen at 1,420 MHz because it is the predominant frequency in the universe due to the overwhelming abundance of hydrogen. That led to Frank Drake's pioneering search on that frequency.

## RADAR WARNING SYSTEMS

Some scientists have suggested that space-age civilisations would possess a system to warn against approaching planetoids, meteorites and comets. That is, anything on course to hit a civilisation's home planet, or planets, and its colonies within its planetary system. The idea of extraterrestrial warning systems, which might be detectable, follows logically from what a few scientists have been urging us to consider. Now that the technology could be developed, supporters of this idea say: 'We don't want to suffer the fate of the dinosaurs when a large meteorite put an end to their tenure on Earth.' Certainly not, but the dinosaurs flourished for a hundred times longer than our species before that meteorite arrived.

Our civilisation *could* be demolished by a large enough meteorite. Some people might survive while the dust clouds hid all sunlight for a few years. No crops would grow. Temperatures would fall everywhere. Livestock would perish and harsh arctic conditions would rule our days. But a much larger meteorite than the one which finished the dinosaurs would probably be needed to extinguish *Homo sapiens*, although one ten miles across (the estimate of that which hit the dinosaurs) could put us back into the caves for a while.

In 1994 we saw the mess relatively small chunks of a comet did to Jupiter, which has 318 times the mass of the Earth. And it is not just the big impacts we should worry about. Some hours before dawn on 30 June 1908, many people in Siberia saw an intense light crossing the sky at a great speed. There followed an explosion which was recorded in several countries, including Britain and the United States. It was a comet, or disintegrating meteorite, which had exploded just above the vast and virtually uninhabited Tunguska forest. The impact killed thousands of trees, and millions of people would have been killed had the comet exploded above one of the world's cities. We can expect an impact such as this every few centuries, so advanced civilisations with several worlds and many space colonies to protect might invest in an early-warning system against the hazards of space debris.

The sort of system the experts favour is a radar system rather than an optical one. Radar provides more precise data on trajectories and is several hundred times better than optical astrometry. Radar can uniquely survey all angles of objects like planetoids with reference to the star of a planetary system, and from reflections can determine the composition of physical objects.

## EVIDENCE OF ET'S TECHNOLOGY
Frank Drake has said:

> The true hope of all search efforts ... hinges on being able to detect *unintentional* signals from extraterrestrials, and not just waiting for them to send us a message. Surely there must be more signals of this kind than signals intended for the benefit of other worlds. We would hope to eavesdrop on escaped television broadcasts, for example, satellite communications, operating instructions beamed to spacecraft, and high-level communiqués between space stations and their home planets.

It is worth being ready for serendipity, but the scientific and technological ceilings for everyone in this universe may have to be very low for evidence of ET's technology to be detectable. Civilisations thousands of years ahead of us would have to be stuck with technologies not much more advanced than our own because Nature fails to provide applicable knowledge for anything better. If this is so, then we may already be near to bumping our heads on that low ceiling and the technological marvels envisaged in science fiction will for ever remain just that – fiction. But if technological marvels are not fiction for super civilisations, then we may be incapable of detecting the effects of their technologies, or, perhaps, be capable of detecting them but not of recognising them for what they are.

## EARLY OPTIMISM
Frank Drake has described how naive attitudes were when he carried out the first SETI search in 1960.[1] At the end of his three-month session with the eighty-five-foot telescope he had failed to detect an intelligent extraterrestrial signal, but at that time he still felt that he might have succeeded, if given a longer period to observe:

> The findings of Project Ozma could not rule out the existence of life in the vicinity of Tau Ceti and Epsilon Eridani [two nearby sun-like stars]. Wasn't it at least possible that we had

126

been looking at the right stars, and on the right frequency to detect extraterrestrials, but at the wrong time? Perhaps their transmitters had been down for repairs those two months, or simply pointed in another direction while engaged in other work.

We realise now that to find a technological civilisation comparable to our own, in our time in galactic history, on a planet circling one of the nearest stars, would be like winning first prize in the national lottery. Their transmitters might have been down for the past *two hundred million years*, rather than the past two months. There may have been life on planets orbiting those two suns, but life as far removed from radio transmitters as were the dinosaurs.

There is one way out of this difficulty of the time factor, which makes the existence of two comparable civilisations existing near to each other at the same time virtually impossible. It is to speculate that knowledge of the universe will make interstellar travel relatively easy. Applicable knowledge might come from an understanding of what gives matter the quality of mass, which makes objects subject to the force of gravity. Particle physicists are hoping to understand this mechanism at the heart of matter in the decades ahead. It is one of the basic and most costly lines of research today.

If physicists did find a mechanism in nature which bestows the quality of mass on matter, then there might be a way of exploiting that mechanism in our systems of propulsion. Without entirely new science to apply, it is difficult to see how travel between the stars can ever become popular with advanced technological beings. Yet if the ultimate in interstellar transport could be developed in a few centuries, civilisations not too far ahead of us technically and intellectually might have travelled to nearby planetary systems. Given time – and there has been plenty of time – every planetary system in the Galaxy might then have an alien intelligence, perhaps non-biological, somewhere in residence, studying and monitoring everything of interest. And we might be seeing the manifestations of this in some aspects of the UFO phenomena. For those in astronomical SETI, however, this line of thinking would provide a serious distraction from their current observations.

If advanced civilisations have been able to find a solution to their interstellar travel problems, there could be more transmitters to detect. They might be sitting on planets in orbit about those two nearby suns which Drake observed for three months in 1960. But that scenario is self-defeating. *Why should they stop at Tau Ceti and Epsilon Eridani?* Would they not have come on to the Solar System where a blue planet with a potentially very interesting biosphere existed?

This shows the unavoidable limitations of the scenario which justifies astronomical SETI. The scenario has to be that civilisations in our era with the capacity and interest in communicating across interstellar distances are well spaced out in our Galaxy, say several thousands of light-years apart. They are unlikely to be much nearer to each other, say tens of light-years apart, without a lot of interstellar travelling. It is statistically unlikely that they could evolve so close together and be active in our epoch. There may be many Earth-like planets, but having two at about the same point in evolution at about the same time is only feasible statistically if we assume a very large number of such planets. And for this we need a vast area of space, a sphere with a radius of several thousand light-years from Earth.

If they have journeyed great distances to the nearest stars to us they would be within 'shouting distance' for astronomical SETI, but we might expect them to come on here if they want to communicate. But, a very important 'but', in a situation where interstellar spaceflight is enormously difficult or impossible, the vastly different levels of development in near neighbours might preclude any communications. It is not a question of where is the nearest ETI but where is the nearest ETI at about our level?

But if we accept the premiss that the nearest civilisation which could communicate with us is a few thousand light-years away, and interstellar travel is enormously difficult or impossible, there is still a lot of ingenious guessing to do. The constant temptation is to try to guess what ET would do in exploring the universe around him. What frequencies would he choose to broadcast messages, if that was the only way to contact and explore other world civilisations? What would his attitude be to his existence and that of other intelligent creatures? All this leads to a lot of entertaining speculation, some of which can point the way to lines of investigation.

## NETWORKING FOR ETs
If the ETs of our galaxy have established a communication system it may be a network. All data would be transmitted to a central station – the source of everything we would like to know about everybody! There might be numerous linked networks within the Galaxy. The advantage of a network is that one only has to make contact with the central station to which many planetary systems may contribute, each one of them then being able to receive data from all the other planetary systems in the network. And since, given a few million

years or so, all the networks within the Galaxy might be linked, it would in theory be possible to acquire all the data transmitted by everyone within the Galaxy in its history, since the first communicating ETs began to transmit.

Call signals, if anyone is calling, would therefore come from the central station of the nearest network. Plug into that and you may be able to receive the histories and wisdom of all contributing extraterrestrials, most of whom may no longer exist. We might not understand what they had to say but we could in theory receive it. Yet there are snags to this convenient set-up: time and stability and the continuing development of communicative extraterrestrials. The networks would have to be established and maintained for hundreds of millions of years. They would require contributions from many civilisations who would need advanced automated technology to run such a system. There may not be enough civilisations evolving to maintain the service. And as each advances in its own way in isolation, it may not have enough in common with its cosmic neighbours to bother to communicate on a regular basis. Change would seem inevitable in any civilisation no matter how advanced; and with change stability could be lost, the stability that would seem essential, to run the networks of the Galaxy.

## THE VALUE OF LONGEVITY

In the 1960s Sebastian von Hoerner, an astrophysicist at Heidelberg, Germany, calculated that if a few civilisations survived for a very long time, say a billion years, then their communications across the Galaxy would have a stabilising effect on other emerging societies. The average lifetimes of technological civilisations would therefore be greatly increased, and there would be more extraterrestrial broadcasters in our era to give astronomical SETI more opportunities to succeed.

Certainly, long-lived species of long-lived civilisations, communicating constantly over hundreds of thousands of light-years, might have a stabilising influence. Though the mind starts to seize up at the idea of any civilisation lasting a billion years. We have evolved from one evolutionary line in fishes to *Homo sapiens* in less than half a billion years. A few million years ago our ancestors were still apes. So one wonders how beings who are further beyond us than we are beyond our ancestral fishes would manage to have a stabilising influence on us.

It is not just the march of biological evolution which comes into this because biological stability in a single lifeform can exist for many millions of years. Scientific and technological development are the great forces for change and can bring drastic instabilities within decades. So how could a technological society remain stable for a million years, let alone for a billion years, a period a thousand times longer? There appears to be only one answer. We have to postulate a technological ceiling above which no technological species can go, no matter how intelligent and able it becomes, because new applicable knowledge, which science provides for new technologies, no longer exists in nature.

If this is not the case and scientific advances and technological developments from new knowledge can go on indefinitely, then all technological civilisations are going to be at different points on a universal scale of developments, the extent of which would be beyond our comprehension. And because, for statistical reasons, we must be at the lowest point on that scale, our chances of understanding those ahead of us cannot be good. Mutual incomprehension may be accepted in the Galaxy. Societies may explore and study – but would they try to communicate the incomprehensible to the uncomprehending?

## NO GIFTS FROM THE GODS
Barney Oliver, one of the founding fathers of astronomical SETI, who headed the NASA Program now run by the SETI Institute, said: 'The pride of identification with this super society and of contributing to its long-term purposes would add new dimensions to our own lives on Earth that no man can imagine.' It sounds fine but Oliver's dream could only become a reality if the brains in the universe, if there are brains beyond the Earth, never reach a capacity much beyond that which we currently possess. Yet as we can already see ways of improving our neurological equipment over the generations to come, we might expect long-lasting ETs to follow this line of progress, especially as civilisations, and the science and technology which they create, become increasingly complex and difficult to deal with. One might expect the human race to be a lot more intelligent in, say, a hundred thousand years from now, if humans are still thriving then. Therefore, how would we, twentieth- and twenty-first-century humans, contribute to a super society whose members are several orders of magnitude greater in intellectual capacity than ourselves, beings more remote from us intellectually than we are from the chimps?

## ET MAY LIKE LASERS
Those favouring optical SETI suggest that the concentration on microwaves during the past few decades may have been a mistake.

They think that ET is more likely to use laser beams and therefore plan to search the spectra of Sun-like stars for unusual emission lines which may have been put there artificially. Using a laser beam to carry your messages saves enormously on the energy bills. The diameter of a laser beam when it reaches its target need only cover the orbits of potentially habitable planets. And if you have the appropriate technology – which we will not in the foreseeable future – you could reach the thousand nearest Sun-like stars in our neighbourhood of the Galaxy by transmitting a thousand beams. The energy involved would be focused on the regions that count. To broadcast with comparable power to a region of sky where a thousand candidate stars exist would need millions of times more energy. So interstellar communications by laser are efficient, providing you have the technology, know your rapidly moving targets and can calculate precisely where they will be in the number of light-years, light-days, light-hours and light-minutes when your beams reach their targets. Also, the beams have to move continuously with their targets while signals are being received. Right from the start, the transmitters would have to be moving in perfect synchronisation with their future targets light-years away.

There would be advantages in transmitting your signals at optical wavelengths, if you were in ET's place. You could choose the wavelength to provide the greatest contrast against the background radiation which would be received. A signal could be made to stand out brilliantly. Another advantage is that optical frequencies, because they are much higher, can carry immeasurably more information than radio or microwave frequencies – and scientists in astronomical SETI anticipate that ET, if he is out there, could have plenty to say. Systems using optical wavelengths are expected to be the main carriers of our communications within the next fifty years because they can carry vastly more information than radio systems, so is ET going to use optical frequencies for his interstellar signals, or will he have something better which we cannot envisage at the moment?

In the 1960s it was suggested that ETs might use lasers to communicate with their neighbours. We had this idea, no doubt, because lasers were then our latest invention. Some people criticised the suggestion, saying that the spectacle of laser beams piercing the night sky would certainly have been noted in historical records when, in fact, there is no mention of them. ET's lasers, however, would not have been like those in discothèque displays.

ET's laser beam, a single frequency beam, would have travelled across the light-years, but when it reached its target it might be only as wide as, say, the orbit of Mars around the Sun. That is a very well-focused beam compared to a pocket torch. The beam would not be powerful enough to be seen, but it could be detected with advanced astronomical equipment. And ETs might transmit laser beams of wavelengths in the ultra-violet or the infra-red, radiation outside the spectrum visible to us.

Nowadays we can appreciate better what may be possible for ET because of the boost to the development of laser technology provided by the Star Wars Program and numerous other projects in optical communications for commercial purposes. Fastening on to laser technology because we have just invented it seems rather chauvinistic. Is it going to be the best method for interstellar communication in a hundred thousand years, which is the sort of time scale we would have to allow for in guessing what ETs might be doing? As scientists of a hundred years ago could not have forecast what the leading technologies of today would be, we are sure to make a lot of wild guesses about anything that the ETs of the Galaxy may be doing.

Nevertheless, this problem does not deter astronomers in SETI. Those pursuing optical SETI believe that ETIs will have the capability to target beams so that they will fall precisely on Sun-like stars and their planetary systems. These beams would be focused very narrowly to avoid loss of transmitting energy, which is a major problem with radio and microwave transmissions where a beam would spread out like any other beam we are familiar with. In optical SETI the famous inverse square law, that the power of a beam decreases in proportion to the square of the distance, does not apply. The inverse square law means that ETIs broadcasting by radio would need an enormous amount of energy to reach far into the Galaxy, though they would achieve blanket coverage instead of specific coverage.

Stuart Kingsley of Fiberdyne Optoelectronics in Ohio is one of the leading figures in optical SETI. It would not be easy for ETIs to hit their targets, but Kingsley thinks they would be up to the job:

> Over millennia they will have developed catalogues for the stars in their vicinity, describing their peculiar proper motions, with full details of each star's planetary system. For them, the ballistic skills (point ahead targeting) required to land photons on a designated target ... will be relatively trivial.

The point here is that the ETIs must know precisely where their target star and planetary system will be years in the future when the laser beam arrives. The photons are travelling at the speed of light, but the target is light-years away and travelling at around fifty kilometres a second, the sort of speed at which stars travel as they orbit the galactic centre. Also, the star's *proper motion*, its exact course in the Galaxy, has to be allowed for. Not easy when you consider that the distance covered by a star and its planets, over a few years, will be thousands of times greater than the diameter of the target which the transmitted beam must hit.

Recent developments in astronomical technology favour the pursuit of optical SETI. Arrays of several relatively small optical telescopes are being built which together offer far greater observing power than the largest optical telescopes of the past, and which will work on the Earth's surface with far less interference from the atmosphere. But small individual optical telescopes can be used to try to detect evidence of ET at optical wavelengths. The scientists in optical SETI want to encourage amateur astronomers in the initial searches, and maintain that any telescope with six-inch optics or larger would be suitable for studying the nearest Sun-like stars.

Stuart Kingsley foresees current developments as a reason to be optimistic about ETs' ability to hit their target planetary systems with data-laden optical beams.

We can be sure that within the next fifty years we will have obtained data on the peculiar proper motions of nearby stars to correctly aim (point ahead of target) narrow optical beams. We presently have lasers powerful enough for the job, but don't know how to aim them precisely, or where to aim them.

In other words, although we know some good candidate stars we don't know precisely where those stars would be by the time our signal reached them. Presumably the sending address in the Galaxy would be in the signal. Like Earthly letter-writers, ET would be expected to give his address along with his message.

The problem with optical SETI is more or less the same as the basic problem with the rest of astronomical SETI. Although it has been a brilliantly conducted exercise, and has provided us with a better view of what may be the status of intelligent life in the universe in relation to the human situation, it does depend on too much guesswork. We are constantly trying to guess what frequencies ET may be using: radio, microwave, infra-red, light or some other band of the electromagnetic spectrum – or some other means, such as tachyons, which could in theory travel faster than light but which have not yet been discovered and may not even exist.

## WHO HAS BEEN LOOKING?

Only a few optical searches have been carried out: in America and Russia in the Northern Hemisphere and in Argentina in the Southern Hemisphere. An optical system called MANIA [Multi-channel Analyzer of Nanosecond Intensity Alterations], designed and built in Russia by Victor Shvartsman, has made two searches from Russia and one from Argentina. The system looks for very brief pulses of pure light – light composed of a single frequency. Because light waves are around a million times shorter than microwaves the pulses can be in nanoseconds, like fantastically short Morse code signals. Monte Ross, of Laser Data Technology in America, has pointed out that, by using very short pulses to transmit data, ETs could send their signals 'great distances with low average power and high efficiency'.

In 1993, Stuart Kingsley opened an optical SETI observatory at his home in Ohio. At the conference on optical SETI in Los Angeles in 1993, he gave a comprehensive account of how amateur astronomers could make a worthwhile contribution to the subject by setting up their own SETI observatories. Anyone can play in SETI research, though some of the necessary technology may be tough to master.

Perhaps optical SETI can be summed up by what Monte Ross said at the Los Angeles conference:

Communication at optical frequencies from extraterrestrial sources many light-years away is considered quite feasible and can be detected with present receiver technology given that short pulses of high energy per pulse will be sent. The reasons for transmitting in this way are substantial, and consideration should be given to searching for such optical signals.

## EXOTIC WAYS TO SIGNAL

According to some ingenious speculators, ETs might not always use radio transmitters to state their presence. A few years ago, one scientist gave a paper at a SETI conference proposing the odd idea that a super civilisation might tip tons of a relatively short-lived (unstable) element, such as *technetium*, on to its sun. The result would be that extraterrestrial astronomers studying spectra of their neighbouring stars would find a very unnatural spectrum, from which they would deduce that it was artificially produced by an advanced technological civilisation. This would work in one way: it would be detectable in all directions. But it is a bizarre idea. What would we do if we discovered such a stellar spectrum? Would we immediately direct radio transmissions to the star, saying: 'Your sun has been tampered with artificially and we are sending full details about ourselves and would welcome an answer in about a hundred years?'

Another speculation from a SETI conference is that advanced civilisations, depending for thousands of years on nuclear power, might look for a permanent way of dumping their nuclear waste. This could be the situation only if civilisations cannot develop a better way of energy generation. The scientist in question has added that spectral modification, the anomalies caused by an unnatural abundance of plutonium-239 and uranium-233, would occur only after geological periods of time, and one wonders if any civilisation depending on nuclear fission for geological periods of time could survive for geological periods of time.

Physicists working today to develop nuclear fusion technology (in which hydrogen nuclei combine to form helium nuclei with the release of energy, as in the hydrogen bomb) say that a nuclear fusion reactor would produce no more radioactive material after a hundred years in use than a coal-fired power station in operation for the same period of time. And we might expect the super civilisations of the Galaxy to improve on that, even if they don't find a better way to supply their energy needs than nuclear fusion.

Another bizarre speculation is that ET could produce a call signal in the spectrum of its star by placing a large quantity of a chemical element, one that could not possibly be present naturally, between its sun and the potential receiver who would be light-years away. The element would then absorb some of the star's energy and re-radiate some of this at its characteristic frequencies. The receiver, say us, could then see these unexpected emission lines and would say: 'That's funny, an ET must have put those lines in the star's spectrum.' This all seems a lot of trouble simply to say, 'We are here if any astronomers with good spectrometers are out there looking in the right direction at this time.' How long such a signal might be made to last, or what techniques could be used is anyone's guess. It does not seem a very good way of looking for life on other worlds.

In SETI, however, very long shots are justified and the optical approach is worth trying, as John Rather of NASA has explained:

Modern electro-optical techniques could be used to examine the spectra of millions of stars per day at high resolution, if a dedicated large automated optical system were built for the purpose. Having found the signal, we must then construct large and sophisticated hardware to gather enough photons to detect the message.

## X-RAY SIGNALS

Some strange ideas have come from a few physicists on ways ET might use X-rays to signal his presence in the Galaxy. In a nuclear explosion about 70 per cent of the energy released comes in the form of X-rays. If the explosion takes place above eighty kilometres, the atmosphere reflects the X-rays into space and a very short pulse of X-rays then heads for the stars.

The physicists have pointed out that the pulse will not broaden much as it goes through space, which is an advantage in signalling, and that receivers on other worlds would just collect a strong X-ray pulse. Civilisations receiving the pulse would not have to worry about ET's frequencies; and the power of the pulse would be much greater than the X-ray background of a solar-type star.

One physicist at a SETI conference got so carried away by these advantages that he proposed that ET might signal to us with a series of nuclear explosions, so spaced out that the signal would be observed as definitely artificial. Not only is the thought that the super civilisations of the Galaxy may still be exploding nuclear devices discouraging to anyone interested in life as a universal phenomenon, but the idea that sane extraterrestrials would use nuclear explosions in this way is bizarre. The signal would be so short it might never be noticed. Can we imagine any ET routinely producing nuclear explosions in space for hundreds of years in order to attract the attention of SETI astronomers on far-off planets?

Perhaps the strangest speculation to come from physicists in SETI is about the use of neutron stars to send signals. The basis of this is sound physics taken to insane extremes. The scenario is that ET travels to the nearest neutron star, which could be many light-years away, and drops a mass of material on it, taking care not to get too near because of the intense radiation and immensely powerful gravitational field. Anyway, disregard the difficulties and let ET drop at least ten tons of matter, of any sort, on to the star. So great is the gravitational attraction of a neutron star that this matter could be travelling at a third of the speed of light on impact. Thus, in a flash, 10 per cent of the matter will emerge as X-ray radiation. One physicist calculated that if you dropped an object weighing 10 billion tons on to a neutron star, the resulting flash of X-rays would be detectable throughout our Galaxy. So the unfortunate, and insane, ET, having carried 10 billion tons of matter to his local neutron star just to signal his presence to the Galaxy, is then wiped out by the most violent burst of X-rays.

One does occasionally meet this sort of speculation which is supposed to support astronomical SETI. If ETs could drop vast quantities of matter on their neighbouring neutron stars, they could more easily, and more profitably, travel to the nearest planetary systems, where blue planets like the Earth may exist.

## ASTRONOMICAL SETI IS NOT ENOUGH

Although it is not possible to free oneself completely from chauvinism when speculating on things extraterrestrial, some scientists in SETI have assumed that our neighbouring civilisations will be more or less at our level, exploiting the technologies that we can currently think about from what we already know. *This is not a reasonable assumption.* If we could now possess, by some wizardry, the science of a thousand years in our future, our thinking about what ET might do would be very different from what we think today. Therefore, as most ETs, if such exist, may be hundreds of thousands of years ahead of us, we must accept that we don't really know what they could do, or what they would be most likely to do. We therefore have to be ready to explore any evidence that looks interesting.

The good thing about astronomical SETI is that many enterprising scientists have been involved, though at their conferences they do seem to agree too much among themselves. And almost all of them would put the blinkers on if someone mentioned the UFO phenomena. Nevertheless, they do have a testable hypothesis and they are testing it, although it can only be tested for a positive finding, and, strictly speaking, a scientific hypothesis should be falsifiable. But SETI brings together those aspects of science which bear directly on the status of our existence and it waves a flag for human culture – the Flag of Earth, designed in the United States some years ago, flies over every astronomical observatory engaged in SETI observations.

However, two nagging questions are unavoidable when considering astronomical SETI:

1. Are we going to discover beings in the Galaxy who are superior to ourselves, or is it more likely that they will discover us?

2. Will such superior beings want to communicate with us or study us?

These questions lead me to think that SETI has to include more than the astronomical approach. Many ingenious scientists have devised hypotheses from the scientific background of SETI which can be tested with the techniques of astronomy. But these hypotheses are almost all based on guessing what ET is able to do, or is likely to do, and our chances of making the right guesses are not good. Things change so rapidly in science and technology that what happens tomorrow could drastically revise our guesses about ET.

The scientists involved with astronomical SETI should therefore not dismiss the possibility that a small proportion of reported UFOs may be extraterrestrial artifacts. They should keep in mind that the North American Indians did not voyage to Europe and discover Columbus, nor the South Sea islanders discover Captain Cook. ET is more likely to find us than the other way round. And the strange and vague evidence reported could – just possibly – indicate that ET has already done so.

# CHAPTER 11
## *Sceptical Scientists*
## *Support Saucers*

Theoretical SETI depends a great deal on science at the frontiers of our understanding to explore the ramifications of the ETH. Many scientists have brought together previously compartmentalised knowledge to provide some stimulating ideas about life and the universe. But what our study of the relevant science reveals is more than most people in astronomical SETI anticipated – or wanted. No enthusiast for astronomical SETI is going to welcome the possibility that some UFOs may be extraterrestrial artifacts. There is no point in scanning the universe for ET if he is already in your backyard.

The irony of this situation has been unintentionally amplified in recent years by a clever group of scientists in the United States who view astronomical SETI as an enterprise with built-in failure. The most articulate of this group is Frank Tipler, Professor of Physics at Tulane University in New Orleans, who decided in the 1980s to make astronomical SETI a target for demolition. In a series of articles in the scientific press,[1] he attempted to demonstrate that we are the only technological species in the universe, which would obviously make SETI a waste of time and government money. He made his case with power and clarity, and anyone interested in the subject should read his papers. But what Tipler has done is far from what he intended, principally because he left out certain biological aspects of the SETI argument. Those who think the ETH may be correct can find a brilliant advocate in Tipler, just by subtracting a few of his assumptions.

What Tipler provided was one of the best arguments yet for the ETH of the UFO phenomena. It seems strange that, to my knowledge, no one in ufology picked up on some of the points made in his admirable articles. One can only conclude that no one who thinks ET may be monitoring our civilisation is checking the scientific press for relevant information.

## OLD COLONIALISM

I remember a leading space technologist once saying that 'More distant space offers the possibility of reaching other stars and their planets and eventually populating some part of our galaxy.' This line of thinking is common in astronautical literature. We have gone forth and colonised the Earth and will therefore go forth and colonise our Galaxy. It sounds almost biblical. These two types of colonisation are, however, quite different, so that human colonisation on Earth cannot be an analogue of galactic colonisation.

What would it gain us to colonise the planets of neighbouring stars? There would be only one benefit: to have a duplicate Earth or two in other planetary systems, as backups in case of disaster. Beyond that there would be no rational gain from what would be a vast investment of resources. Exploration, though, would be a different matter, and we are already thinking about that ourselves by inventing interstellar probes on paper. We want to know about other worlds and the wonders they must possess. That would be our motive for going to the stars, and, we hope, the motive for those technological beings who might have preceded us.

Let us speculate that we have a revolutionary advance in interstellar transport and it becomes possible to face the hazards of space and visit other planetary systems. After a while we discover in one of them an emerging technological civilisation, at something like our present level of development. What would we do? Would we land and destroy that civilisation with our advanced technology, and take the planet for ourselves with all its potentially dangerous biological features? I don't think we would. Thus we should not expect exploring ETs to interact directly with us and wreck our civilisation. They may or may not be out there monitoring us, but they are going to monitor secretly if they can.

So the argument put up by Tipler that if other technological species exist out there they would be here by now, displaying themselves and their technologies for all to see, is not the most reasonable contribution to the subject of SETI. Yet Tipler and his colleagues received world-wide publicity in the 1980s for this argument, firstly in the pages of distinguished science journals and then in the general media.

## HIGH STREET ALIENS

I remember Professor Michael Hart, a severe critic of SETI, once saying that we don't see any aliens when we go into town, as if the aliens – if they had come – would be shopping in Sainsbury's. For practical and biological reasons ETs will not cross interstellar space to go into town, even if they could without creating hysteria in the streets.

It is a reasonable assumption that ETIs are going to be most interested in information about the Earth and its life and civilisation. They will not want our resources – minerals and oil – or our food, which would probably wreck the best maintained alien metabolisms. And they are not going to eat us, like the aliens in the film *Alien*. They could meet their needs from the resources of the Solar System and the constant energy supply offered by the Sun. In short, they are not going to colonise the Earth, and that is why Michael Hart has never seen them out shopping.

## TIPLER AND COLONISATION

Frank Tipler maintains that colonisation in the Galaxy would be self-perpetuating. Colonisation might be seen as such with biological colonists, providing other lifeforms did not get in the way. Once they got going they would support themselves and multiply. They would not need continuous support from the home planet. This pattern of colonising other worlds has been suggested many times in the literature. But Tipler's vision of theoretical colonisation is based on the existence of self-reproducing von Neumann machines, so named because the idea was proposed years ago by the great mathematician John von Neumann:

> One need only construct a few probes [von Neumann machines], enough to make sure that at least one will succeed in making copies of itself in another solar system. Probes will then be sent to other stars of the galaxy automatically, with no further expense to the original species.

This does not seem impossible, given a successful future for computer technology, but if our descendants make robots which can make other robots they could be heading for a nightmare situation. All lifeforms on Earth, including ourselves, are von Neumann machines in that they use materials from their environment to make more individuals similar to themselves. But advances in human abilities, like advances in all lifeforms, depend on basic biology, the way we are put together, and it has taken a million years of Darwinian evolution to advance from caveman *Homo erectus*, with two-thirds of our cranial capacity, to *Homo sapiens*. We are a product of Darwinian evolution, which is a very slow builder of new lifeforms.

But robots which make new robots – that is an entirely different ball-game! They could produce significant improvements with each generation, and within decades could cover the ground which would take Darwinian evolution millions of years to cross. Tipler does not face that possibility because he sees intelligent robots as racially indistinguishable from biological lifeforms:

> I personally feel that advanced civilisations would be non-racist ... and would consequently see no distinction between intelligent robots – the von Neumann probes – and intelligent beings produced by natural evolution.

Not to make the distinction which Tipler does *not* make would be a terrible mistake for anyone contemplating the construction of a von Neumann probe. Self-reproducing robots would be capable of Lamarckian evolution, which was put forward by the French biologist Jean Baptiste de Lamarck some fifty years before Darwin's *Origin of Species*, published in 1859. His theory stated that animals evolved by passing on to their progeny the characteristics which they had acquired. Thus Lamarckian evolution could be a million times faster than Darwinian evolution in whatever significant changes it brought about. It cannot operate in biological organisms because there is no way by which acquired characteristics can be passed on. But it could operate in robots. The character Data in *Star Trek* comes to mind. He seems a very nice chap, the most capable member of the crew on board the *Enterprise*, but if he could replicate he could make the human crews of all starships in the Federation totally redundant within a couple of generations. And his offspring could soon rule the Earth – probably a lot better than the *Homo sapiens* who were replaced. Therefore, unless we pulled the plug soon enough, the self-reproducing robots might take us over.

Tipler has suggested that advanced civilisations would send such robots into other planetary systems where they would build more von Neumann machines, improved versions of the old model. These would then go on to the next planetary system and repeat the process. Given that this scenario is possible, then the Galaxy would be taken over by von Neumann machines within several million years, and we would see them busily reconstructing everything in sight in line with projects and ideas unimaginably remote from our own. 'The person who was responsible for the construction of a von

Neumann probe would be the father or mother of galactic civilisation,' said Tipler. But it would be a civilisation of incredibly advanced robots, and that distant 'person' would be about as much a 'father or mother' as our ancestral fishes which scrambled over the Devonian mud some 400 million years ago to give rise to all land vertebrates.

So self-reproducing robots could be a phenomenal danger, a potential catastrophe for life and civilisations everywhere. And they could come back after a few generations and eliminate their creators. No responsible society is going to launch them into space.

Tipler counters this argument with typical adroitness:

> Most writers who consider possible extraterrestrial societies tend to regard a society as a single individual. Their articles are filled with such sentences as *Society would not wish to squander its resources on an interstellar probe*. But a society is not a single intelligent creature with a single will. It is instead a rather loose organisation of different individuals, each with a different amount of resources under his or her control, and each with a different opinion about how these resources should be used.

This is so, but building an intelligent von Neumann machine and setting it free could have disastrous consequences for the builder, as well as the rest of society. That would be a deterrent. And if one *did* escape, I guess the resources of an advanced society would be used to destroy it. There will be a *prime directive*, to use *Star Trek* jargon, which forbids the building of any kind of self-reproducing robot.

Also, it is difficult to envisage any group building a von Neumann probe in secret. If we built one in the future, we would have to provide a lot more than the propulsion system, the sensors and communications systems. The probe would have to be able to repair itself when necessary as it travelled across the light-years, and on arrival at a planetary system, it would need the equipment to mine and process raw materials from asteroids and space debris. It would then have to use the processed materials to manufacture many high-tech mechanisms for its upkeep and reproduction. What we could be sending, if we built a von Neumann probe, would be more like a large factory than a probe – and it would have to function for thousands of years in space. To be fair, Tipler does suggest that 'the intelligent species which constructed the initial probe could reduce the initial investment by building the initial probe small, but programmed to construct larger probes in the target systems'.

Frank Tipler goes on to refer to the vast number of planets which those in SETI believe exist:

> If intelligent life with technology comparable to ours ever evolved on any of these planets within five billion years after the formation of their planet, as we did, then ... they would have a von Neumann probe in our system.

This does follow from Tipler's scholarly analysis – except for one thing: *the probes may be here*, manifesting themselves in certain aspects of the UFO phenomena. If so, they don't seem to be von Neumann probes, otherwise our world would have been taken over long ago, according to Tipler's argument.

## *EXPLORATION VERSUS COLONISATION*

The key to the extensive controversy which followed the publication of Tipler's papers was simply the difference between *colonisation* and *exploration*, but no one seems to have been vociferous enough to pull the plug on Tipler. Those in astronomical SETI seemed somewhat short of advocates to counter such a competent analysis of astronomical SETI and the widespread publicity it received.

The point to make is that exploration would have left everything unchanged. The Solar System could have been alive with intelligent robots at times during the past few hundred million years, yet evidence of their activities might be impossible to discover. Even if our astronauts find nothing after exploring every part of the Moon and Mars, and the thousands of asteroids which orbit the Sun, the area left which could hold evidence of ET is still vast.

Tipler has said:

> Virtually any motivation we can imagine that would lead ETIs to engage in interstellar radio communication with us would also motivate them to engage in interstellar travel.

This is powerful support for the ETH. Yet there *are* two reasons why ETIs would not be here. Either technological civilisations capable of interstellar spaceflight are too rare in the Galaxy, say thousands of light-years apart, or the light-years are not crossable, except at costs which are unacceptable.

In no way is past colonisation on Earth the same kind of activity as the colonisation of other worlds. Colonisation on Earth was within one unified biosphere and took place naturally as an extension of human evolution. The colonisers breathed the same air as those being colonised, ate the same food and dealt with the same hazards to life and health. A few biological hazards, like yellow fever and malaria, may have laid low for a while the European colonisers of recent centuries, but most acquired immunity and dealt with these attacks on their biological integrity as well as the natives. But the idea of colonising a different world biology which is light-years away does not make much sense to us, and would probably seem even less sensible to more advanced societies.

What Tipler does not bring into his argument is that all biospheres will be different in fundamental ways at the molecular level, which is the essential interactive level as far as food and health are concerned. To make a new biosphere for ourselves on Mars, a stable complex ecosystem on a planetary scale, might take thousands of years. We might begin to colonise Mars in the opening decades of the next century. We could do this without disturbing the wildlife! The best we can hope for there is the Martian equivalent of our bacteria, obtaining their energy chemically deep beneath the planet's surface. But if Mars had a flourishing biosphere, like the Earth's, we would not sterilise the planet to impose our own biosphere. Therefore, we should not expect that ETIs would sterilise life-bearing planets in order to colonise them, especially as there is bound to be plenty of lifeless real estate for the taking.

If our descendants properly colonise Mars, a replica of Earth's biosphere would have to be formed – the ultimate in ecological engineering. Think of the number of journeys needed. It could not be done with our current system of propulsion, so much would have to be transported to the red planet. But even with a revolutionary advance in our spaceflight capability, the problems of colonising Mars may take a thousand years to solve, according to one optimistic estimate. Yet Mars is a quarter of a million times nearer than our nearest star. The colonisation of a suitable planet orbiting one of our nearest stars thus appears to be a venture to be undertaken only out of the greatest necessity, perhaps to ensure survival in the long term. It would be the same for all technological species in the Galaxy.

## ONE MAN'S MEAT IS AN ALIEN'S POISON

Basic biology does not contribute to Tipler's argument at all. Life on other worlds may be composed of the same biogenic elements as life

145

on Earth, including hydrogen, oxygen, carbon, nitrogen, sulphur and phosphorus, which, with the exception of phosphorus, are the commonest elements in the universe. These elements can automatically form many of the molecules of life, even in interstellar space, and they may form the basis of all life, no matter where that life exists in the universe. But there will be differences in the ways in which these components are put together. Different amino acids may be used along with some of the twenty that form the proteins of Earthly life, and the nucleic acids of the genetic system could be different. Our genetic code, the molecular structures of our genes and the intricate chemical pathways of life's metabolic processes will hardly be the same on other worlds.*

All this is basic to colonisation by aliens. What is food to us could bring death to them. There wouldn't be all the amino acid building blocks in our food to make the proteins needed for the repair of their bodies. For the same reason, they would not be able to synthesise the vast number of enzymes needed to run their alien metabolisms – not if they needed large numbers of enzymes, as life does here, for the functioning of their biochemistry. That is bad enough, but they would also have to be permanently sealed within a spacesuit, and thoroughly decontaminated every time they set foot on Earth because micro-organisms are everywhere, outweighing in protoplasm all other lifeforms put together. And they would have to do all this while preserving their own ecosystems of micro-organisms within their bodies because like us, if they evolved in a biosphere, they would probably depend on billions of internal micro-organisms for their existence.

Sadly the scenarios of *Star Trek* are wrong. Spock reports to Captain Kirk that the planet's atmosphere is breathable, and out the landing party goes to freely explore 'where no man has gone before'. In reality, one whiff of that 'breathable' atmosphere could end a promising career in Star Fleet Command. And maintaining control of our bowels on Planet-X could be an embarrassing problem never faced by Captain Kirk and his crew. The careless ingestion of the local microbes might disrupt the balanced populations of micro-flora in our gut and wreck any diplomatic close encounters of the third kind. We are beginning to see why Tipler's extraterrestrials have not colonised the Earth.

But we have to allow for robots who would be immune to disease

* Helium is the next in weight and abundance in the universe to hydrogen, but it does not combine with any other element and is therefore not a likely component in any living system.

146

and perpetually powered by energy instead of food, with no worries about extraterrestrial dysentery. However, we live in a very corrosive environment – we would soon be dead without our corroding oxygen – but rain and oxygen and other chemicals in our environment might not be good for robots. If you were an intelligent robot you might be very unhappy about being corroded and prefer a lifeless world with little or no atmosphere, away from corrosion and interfering organisms, especially intelligent ones.

So let us not worry about invasions by biological beings or intelligent self-reproducing robots. One can envisage super societies taking out insurance policies by colonising a few planetary systems, but my guess is that this is about as far as colonisation would go. Exploration would be the main interstellar activity.

## OTHER CANDIDATES FOR TECHNOLOGICAL STATUS

Tipler believes our technological abilities are unique.

> The biologists argue that the number of evolutionary pathways leading from one-celled organisms to intelligent beings is minuscule when compared with the total number of evolutionary pathways. Thus, even if we grant the existence of life on a hundred billion planets in the Galaxy, the probability that intelligence has arisen in our Galaxy on any planet but our own is still very small.

Biologists would agree that each of the several million species on Earth today has its own genetic pathway going back and joining other pathways that go back to the dawn of life, and that only one of those pathways has led to a technological species. But the assumption Tipler draws from this fact cannot be justified.

Let us imagine that the primate line in evolution that led to humans had never existed on this planet, but that apart from this everything else was more or less the same as it is today. There would exist a wild Garden of Eden without Adam and Eve. In this situation there are several lines in mammalian evolution that might evolve bigger brains and more intelligence, given another fifty million years, such as certain marsupial possums, rodents and mongooses. The potential for the evolution of technological intelligence has increased greatly with time since, say, the days of the dinosaurs. We have evolved from shrew-like animals in about sixty million years, so one of the currently existing species of mammals might lead to a technological creature given about the same amount

147

of time to evolve. We can see that the potential for the evolution of big brains is present, and our own evolutionary history, driven by a series of chance events like all evolutionary histories, may not be the only way to technological intelligence.

## MOST VALUED POSSESSION

As a general rule, the brighter people are, the more importance they attach to information. If this applies to the super brains of the Galaxy they are going to be great collectors and analysers of information, maximising their amassing of data by a task force of robots. The risk to life and the enduring boredom of interstellar space – probably the most boring place in the universe after a while – would not be for *them*. They would stay at home with their three-dimensional smell-and-feel interactive television sets, receiving data from thousands of robotic explorers as they voyage from planetary system to planetary system. For a being whose life expectancy is thousands of years this could be a good way to pass the time. Let indestructible machines, but not von Neumann probes, deal with the dangerous aspects of space exploration.

That is my scenario. Right or wrong, we shall never know, but it does reconcile the contradictions of the scientific rationale for SETI and the arguments of Tipler and like thinkers, whose case for our being the only technologists in the universe tends to fall apart when one considers the basic biology involved and the difference between colonisation and exploration.

That Tipler's line of thinking gained so much space in reputable science journals is surprising, especially as his hypothesis cannot be tested. No one can prove a negative about life outside the Earth. The universe is too large for that. But it is hard to believe that the human cranium houses the ultimate in brain power; that no brains anywhere else have reached such a lofty level. This will not be so if the ETH of ufology is correct.

## WOOLLY OCTOPOIDS

One more point worth consideration is that all the advanced brains belong to mammals, and to a lesser extent to the other vertebrates – the birds, the reptiles and amphibians. No other group has much of a brain except certain cephalopods – octopuses and their relatives. This situation probably developed because the first vertebrates, in the form of fishes, overwhelmed the competition when all creatures lived in water – in the sea, lakes and rivers. The fishes became the most successful lifeform, so it was from this group that all four-limbed animals evolved. No hungry carnivorous competitors were around as they struggled on to the land in the early days of fish–amphibian evolution. Dry land was free for a take-over with plenty of nourishing insects and the like already in residence. But it might not have been like that. Had the vertebrates not evolved or had they become extinct before the evolution of fishes really got going, then all the niches occupied by them could have been occupied by another lifeform.

The opportunities taken by the early vertebrates on land would then not have been taken. Another lifeform would have dominated land life. So great has been the dominance of vertebrates that we tend to accept the reality without much thought about what might have been. Actually, when you look for a lifeform to play the role on Earth that the vertebrates have played, there is not much choice. The only other group which might have done so are the octopoids. If fishes had not evolved as the first vertebrates, the octopoids, which were doing well in the Cambrian Period (570 to 500 million years ago) when there were no fish around, might have taken their place and eventually become the dominant land form. If the octopoids had come ashore 400 million years ago instead of certain bony fishes which gave rise to the amphibians, reptiles, mammals and birds, then land life could have been dramatically different, though all the available niches would have been filled with the octopoid counterparts of past and present mammals from mice to elephants. I sometimes look out from my office window at the sheep grazing on the Pembrokeshire hillside opposite and try to imagine what they would have looked like if they had evolved from an octopoid ancestor instead of a fish. Their resemblance to an octopus might have been about as close as the sheep's resemblance to a fish, but they would have been astonishingly different. Would they have had woolly coats, I wonder, which *our* octopoid counterparts used to make garments? A world full of different octopoid species, as rich in variety as the vertebrates, would take some imagining – especially a feathered flying octopoid. And would the technological species among them, our octopoid counterpart, look as little like an octopus as we resemble our distant fishy ancestors?

## POINT TO PONDER
All this I put forward to counter the assumption that the path followed by the anthropoid apes and humankind has been the only way to the evolution of a technologically intelligent species. And to counter the widely accepted belief that the primate lifeform alone will house the technologically intelligent brains throughout the Galaxy.

149

I invite you to decide which of the following two statements is more likely to be correct:

1. (Tipler's conclusion): We have not yet found any evidence of an ETI presence in the Solar System because we are the only technologically intelligent beings in the Galaxy.

2. We are not the only technologists in the Galaxy. The evidence of ETI's presence exists, although we have not yet been able to confirm its existence, either because we have not yet explored space sufficiently, or adequately investigated certain unexplained phenomena in our environment, or because the evidence is too far away and can never be accessible to us.

I choose the second alternative.

15. The surprising capture of a UFO in a photograph of a mountain taken on 8 October 1981 on Vancouver Island in British Columbia – see pp. 164–5. (© *Hannah McRoberts*)

16. (Inset) A digital enhancement/enlargement of the Vancouver UFO shows that the object was part of the original scene taken by Mrs D. M. – see p. 160. (© *Dr Richard F. Haines*)

17. and 18. The two photographs of a UFO that glided over the Trents' farm near McMinville on 11 May 1950. Judging by the camera used by Mr Trent (see photo 21) to take these exhaustively studied photographs, at least a minute must have elapsed between each shot – see p. 164. (© *Paul Trent/Quest Publications*)

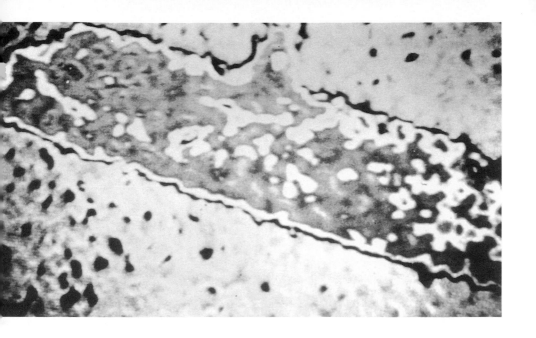

19. and 20. Two high-resolution computer enhancements made by Ground Saucer Watch in their study of the Trents' photographs. Note the orientation of the UFO in one shot shows its nearly flat base, while both shots show the UFO's off-centre tower. (© *GSW*)

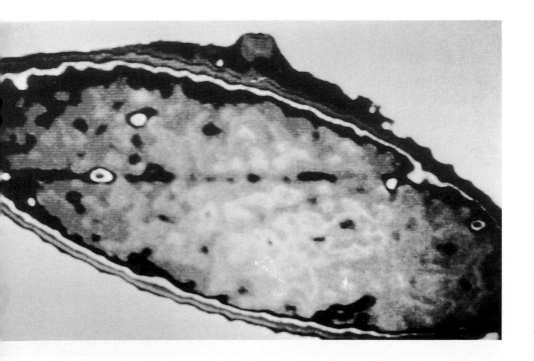

21. Paul Trent in 1950 with the camera that took the two famous photographs. (© *Paul Trent/Quest Publications*)

22. This photograph was taken with a telephoto lens by Akira Meazuka on 27 September 1986. First spotted at around 11.30 a.m., the UFO hovered noiselessly for about 25 minutes over Shiogama City, Miyagi Prefecture, some 180 miles north of Tokyo. The first witness gathered a group of sixteen people, including Meazuka, to observe the UFO, which was also seen by a group of people at a nearby school. The UFO appeared to be rounded, matt black, with no windows, and seemed at times to be rotating. Eventually it rose slowly upwards and disappeared from view. Subsequent investigations showed that no balloons had been released in the area. (*Akira Maezuka/JSPS/Fortean Picture Library*)

# CHAPTER 12
## *Who's Making Waves?*

When large numbers of people in a region or country begin to report UFOs, the ufologists start talking about waves. But who or what is making the waves and how do we separate hard data from imagination and hysteria? UFO waves ought to provide support for the extraterrestrial hypothesis and opportunities to test it. But do they?

The wave effect is a well-known psychological–sociological phenomenon. It is not restricted to UFOs, but in the UFO literature you can find many references to waves of reports. Often they are described in a way which implies that the ETIs behind UFOs (or whatever is behind them) are visiting us in waves. Not only are they visiting Earth in waves, they are visiting individual nations in waves. One year it is the turn of France, another year Britain, another Spain, and so on.

What is happening? The psychologists say that just one interesting and well-publicised UFO case makes certain members of the public sensitive to the subject. Therefore, when they experience something very unfamiliar, a phenomenon which is to them quite unrecognisable, their minds bridge the gap in comprehension with what they have read in newspapers and discussed with friends. If UFOs are in the news, they see UFOs. If a strange animal is in the news, they see a strange animal. There have been plenty of strange animal myths with whole neighbourhoods convinced that a dangerous beast was on the loose. And sometimes they have been right.

The wave phenomenon was evident in the early days of ballooning. When ballooning became a major activity in the latter half of the nineteenth century, many adventurous flights were made. They became headline news at the time and more people reported the balloons than could possibly have seen them. The hot news of the day simply made some people interpret what they saw in the sky as a balloon.

Just before the First World War airships became news. And the widespread interest in them intensified in Britain with the outbreak of war. Official records show there was a wave of airship sightings during that period. As the power of the media is now much greater than it was during the First World War, it is only to be expected that its effect will be greater. Therefore, when a UFO event gets wide publicity many people will start seeing UFOs. They have been psychologically conditioned to do so and feel supported in their interpretation of what they see. It is an established psychological characteristic of the human mind which must have been responsible for a large proportion of all UFO reports, and we have to balance this against what may be hard evidence.

## HARD EVIDENCE FROM WAVES
Let us look at what happened in the major waves in Belgium and Mexico.

These UFO waves followed the expected pattern. Two policemen in a patrol car provided the first credible report of a UFO in the Belgian wave, though a few odd accounts were received earlier from the public. A convincing report spreads through the media, because no editor will turn down a story involving two policemen and a UFO, so the event gets plenty of coverage. Other people then confirm the first sighting and report additional UFO events. Some newspapers send journalists to investigate, which induces more people to see UFOs. The public get increasingly interested in what may be going on and editors feed that interest. The wave builds up. In this situation there are obvious questions: how is the wave being generated?; and if reliable data are being reported, how can they be separated from what is not reliable?

If a landing is reported, we might expect it to be properly investigated when everyone is aware that a wave is in progress. No landings were reported in the Belgian wave, but there were plenty of reports of UFOs which lingered long enough to be well photographed. Surprisingly, only one UFO was recorded on video tape. (See photographs 10 and 11.)

## MYSTERY OVER BELGIUM
The Belgian wave began on 29 November 1989 with some strange sightings at Eupen. On that day, Heinrich Nicoll and Hubert Von

152

Montigny, both sergeants in the Belgian *gendarmerie*, reported two triangular-shaped objects, which were moving slowly or hovering at a very low altitude.

Von Montigny relates how the action began at 5.50 p.m.

We were driving on the road from Eupen to Kettenis when my attention was drawn to a slow-flying object. It hung nearly 200 metres away above a field at a height of about 300 metres. It was twilight, but still light enough to see. Below the object I saw three powerful searchlights directed to the ground and one orange-red flickering light. As the thing hung in the sky, the searchlights moved across the ground. When the object flew in our direction and came right over our patrol car, we could clearly see that the object was a triangular platform. The sighting lasted until 20.00 when the object disappeared in the direction of Spa.

The two policemen heard only a 'soft buzz' during this sighting. They could not identify the object as a plane or helicopter.

People in Eupen also reported the object. The Air Force base at Bierset reported an unidentified target on their radar screens. A plane took off from Gelsenkirchen, a NATO base, but failed to find the UFO. Later in the evening of 29 November, the two police sergeants, still on patrol, saw a second and larger triangular object 'which seemed to rise from a wood'. They said it appeared to be turning on its axis as it flew slowly over the countryside.

More sightings were reported during the following days. The media became interested, as did the main Belgian UFO society, SOBEPS. A police patrol in Battice reported 'a triangular-shaped object and a red ball descending perpendicularly from it', but discs and balls of light were also reported by members of the public.

And so the wave of reports continued. No one knew what the objects were. The most rational guess was that secret American aircraft were involved but this was strongly denied by the American Air Force: no AWACS, or the high-tech Lockheed F-117a, or any remote-controlled aircraft had been flying in the region. On 21 December, Defence Minister Guy Coëme told the Belgian Parliament that 'the reports were not due to spy planes or other military experiments'.

The UFO societies were busy and soon had a dossier of over 400 reports. The Secretary of SOBEPS, Monsieur Clerebaut, felt certain that unexplainable objects had been observed.

153

Don't tell us that this is all a fantasy. I have statements of twelve policemen who saw things at a distance of less than 200 metres. We have received reports from pilots, judges, an engineer, a lieutenant-colonel, and a trainee air-force meteorologist – all serious people who saw the thing sometimes from a distance of less than fifty metres.

High-ranking officers in the Belgian Air Force maintained that no Stealth aircraft, or new high-tech planes could have been responsible for the sightings. Firstly, they had not been present in Belgian airspace and secondly, no plane could hover or fly at a few miles an hour, as many of the reports claimed, without crashing. So there were lots of seemingly reliable reports but no explanations.

Events came to a climax during the night of 30/31 March 1990, when the Belgian Air Force scrambled two aircraft to investigate a UFO which had been detected by their radar, while both civilians and the police were reporting sightings. Upon interception the pilots reported 'a structured UFO'. This was the first encounter the Belgian Air Force had with UFOs.

To placate public enquiries, the Chief of the Belgian Air Staff, Colonel W. DeBrouwer, made the following statement on 11 July 1990.

On the night of 30th and 31st March, we had an observation on the radar and in addition a visual observation on the ground by the police. What the pilots detected was well outside the normal flying envelope of an aeroplane. Sometimes they had what we call lock-ons, which gave parameters varying from speeds between 150 knots to 990 knots, an acceleration which occurred in a few seconds. The speeds would be impossible to tolerate for a human being, that's the first point. The second point is, the visual observations always describe a system, a machine, which hangs and hovers above the surface at quite a low altitude without making any noise. Now with the current technology that would be impossible.

So the Belgian government, air force, police and many worthy members of the public were involved in the Belgian wave. Objects and events were reported that could have an extraterrestrial explanation. But after such events one needs hard evidence to study. And what evidence is now available? Only the radar recordings and the verbal reports of the many witnesses. That is not enough to confirm the extraterrestrial hypothesis.

## THE MEXICAN WAVE

During the Mexican wave, which started in 1991, hundreds of witnesses in Mexico City and other areas reported UFOs. Photographs were taken, including some by the police, and video recordings were made by many members of the public. The wave started to surge after the total eclipse of the Sun on 11 July 1991, when thousands of people gathered in Mexico City to observe the spectacle. As they watched, a UFO appeared by the eclipse. Some people had come with camcorders to record the eclipse, and seventeen independent individuals at different locations recorded the UFO. Jaime Maussan, the presenter of the television news broadcast called '60 Minutes', was the person mainly responsible for bringing this video material together for journalistic examination. We still await a report of a scientific examination.

Mexico City then enjoyed one of the longest-lasting UFO waves in UFO history. One day three UFOs hovered above a motorway in Mexico City, causing traffic chaos as motorists left their cars to view the visitors. On another day a small fleet of UFOs flew over Mexico City. Whether or not these were sightings of what could be extra-terrestrial artifacts or something else has not been clarified. Misinterpretations were bound to occur after the mass sighting of 'something' at the eclipse, a story sensationally covered by the media – reasonably so, perhaps, because it was a sensational story.

It was claimed that computer enhancements of some of the video frames showed that each of the seventeen camcorders had recorded the same object. A 1994 press release from AAC/ORTK, an international 'right to know about UFOs' organisation first established in the United States, reported:

That in Mexico City on July 11th, 1991, during the total eclipse of the Sun, tens of thousands of witnesses observed a UFO, and 17 independently operated camcorders, at varying locations, recorded the event for a total of 25 minutes. Upon enhancement each camcorder had recorded the same silver disc-shaped object. At a time when all eyes would be focused on the sky, this was undoubtedly an attempt to raise human awareness to the reality of the UFO.

Strong scepticism is the only rational response to reports of this kind. Confirmation of the taped UFO at the eclipse could only come from physicists who could assess the physical elements involved in the observations, and from photographic experts. This would apply to all the other video tapes and photographs of UFOs in Mexican airspace. (See photographs 7, 8 and 9.) So far no research report is available from competent scientists.

## ASTRONOMERS AND UNIVERSAL LIFE

What has been reported does show the possible potential of the camcorder to probe the UFO phenomena. The Mexican reports show how the solar-eclipse event might have confirmed the universality of life in an unexpected way. And in the next chapter (on photography and UFOs) we can see *what might have been*.

But let us speculate for a moment and reflect upon future solar eclipses. They are certain to be astronomically observed, so perhaps we could ask astronomers to keep a look out for the odd UFO: 'Never mind the solar eclipse, get the UFO!' This stratagem is more science fiction than science, of course, but it might be used by an astronomer or two who could spare a moment while observing future eclipses. However, no astronomer during the past century has detected a UFO at a solar eclipse, so why should a UFO turn up at these astronomical events sometime during the next century?

How would the science community react to a paper on the study of those seventeen tapes of a UFO? If the photographic material was good enough and the study rigorous enough, then international science journals would probably publish, unless the UFO could be dismissed as an atmospheric or optical effect.

## MOON MYSTERY

Before we leave this subject, we should examine an idea which has sometimes been dragged into the ETH debate. It is that only in our epoch has the Moon precisely covered the Sun's disc to produce total eclipses. Is there something odd about this, as some people have suggested?

Let's look at a few facts. Complete eclipses of the Sun are observable somewhere on Earth about twice in every three years. The shadow of the Moon on the Earth as it passes in front of the Sun is about 300 kilometres wide. But for much of the time the shadow will be travelling over ocean which covers seventy per cent of our planet. These days eclipses are not as astronomically important as they once were because astronomers have equipment to mask the Sun and provide an artificial eclipse. But total solar eclipses are the real thing, so astronomers will always take any opportunity to observe one.

In the early days of the Solar System, the Moon would have been much closer to the Earth. But its gravitational interaction with the Earth throughout its history has constantly been slowing it down in its orbit. Consequently, it has drifted slowly into a larger orbit and moved further from the Earth. Is it a coincidence that in our time, when civilisation is able to observe solar eclipses, that the distance of the Moon from the Earth is such that its disc precisely blocks out the disc of the Sun? Actually there is nothing coincidental about this. Astronomers have calculated that even in the last days of the dinosaurs, some sixty-five million years ago, the Moon's orbit was only one per cent less than it is today, which would have made no discernible difference to a total solar eclipse.

For practical purposes, the earliest known record of a solar eclipse is in an ancient Chinese document – the solar eclipse of 22 October 2137 BC. Astronomers, of course, can calculate eclipses for the past and the future, and events in distant history can sometimes be dated if a solar eclipse is mentioned in the record.

If ET has been studying us throughout our history, he might have seen some surprising changes of behaviour in response to an eclipse. There is an account in *The Persian Wars* by Herodotus which supports the belief that the ancient Babylonians were able to predict eclipses. Thales of Miletus, a Greek who lived some time between 640–546 BC, is supposed to have applied their knowledge to good purpose. In *The Persian Wars* Herodotus tells of what happened in response to the eclipse of 28 May 585 BC:

> Just as the battle was growing warm, the day was on a sudden changed into night. This event had been foretold by Thales of Miletus, who forewarned the Ionians of it, finding it for the very year in which it actually took place. The Medes and Lydians, when they observed the Sun's demise, ceased fighting, and were alike anxious to have terms of peace agreed upon.

I wonder if a few UFOs hovering unambiguously over our cities would have a similar effect on the wars now in progress on our planet?

# CHAPTER 13
## *Photographic Evidence of UFOs*

There was a time, not that long ago, when publishers and the public were ready to accept photographs and movies of UFOs without any expectation that the material had been examined by suitably qualified people. And the good fakes have haunted ufology for years and still linger in the literature. There are photographs of UFOs which are undeniably photographs of UFOs, such as those taken by the teams of researchers in Hessdalen, but whether or not they have any extraterrestrial connections is another question.

The investigation of UFOs on film is a very technical and time-consuming business. Experts *are* available in photographic science and technology in the universities, but the UFO societies seldom ask for their help, though some academics I know would freely provide their expertise, if asked. Most of the work has been carried out by a few well-qualified people in ufology.

Great differences exist in the photographic material available. Photographs of the BOLs at Hessdalen, taken by research scientists, obviously come into a different category from a photograph of a distinctly structured flying saucer taken by an individual while on holiday in some isolated part of the planet. The importance of authenticity increases enormously as we move from photographs of probable natural phenomena to photographs of possible extra-terrestrial artifacts, while the evidence is generally less credible as we move from the one to the other.

Television occasionally shows programmes on UFOs which include video tapes of UFOs. But do the producers of such programmes have the photographic material examined by experts? They are offering it as evidence of the physical reality of some UFOs, but the television producers do not know for sure, any more than we know for sure. What they *do know for sure* is that a proportion of their audiences will be convinced by the photographic evidence they offer. So where are the experts in these programmes to give their unbiased opinions on the genuineness, or otherwise, of the photography? They have not appeared in any of the programmes I have seen.

Although photographic evidence may never provide conclusive proof that flying saucers have a physical reality, a collection of well-studied photography from all parts of the Earth, together with the analyses and conclusions of the numerous experts involved, might encourage some scientists to take an interest in the phenomena. A multi-disciplinary team of experts might be asked to analyse each photograph, film and tape. The public would certainly be interested.

## WHAT TO LOOK FOR

So what would the experts look for in UFO photographs? Prints are very easily faked. Shadows must match up and be consistent with all light sources. Also, grain densities and the diameter of grains forming the image of the UFO and the background must be the same for the same amount of light reaching the film emulsion. We can see that this was indeed found in the photographic enlargement (see photographs 15 and 16) made by Dr Richard Haines of California. Haines was a research scientist with NASA until his retirement in 1988, and is a leading authority on the UFO phenomena, including the technical aspects of analysing UFO photography and video tapes.

Movies are easier to verify because movement provides significantly more information, but few people have had movie cameras at the ready when UFOs have passed by. However, these days they may have a camcorder. The camcorder could be an important tool for gathering evidence in the future, as it becomes as widespread a possession as the camera. According to Haines, it is not easy to fake a UFO on video.

Camcorders and tapes match up like bullets and guns. The signature of a camcorder is on the tape, so if, for instance, it were claimed that a number of tapes showing the same UFO event came from different camcorders at different locations this could be checked. Such checking might be relevant to the reports that numerous individuals with their camcorders photographed the same UFO in Mexico City, when crowds gathered to witness the solar eclipse on 11 July 1991. (See Chapter 12 for details of the wave of UFO sightings in Mexico.)

## UNIQUE OPPORTUNITY

During the eclipse thousands of people observed a UFO, and seventeen of them, from various locations, independently recorded it with their camcorders. Later computer enhancements seem to confirm that at least some of the camcorders had photographed the same disc-shaped UFO. Unfortunately the photographic evidence available from the event lacked detail, but what is theoretically interesting, and of possible scientific importance, are the different angles of view that seventeen separate camcorders might provide, if we were lucky. Because of the great distances of the Moon and Sun from the Earth, everyone in Mexico City would have had the same view of the Moon passing between them and the Sun. But the UFO was nearby – near enough to provide different angles of view. Therefore, if the evidence was good enough, a composite picture of the UFO might be built up from various frames from the different tapes. This could have been done with precision if the UFO and the eclipse had come within the same frames.

Astronomers observe and monitor solar eclipses and every phase of such events is recorded with considerable time-keeping precision. Therefore, given that the video material were adequate (which, unluckily, it is not) all the tapes could have been synchronised and the times at which the UFO was photographed precisely determined. We could then move on to study frames taken at the same time to see if the moving UFO was in exactly the same position in all the frames taken at the same time. We could even have developed a three-dimensional model of the UFO. The Mexico City video tapes would have provided a unique opportunity of testing the ETH – or detecting a terrestrial craft. The solar eclipse over Mexico City was *almost* a unique opportunity to make progress had the tapes provided the necessary data.

Most video tapes of UFOs are taken by unaccompanied individuals, so what can we look for in them? With the camcorder lens focused on infinity, any blurring through motion of the camera must be the same for the background and the UFO, unless, of course, the UFO itself was moving fast. The frames must have the same level of noise as the image of the UFO. A doctored tape could make the noise level of the UFO double that of the rest of the frame, but experience and expensive equipment would be needed to measure this. Background and UFO will go together, what affects one will affect the other.

It is obviously important that numerous photographic experts participate in the examination of recorded UFOs. But apart from a few well-qualified investigators, all with many years of involvement in ufology, hardly anyone is named in the literature. Photographic experts need to be brought in who have had no connection with ufology, and what they report needs to be checked by other experts. In particular, the need to verify should be part of the job of any producer preparing a television programme on UFOs. Viewers have a right to know who has checked the tapes for their probable authenticity. Probable authenticity is about the best any expert could provide.

## THE NEW ZEALAND ENIGMA

The participation of two pilots and four other people in New Zealand in the filming of UFOs for television is unquestioned. The UFOs they witnessed remain unexplained though they were described on audio tape as they were filmed and were detected by both air and ground radar. The cameraman took 23,000 frames on 16mm colour film. It has been examined by numerous experts, though only one detailed analysis was published.

The story began at the end of 1978 when pilots on the route between Wellington and Christchurch started reporting seeing unidentified lights above Kaikoura on the east coast. Ground radar in Wellington confirmed the sightings, which made for an interesting story. Television journalist Quentin Fogarty from Melbourne, on holiday at the time, became curious and persuaded his company to have a camera crew and himself make a routine flight on an Argosy cargo plane between the two New Zealand cities.

On board were the two pilots, photographer David Crockett and sound recordist Ngaire Crockett, a husband-and-wife team, plus Fogarty himself. They flew to collect a cargo of newspapers at Wellington and took off for Christchurch. It was the last day of 1978, just past midnight. As they neared Kaikoura, the radar staff in Wellington reported the detection of UFOs. Then, for about thirty minutes, they witnessed a number of red and white lights which vanished and reappeared and generally behaved in a frisky fashion. Fogarty kept up a live commentary for his listeners while the cameraman tried to capture the UFOs on film.

At about one o'clock in the morning the plane landed at Christchurch. An hour later it took off again to fly north to Wellington. The same people were on board except Ngaire Crockett whose place was taken by a local journalist. As they passed over Kaikoura again heading north, they met the UFOs performing their strange manoeuvres. Fogarty again provided commentary while David Crockett took more film. There were 'bright pulsating lights

162

appearing and disappearing . . .', plus a UFO which was tracked by the plane's radar and reckoned to be ten miles away. It was described as having a 'brightly lit bottom and transparent sort of sphere on top'. If it was ten miles away it must have been large. Later, Dr Bruce Maccabee, an optical physicist who worked for the US Navy, examined the film and calculated that if the UFO was ten miles from the plane it was between sixty and a hundred feet across and emitting light radiation equivalent to an incandescent light bulb of 100,000 watts.

The film was analysed by others but disappointed everyone. It did not show the UFOs clearly enough, probably because of the difficult conditions for filming on board the plane. But the general conclusion from the photographic experts was that the UFOs were not planets, stars, balloons, satellites, atmospheric phenomena, or reflected lights. John Cordy, who was the senior air traffic controller when the first detections were made by radar on 21 December, is on record as saying that although the newspapers greatly exaggerated the radar evidence, the good echoes did seem to come from solid objects.

This was a major UFO event, and like other major UFO events it provided a lot of data, yet everything remains unexplained. People in the UFO societies examined the evidence and had outside authorities look at the film. A spokeswoman for Kodak told me that it was studied by two experts at the company's headquarters in London, but that *no report was written on their work*. The basic problem is that the science community is not going to take much notice of what experts from the UFO societies have to say. This may be unjust, but it is a fact. But if those at the heart of the science community could be persuaded to do the research, and they could be if the data were good enough and if their career promotions were not put in jeopardy, then what they have to say would probably be widely reported in the scientific press and therefore available for the consideration of scientists in general. The New Zealand incident, like other major UFO events, was another missed opportunity to either support or weaken the claims of the extraterrestrial hypothesis.

## GENUINE PHOTOGRAPHS
Few still photographs of UFOs have been seriously considered as possible evidence of ET's spacecraft, but at least two have withstood the test of time and numerous detailed studies. They were taken on 11 May 1950 by a farming couple in the state of Oregon, the Trents, as the flying saucer glided over their farm. (See photographs

17, 18, 19, 20 and 21.) These were the only photographs to with-stand the scrutiny of Colorado University's 'Condon Investigation' – the only ones analysed which were not declared to be fakes or of natural or man-made objects. In the Trents' photographs, the building, post, plants and overhead wires in the foreground made an acceptable analysis possible. One of the Condon investigators, William Hartman, has stated that the photographs show that 'an extraordinary flying object, silvery, metallic, disc-shaped, tens of meters in diameter, and evidently artificial, flew within sight of the two witnesses'.

## A SURPRISING CAPTURE

Richard Haines has provided one of the best studies of a flying saucer photograph.[1] The possible significance of the photograph is comparable to that of the photographs taken by the Trents, but the circumstances in which it was taken were very different. The photograph was taken by a Mrs D. M. who has remained anony-mous and made no profit from her unexpected capture on film of a saucer.

On 8 October 1981, at about eleven in the morning, Mrs D. M., on holiday with her husband and young daughter in Vancouver Island, British Columbia, took a single photograph of a nearby mountain. After her colour film negatives were processed and printed she was astonished to see a flying saucer-shaped object near the mountain. (See photographs 15 and 16.)

Richard Haines has said that

> one must be careful to fully document seemingly unimportant details concerning the person taking the photograph, the social situation which surrounded the photograph, the camera–lens–film data, the developing–printing–enlarging activities and the manner in which the photograph came to the attention of the investigator.

Apart from the technical investigation, Haines himself visited the photographer in her home, spending a week in Canada. And with his father, who was a surveyor, they together examined the location and its relation to the photograph on the very day of the month the photograph was taken – though two years later.

When Haines examined the original negative film he found the frames on either side of the UFO photograph were simple holiday snaps. This meant that if the photograph *was* faked, only one shot was taken. If a faked saucer had been thrown into the air, the thrower and the photographer must have been exceptionally adept or exceptionally lucky to get such a shot first time. Nevertheless Haines was cautious. Could a Frisbee have been used? The family did have one, a black one which Mr D. M. readily produced when questioned. But their Frisbee could not have produced the image of the domed disc. Nevertheless, Haines commenced a research project on Frisbees, talking to the experts and making a model with the dome, as the saucer appears in the photograph. He could not produce the necessary results for a fake.

His final conclusion was that the people involved were apparently honest and trustworthy and that the photograph is apparently genuine. His final words: 'The disk's identity has not been identified to date.'

My view is that we might dismiss such a photograph as a probable fake if it were the only photographic evidence of an extraterrestrial artifact. But it is not alone. It is just one item of possible evidence among a great many, which would include the Trent photographs, the incidents at Rendlesham and Trans-en-Provence, and the Belgian Air Force information, plus many other unexplained events.

## UFO VISITS THE HILTON HOTEL

Richard Haines has also investigated an unusual opportunity to capture a UFO on video tape which was missed in a most extraordinary way. On the Wednesday evening of 7 November 1990, a UFO parked itself high above the roof of the seventeen-storey International Hilton Bonaventure Hotel in Montreal, Canada. Over fifty people witnessed the UFO from the top of the Hilton including two policemen, several other officials, one journalist from the local newspaper, *La Presse*, hotel staff and guests. People in the city also saw it, including Bernard Guénette, a computer graphics specialist with an interest in UFO phenomena, who later collaborated with Haines in his study of the event.

The UFO stayed to be photographed for two and a half hours while people came and went, puzzled by the hovering lights in the sky. Yet only two photographs were taken, and those by the journalist who was not a photographer – and with an ordinary short-focus lens completely unsuitable for the task. One wonders what photographic journalists do for a living in Montreal when so many people were looking at a UFO for a couple of hours without the assistance of a photographer. The journalist who took the photographs had to phone his office for one of his staff photographers to tell him how long an exposure to make. A short journey from the newspaper, a sturdy tripod and a long-focus lens might have helped to solve the enigma of the Hilton UFO, but no one was awake to the opportunity – not even the press.

The UFO was first noticed at about 7 p.m. A guest swimming in the outdoor heated swimming pool on the roof of the Hilton saw a luminous, oval-shaped object hovering in the sky above. She pointed it out to the lifeguard on duty who notified the hotel's security officer, Albert Sterling. He arrived to see the large hovering object in what he described as 'an almost cloudless sky' and phoned the police. He couldn't at that time get through to the local airport to check on air traffic in the area. Meanwhile, people in the city had also seen the UFO and notified the local newspaper, *La Presse*. By about 8 p.m. the object had become brighter and Sterling phoned the police a second time.

Journalist Marcel Laroche, who wrote an article on the event, arrived from *La Presse* and Police Officer Lippé from the police station. Lippé later reported a luminous round object with three yellow lights, each radiating a distinct beam. Later, Lippé, Laroche and the lifeguard saw a small private plane flying at a lower altitude than the UFO, but no other aircraft were seen. The minimum height for that plane would have been 1200 feet to meet local regulations, so the UFO was higher, although the UFO appeared large compared to the plane.

At about 8.30 p.m. Police Sgt Masson arrived on the Hilton roof. He was so impressed by what he saw that he called the Royal Canadian Mounted Police – though flying police might have been more useful. Dorval International Airport then reported that those at the Hilton were not alone in witnessing the UFO. Calls had come in from the public but nothing had been seen on the airport's radar.

At this time, journalist Laroche decided that a photograph of the phenomenon might be useful and collected a 35mm camera from his car. Police Officer Lippé had the lights on a high building under construction across the street turned off, but this made no difference to observing the UFO. At 9 p.m., police reinforcements came in the form of Officer Denis Pare. Laroche took several photographs on ordinary colour film, using a thirty-second exposure. The complete roll of film was subsequently studied by Haines.

At about 9.30 p.m. Inspector Luc Morin of the Royal Canadian Mounted Police, who had been assigned to the case, arrived. He had phoned the Department for National Defence and had been told there were no military flights in the Montreal area that night. His later description and drawing of the UFO matched those of the other main witnesses. At 9.45 p.m. the police decided that a video recording of the UFO might be desirable, and at 10.20 p.m. Police

Officer Michael Cote arrived with a camcorder. However, Inspector Morin has stated that at 10.10 p.m. the UFO was no longer sufficiently visible for photography as heavy clouds had formed, and that was the end of a very unusual evening.

The principal witnesses have drawn the UFO. Their drawings are more or less consistent, as are their verbal accounts. But above all, good photographs were needed. Reports and drawings from the most reliable of witnesses are not going to advance anyone's understanding of the Hilton UFO. Richard Haines, who applied his expertise to the photographs and who investigated the details of this case, has been bemused by the way the event was handled. The UFO was hovering over the Hilton for two and a half hours, observed by police, the press, the general public, and hotel staff and guests, yet no aircraft was alerted to investigate and no proper photographs or video recordings were made. The Hilton UFO therefore remains a mystery.[2]

# CHAPTER 14
## *How Do the Saucers Fly?*

Although our systems of propulsion have taken humankind to the Moon and back several times, the costs in energy are so high that spacecraft will not easily go further with human astronauts on board. The ways we overcome gravity and the inertia of matter also produce all sorts of problems for us. Fossil and chemical fuels pollute – and ignite and explode in car and aircraft accidents. They are heavy and hazardous and not ideal sources of power. Future routine journeys within the Solar System – thousands of times more demanding in energy than were the Apollo flights to the Moon – will remain an impossible dream until a new propulsion system for spaceflight is developed.

The dream is to colonise neighbouring space and to explore the worlds of the Solar System – and then to send exploratory probes to the stars. But this will require a method of propulsion that we can barely envisage at present because the basic science for its development, which has to be fundamental physics, has yet to be discovered.

Those future spaceships, designed in theory and proposed in technical journals, are propelled by systems we can already envisage in the twentieth century. That is not a realistic scenario. They would either be horrendously dangerous or need so much fuel that they cannot be seriously considered.

One example, the interstellar probe Daedalus, was an enthusiastic exercise in showing what will *not* be developed in the future. It was planned in technical detail by members of the British Interplanetary Society in 1977. The Daedalus plan calls for a two-stage craft, 54,000 tons in all, most of it fuel to enable the craft to travel at 24,000 miles per second on its way to Barnard's Star almost six light-years away. At that speed it would reach the star in fifty years and fly straight through any system of planets which may be there. No fuel would be left to slow down Daedalus or put it into orbit. Yet to achieve this mission it has to carry, at take-off, some fifty thousand tons of fuel. That would be the cost, with current technology, for a quick look at one of the nearest stars and whatever may be in orbit. Is anyone going to use current technology in such an expensive and cumbersome way?

It must now be admitted, with respect for those imaginative people who conceived Daedalus, that this is definitely not the way to the stars. Something quite different and more practical is needed, something we can use routinely. Without this *something* for future space propulsion, no one is going into the interstellar spaceflight business – and even exploratory flights by astronauts and scientists to the more distant worlds within the Solar System will not become routine. We need a propulsion system that does not require colossal amounts of fuel to transport payloads and people to the outer planets and their moons in a matter of weeks rather than years. And we would need a system to take exploratory probes to the nearest stars in a relatively short period of time compared with the human lifespan – which may have been considerably extended by biology by the time we start launching interstellar probes.

The absurdity of using currently conceivable means of travelling to the stars becomes plain when we consider what is basically involved. Our spaceship, built in orbit to make things easier, is ready and has enough fuel to visit the nearest star some four light-years away. The energy needed for this exploit would drive the world's current industries for many years. Off we go, steadily accelerating as we use up half our fuel. The difference in the spaceship's mass which decreases with the consumption of fuel is disregarded here in order not to complicate the point.

We near our destination after several decades and fire our engines to slow down. There would be a lot of slowing down to do before we could go into orbit at a convenient point in the alien planetary system. The remaining half of our fuel is used in this manoeuvre. After we've thoroughly explored the planetary system, we have the tiresome task of manufacturing the fuel for the return flight, using local resources. We then head back to Earth, following the same flight procedure.

What would we have done in terms of our use of energy? We would have used X amount of energy to accelerate to our speed through interstellar space, plus an equal amount of energy to stop. The energy at both ends of this exercise would be lost into space. So can we expect civilisations thousands of years ahead of us technologically to be travelling around the Galaxy in such an inefficient way? I do not think we can. If we are serious about the exploration and use of the Solar System by human beings as well as by probes, we should encourage research in fundamental physics because it is only from that area of science that the basis of a new technology of propulsion could come.

## GRAVITY FOR SPACEFLIGHT

Numerous technologists have carried out theoretical research into how to use advanced energy sources for journeys within the Solar System and to the nearest stars, and have published their results in scientific journals. The means of propulsion have ranged from the chemical fuel currently used in rockets to nuclear fission and nuclear fusion, and onwards to matter–antimatter annihilation. The use of antimatter seemed the ultimate energy source because all the fuel is transformed into energy when equal quantities of matter and antimatter come together, when matter–anti-matter annihilation takes place. (This is already happening in the accelerators of particle physics, but only atomic particles are involved.) In contrast to the 100 per cent efficiency of matter–antimatter annihilation, only 0.7 per cent of hydrogen is trans-formed into energy in nuclear fusion, the energy source of the Sun, stars and hydrogen bombs.

Would antimatter be the ultimate fuel for star trips once a technology for producing and handling it could be devised? At present all the antimatter in the world, produced in the accelerators of high energy physics, would not be enough to cover a pin head. But production of antimatter in quantity is not the only problem. Any future containment of antimatter during its production and storage looks about as dangerous as anything could. One slip, an accidental contact with the product, and good-bye!

Will antimatter take us to the stars? It looks an unlikely can-didate, even though it drives the *Enterprise* across the Galaxy in *Star Trek*. A simple but elegant solution is needed, something which is ready to use wherever you are in the universe, something which costs nothing, is always available and will take you anywhere at any speed you choose, something which is safe to use. That energy source is always with us – it is gravity.

## THE MYSTERY OF GRAVITY

Gravity is the mystery force of the universe. The apple that hit Isaac Newton on the head did not clarify the nature of gravity in his mind nor how it is produced, as the myth proclaims. He simply suffered *its effect* and went on to describe it in mathematical terms. Only now are physicists with their sophisticated technology approaching a level of understanding that may in the decades ahead enable us to discover the source and mechanism of gravity.

When travelling about the planet in vehicles we use vast amounts of energy to overcome gravity and also the *inertia* of vehicles and their contents. Inertia is a very strange attribute of matter, and together with the nature of mass may hold the key to the future of spaceflight. When Galileo climbed the Tower of Pisa in the six-teenth century, he took with him, so the story goes, a cannon ball and a wooden ball of the same size to drop at the same time. Everyone at this demonstration of fundamental physics expected the cannon ball to hit the ground first. But Galileo knew this would not happen. Both balls hit the ground simultaneously. Why was this? The gravitational attraction between the Earth and the cannon ball was certainly greater because the cannon ball had greater mass than the wooden ball. However, the inertia of the cannon ball (its resistance to the gravitational force) was also proportionally greater than the inertia of the wooden ball. Mass and inertia are always equivalent – more mass, more inertia. Therefore, as the ratio of mass to inertia of both balls was exactly the same, they hit the ground at the same time, much to the satisfaction of Galileo and the distress of his professors, who had been reading too much Aristotle instead of pursuing experimental science.

Gravity is a local phenomenon. It is less on the Moon and Mars, for instance. But inertia for any one object is the same everywhere in the universe. It is determined by all the matter in the entire universe. Nevertheless, if a way could be discovered of temporarily removing from matter the attribute we call mass, the same process would also remove inertia because mass and inertia are equivalent. In a hypothetical situation where the inertia of a spaceship and its contents had been removed, or, in other words, all its mass had been removed, it would automatically travel at the speed of light. This is decreed by the nature of the universe: all massless particles, photons, travel at the speed of light. If we remove only most of the spaceship's mass and inertia it would need little energy for rapid acceleration. Saucers observed on the ground which take off and quickly disappear from view might possess a technology to control mass and inertia. It is one way to explain otherwise inexplicable reports.

## BEYOND THE SPEED OF LIGHT

Dr Robert Wood, an aerospace engineer at the McDonnell Douglas Corporation, has been thinking about faster-than-light travel. He has pointed out that most scientists encounter a problem in accepting the possibility of a large number of UFO visitations because they assume that our current science, and all science of the future, will never permit travel faster than the speed of light. He says:

> This is the linchpin assumption because it is immediately clear that, if the opposite assumption is made (such as *it is very simple to travel at a million times the speed of light if you know how to do it*), then it is hardly necessary to go through the details to imagine that one would expect a lot of visitors to Earth.
>
> It cannot be *proven* at present that it is possible to travel faster than the speed of light. However, what we *can* say is that all experiments accelerating particles to high speeds (but never faster than the speed of light) have always used electromagnetic radiation to do so. This is like trying to use sound waves to propel a vehicle to supersonic speeds.

He concludes from this that it is not surprising that sub-atomic particles accelerated in the accelerators of high-energy physics cannot be pushed to speeds faster than that of light. But I was left wondering what energy, what propulsion system, we might use to send sub-atomic particles through the 'speed of light' barrier.

One major obstacle stands in the way of faster-than-light travel. Einstein showed that objects nearing the speed of light greatly increase in mass, so that at the speed of light an object would theoretically possess infinite mass, which at the best of times is difficult to shift. Apart from that, one can accept Wood's argument. We certainly have nothing that moves faster than the speed of light which could propel anything faster. Wood suggests, however, that gravity might one day make space travel faster than light.

Maybe, if science has a successful future, the physicists will find a way around Einstein. Indeed, the major research line in particle physics which bears directly on the model of the universe, as currently understood, is moving in that direction. It involves the search for a particle known as the Higgs boson. The Higgs field, thought to be an energy field pervading all space and a left-over from the Big Bang, should manifest itself in the presence of Higgs bosons. The Higgs boson is thought to give mass to matter, and is needed to explain the nature of the W and Z sub-nuclear particles which play an essential part in the scheme of things. In some way as yet unknown it bestows mass upon these particles.

The Higgs boson is expected to be detected in CERN's particle accelerator in the near future – the only place it can be detected now that the Americans have given up the building of their huge accelerator in Texas. High levels of energy need to be produced by colliding beams of particles to create the Higgs boson because it is a very massive particle, perhaps eighty to ninety times the mass of the proton. This is a costly exercise and, in general, government support is declining. But revolutionary technology could come from this research as we gain a deeper understanding of the ways in which the universe works at its most fundamental level. Physicists believe the Higgs boson exists and we can only wait for its discovery which will make front-page news throughout the world.

If interstellar travel could be possible for us by the application of future physics, it would have been possible for technologists who evolved in the Galaxy long ago. This is a key point. In SETI much depends on the practicality of interstellar travel. If it is impossible or very difficult, then there will not be any flying saucers outside the heads of those people who report them, and no extraterrestrials will have visited the Solar System in its four billion years' history – since the Earth has been in a fit state to receive visitors. But if flying to the stars is no more difficult for *them* than flying to the Moon or Mars would be for us, then the Solar System, and especially the Earth, will have attracted many visitors.

## REPORTED CLUES TO ET'S POWER SOURCE

The witnesses of close encounters with flying saucers, in many parts of the world, have reported certain effects and observations with a curious level of consistency. It seems that the physical effects upon witnesses could result from the propulsion system used. James McCampbell, a physicist-engineer who used to work for NASA, has a neat way of handling UFO data which he has used to obtain at least a vague theoretical insight into the nature of the saucers. Given that flying saucers have a physical reality, McCampbell believes it possible to gather data that are scientifically interesting from the thousands of reports available, and from this to construct a consistent idea of what we might call the physics of flying saucers.

McCampbell makes the point that much of this data would be inexplicable to witnesses, almost all of whom are non-scientists. He gives one example where a witness said that a saucer occupant in a spacesuit had his face covered by wire mesh. McCampbell suggests this could have been shielding against exposure to intense microwave radiation which he thinks may be associated with the power system of saucers. But this would indicate a biological saucernaut. An enlisted *Homo sapiens*?

In close encounters with saucers, a common effect reported is a loss of electrical power, especially in cars. Physiological symptoms in witnesses have included radiation damage and burning which are consistent with exposure to high levels of microwave radiation. Also, the sensation of being warmed up, humming and high-pitched noises, certain kinds of odours and a metallic taste could all be produced by exposure to microwave radiation.

McCampbell has studied the effects of microwaves on hearing.

> Experiment and theory show that the pitch perceived from impinging microwave pulses result from two, distinctly different, mechanisms. At weak intensities and pulse rates, in the low audio range, the pulses directly stimulate the inner ear and are interpreted as humming sounds. For very intensive radiation the pressure waves reverberate inside the head, creating the impression of high-pitch whistles. No known mechanism produces tones of intermediate frequencies. Thus the sounds stimulated by microwave radiation from UFOs would be discontinuously dependent upon the distance to the UFO.[1]

He goes on to point out that microwave radiation could account for most of the physiological effects reported; that the humming sound is consistently mentioned and that the threshold for hearing the high-pitch sound of microwaves is 22,000 times greater in intensity than that needed to produce the humming sound. Any witness hearing the high-pitched sound should escape immediately before being cooked alive.

The smells reported are typically of sulphur dioxide (the rotten-egg smell), benzines and ozone. McCampbell points out that such compounds can be produced by discharges of microwaves into the atmosphere. There is also the matter of taste. Some witnesses have experienced 'a funny metallic taste' which can be induced by low-level microwave radiation. I know someone who had that experience on and off for weeks. I suggested the misuse of her microwave oven as the possible cause, since when the symptoms have disappeared.

On a few occasions, very close proximity to saucers in flight has reportedly caused witnesses to be cooked from the inside out, according to the autopsies. In these few extreme cases it would be difficult to substantiate the details. But many hundreds of reports of less dramatic heating and burning effects do show a pattern which could be explained by the presence of microwaves. Witnesses in cars have had the exposed parts of themselves burned red; metal watch bands and rings have become hot, as have car bodies.

It therefore seems reasonable to accept that there is enough evidence to conclude that there may be something of great scientific interest to investigate. Reports of physiological effects should be more reliable than reports of strange lights and objects. Are intense fields of microwaves in some way associated with a technology that controls mass and the effects of gravity?

McCampbell believes that a hypothesis for the power source of flying saucers can be conceived that is consistent with the reported observations. He thinks it safe to gather scientifically interesting data from the thousands of reports available. He emphasises that most reports come from people with no scientific background, which ensures that the interesting information cannot have been invented or imagined, or be the result of poor observation of the reported event. According to McCampbell:

> A vast reservoir of technical data on UFOs lies in the published reports of witnesses. And it can be tapped by the careful study of details in single, well-documented events or in the composite from many similar cases. Validity of the data is assured when the reports contain technical information that could not possibly have been known to the witnesses. Ironically, testimony from simple, ordinary folk can therefore be the most valuable. It is essential to focus attention upon the phenomenon reported rather than the identity of the witness or other diversionary issues.

A critic might say that McCampbell and others have read the scientifically interesting data into the reports. It could be so, although the reports and the science look too detailed for this.

## DO SAUCERS CONTROL THEIR MASS?
The flight characteristics of saucers, described in hundreds of reports, have puzzled people for a long time. There is an uncanny consistency in accounts which seems to indicate that the saucers control their mass and inertia, and various levels of microwave radiation appear to be associated with the propulsion system.

The saucers show no system of propulsion, yet they hover and descend slowly, apparently under control. They are often described as fluttering downwards, like a leaf, as if almost weightless. And they travel through the atmosphere with skimming, bouncing movements. These flight characteristics are well understood by aeronautical engineers. What is not understood are the fantastic rates of acceleration, the sharp-angled turns at great speed and the instantaneous stopping in flight. It looks as if this could only be done in vehicles which have little or no mass and therefore little or no inertia. They also have no, or little, effect on the atmosphere as they take off rapidly through it. There is no rush of air. This cannot be explained.

A brief return to Einstein is relevant here. Einstein's principle of equivalence shows that gravitational force and acceleration have an identical effect on matter. To take a modern example, when astronauts are accelerated into orbit they experience a force of several Gs, the same as they would experience if on a massive planet with a gravitational field of the same number of Gs. The gravitational effect produced by the gravitational field of a planet and the same effect produced by appropriate acceleration would be identical.

We cannot expect to duplicate saucer technology. It would be like asking medieval craftsmen to build Concorde. So we cannot do anything at the moment to test the hypothesis that ET's spacecraft control gravity. The first hypothesis to test – and one which we can test – is that flying saucers are landing on Earth. To obtain either a positive or negative answer to that hypothesis is enough for the moment.

## FUTURE NEED
It is hard to believe that our civilisation with all its dynamism can survive more than a couple of centuries if restricted to the Earth. Two million years of struggle for survival have conditioned humanity too strongly to exploitation and expansion. We look like the last sorcerer's apprentice – at least on this planet. Our partial control of the effects of civilisation will not be enough. Pressures on the Earth will increase. Release from this problem might be found by moving into new environments in the vastness of the Solar System, but this would only be possible with a revolutionary advance in space transport. In the foreseeable future, we will not be able to take advantage of what is on offer out there because we are stuck with primitive propulsion technology. One would think that nations with the scientific and technological capacities to move forward in this area would support research which might, in the decades ahead, begin to produce the science for a practical system of propulsion for

177

space exploration. Yet the opposite is actually happening. Those governments with the capacity to act are cutting back on their support for what would be the essential research. Fundamental physics appears to be the only science from which we may gain the knowledge to advance the technology of space propulsion, and this area of science is not getting the support that it once enjoyed.

Space offers the only environment for virtually unlimited use. If we could take up the offer, the growth of civilisation could continue unfettered by building space colonies and using the energy from the Sun to drive industries and manufacturing with material resources and energy outside the Earth. Polluting residues could be safely dissipated into space. What is now impossible could be accomplished with relative ease with a revolutionary new level in propulsion technology for spaceflight. It could save civilisation. The alternatives would be catastrophic conflicts or the most rigid controls ever known on human activities.

We may not be the first among technological species to run into this situation. High technology may often be too successful for the good and survival of civilisation. The warning symptoms may be slow to appear but serious environmental sickness is fast in developing. It could be a common problem. If so, there would be inevitable pressures to drive technological species to use the space of their planetary systems. And if flying saucers are extraterrestrial spacecraft powered by the control of mass and gravity, then we may one day be able to exploit this same means of celestial transport. Our Earth-based civilisation would then be saved and our space age future could expand and begin to explore the Galaxy, as perhaps many civilisations have done during the past few billion years.

## A VOYAGE INTO FANTASY?

A few people have anticipated what the present trend in physics to discover the nature of mass and gravity might lead to. In 1981, in the United States, Dr Frederick Alzofon suggested a way of exploiting gravity to propel spacecraft. He thought it might be possible to weaken the Earth's gravitational force on a spacecraft by manipulating Nature at a sub-nuclear level. He proposed that the Earth's gravity is produced by the mass of our planet interacting with an energy field formed of what are called 'virtual processes'.

The temptation with all such speculative exploration of Nature is to go on to show how knowledge that we do not yet possess, and may never possess, might be applied to create revolutionary technology. However, the spaceship which Alzofon proposed consisted

178

of panels of aluminium and iron incorporated in a symmetrical way around the hull of the craft. When the propulsion system starts, the nuclei of the iron atoms are all oriented in the same way by pulses of microwaves in a magnetic field. This effect is supposed to spread to the nuclei of aluminium in a domino fashion – and then to the 'virtual processes'. If these are involved in the creation of gravity, then as they interact with the oriented nuclei of the iron and aluminium they will lose energy and the gravitational field will be reduced.

Kenneth Behrendt is another scientist, a chemist in New Jersey, in the United States, who since the early 1980s has been working on the possible theoretical basis of UFO propulsion. He has tried to rationalise the technical data contained in the reports, the technical data to which McCampbell has drawn our attention. And he has been especially concerned with how saucers may fly, the effects on witnesses and the environment of the propulsion system which ET may be using.

Behrendt's starting position is that saucers in flight must be massless, or nearly so, to have the flight characteristics that are constantly reported. He puts it like this:

> Suppose a witness reports a saucer, thirty-two feet in diameter, hovering near ground level. Suddenly it rises and disappears into a cloudless sky in only ten seconds. To do this the UFO would have to reach an altitude of 20.83 miles in ten seconds where it would become a point too small for the human eye to resolve. If the craft's acceleration was constant, its crew would have felt an inertial force of 68.38 Gs, and at the end of its ten-second climb the craft would be moving at 15,000 miles an hour.
>
> If the UFO weighed ten tons its engines would have to produce a force of 1,368 million pounds. The power output of its engines would have had to be 27.36 million horsepower or 20,000 megawatts. Thus its power output would be equivalent to about twenty 1,000 megawatt nuclear power plants operating at peak output.[2]

Behrendt points out that we cannot expect such immense power to be generated within the small closed craft that are reported. Therefore, any hypothesis on the UFO propulsion system requires a more or less massless craft.

It is fun to develop such ideas. They may lead forward or round and round in fascinating circles. But even given that UFOs do have a physical reality and do exploit gravity to cross interstellar space and to explore the Earth, we cannot expect to be able to copy their technology.

Let us go back in time to eighteenth-century London and leave a jet aircraft in one of the fashionable parks. There were plenty of technologists living in London at the time who would hurry along to examine this wonderful object which had suddenly appeared. They would soon see it was not made to be drawn by horses, and might guess from the wings that it was made to fly, but they would not be able to duplicate the technology because they would not understand the principles involved in its construction and function, and they would not be able to produce the materials needed. It would just remain on the ground, a mysterious monument for all to marvel at.

If a gap of 200 years cannot be bridged within one planetary biology and one species and one civilisation, how can anyone expect the gap between two planetary civilisations to be bridged? If a flying saucer landed tomorrow and our best scientists and technologists had full access to it for an unlimited period, they would not have a hope of understanding its propulsion system and duplicating the technology – and building another saucer.

## TOWARDS A QUANTUM LEAP
We cannot foresee what is likely to come from future research in fundamental physics, no more than the Victorians in the middle of the last century foresaw our communications and electronic technologies in the basic research then in progress. But there are indications (let's put it no stronger than that) that our counterparts have mastered the mechanism of mass and are controlling mass and gravity in their spaceflight technology. Therefore, if we prove that some UFOs are extraterrestrial artifacts, we will have confirmed that mass and gravity can be controlled. Not only would we know that a new space age of exploration and colonisation of the Solar System is possible, but we would know that with the new understanding we might also solve all our problems of propulsion on land, in the air and on the sea. This might be one of the quantum leaps that all successful civilisations make in time.

# CHAPTER 15
## *A Theory to Predict Close Encounters*

----

**W**hen are close encounters with UFOs most likely to occur in any given location? This seems an unanswerable question, but Roy Dutton, an aerospace engineer who worked for British Aerospace until his retirement in 1991, proposes that his Astronautical Theory can answer it, and he invites any qualified person to test the theory. This is a unique opportunity for scientists and technologists, who are justifiably sceptical, to test an actual theory of UFOs.

Roy Dutton began his spare-time research after the UFO wave in Britain in 1967, having been intrigued by the strange aerial craft that were being reported. He studied the reports from a professional point of view, and went on to develop what must be the only fully developed theory to predict a definite pattern for the arrival of extraterrestrial artifacts in our environment.

Like all scientific theories it is *testable*, but so far Dutton himself has had to do all the testing, using the most credible reports from Europe and America. It is not a difficult theory to understand as it now stands, although its development over more than twenty-five years is not so easy to comprehend.

### THE AERODYNAMICS OF UFOs
The first thing Dutton did in 1967 was study the reports to see if they made sense in engineering terms. He sketched the reported UFOs and made notes on their flight characteristics, their sounds and lights. 'The reports contained enough common features to convince me that there was something to investigate – and this launched me into the research which I've continued until this day.'

He realised that the apparently credible reports of UFOs in 1967, when not simply lights in the sky, were *bodies of revolution*. Their shapes (discs, conical-like craft and long cylindrical objects) could be produced by rotating a line about an axis. He found the shape of the discus-like variety

> reasonably efficient in terms of drag when moving edgeways through the atmosphere, but not efficient if aerodynamic lift is also required. But if lift is provided by some other means, it is logical that these discus-shaped objects are usually witnessed moving edgeways in level flight.

He soon found that the aerodynamic behaviour of what had become known as flying saucers was consistent with what was being reported.

> My interest in UFO behaviour was aroused by a report in which the witness described a low-flying disc which sounded like the wind as it passed overhead. Anyone who has stood beneath a low-flying glider in calm conditions will know how much noise is generated, even by the wake of a good aerodynamic shape. The object described by the witness would have had a much noisier wake, which in humid conditions might become a visible vapour trail.

It seemed to Dutton that if UFOs are solid bodies moving through our atmosphere, no matter what the source of propulsion, their flight characteristics would be familiar, such as the bouncing flight pattern when in level flight:

> It's reminiscent of a dynamic form of speed instability affecting conventional aircraft which is known as Phugoid Motion. After an aircraft encounters a disturbance, it can sometimes drift in an alternating manner, above and below its flight path, losing speed as it rises and gaining speed as it descends until the oscillation is damped out.

He also pointed out that the spiralling descent of discs, reported by many witnesses, is the pattern of free-fall descent for a rotating disc. And the falling leaf descent, an oscillation from side to side also reported, is what would happen when a disc is descending but not rotating. Dutton built a six-inch model of a disc with a dome to confirm that such a structure would behave in these characteristic ways. 'When dropped flat from a high balcony in still air the model behaved as expected, and consistent with eye-witness reports.' He was satisfied that the aerodynamic behaviour being reported was correct for the type of vehicle being described. The discs, he concluded, were solid objects and had mass.

## TRACKING CLOSE ENCOUNTERS

His next step was to search for any order in the reported UFO activity of 1967. Looking at the geographical distribution of the close encounters, he found that a band thirty-five miles wide contained most of the events in the northwest and north Midlands. In 1971 another wave of reports occurred, including some of fireballs travelling through the atmosphere. When Dutton plotted the geographical distribution of this second wave of reports, he was surprised to find it very similar to the 1967 wave but skewed south-east to north-west. Either something strange and orderly was happening or those particular bands across Britain were inhabited by a lot of fantasy-prone witnesses.

During Dutton's study of the most credible events in Britain between 1967 and 1973, he noticed that numerous witnesses had reported brilliant balls of light which could not be explained away as satellite re-entry debris, meteorites or meteors. They were too bright and their reported trajectories were generally not right for these conventional explanations. They were reported as stable balls of light, not as objects that were burning up in the atmosphere. Dutton began to wonder if they might be extraterrestrial craft coming into the atmosphere and linked with the close-encounter UFO phenomena. He was surprised to find that these balls of light had been 'almost mechanically cyclic in their frequency'. The majority had been witnessed within six days of specific dates which divided each year into ten equal parts. 'This observation,' says Dutton 'was used to good effect during the subsequent review of historical global UFO reports.'

## GLOBAL REVIEW

The study of close encounter events in Britain led Dutton to a global study, using certain international catalogues of UFO reports, selecting data covering the period from 1885 to 1971, including twenty-six reports, spread over almost a century, of objects flying into or out of large expanses of water – lakes and the sea. These reports seemed so unusual as to make them credible. 'I thought that if high-tech spacecraft were arriving here, they might find large expanses of water the best places to hide temporarily.' He found that approximate Great Circles linked these events around the world. This discovery led to the idea of trying to link the global events with similar circles on the celestial sphere. (Great circles can be plotted on the Earth's surface and on the celestial sphere – see Figures 2 and 3 on pages 186 and 187.)

## PERMANENT TRACKS IN THE HEAVENS

We have to consider here how it was possible to get to grips with an extraterrestrial monitoring program which the Astronautical Theory describes. A spacecraft in a *short-term* orbit of the Earth retains its orbital position in space relative to the heavens. (Long-term orbits will drift with time.) While the orbit is maintained, its reference to the stars remains constant. But the Earth is rotating beneath the orbit. Therefore, the track of a satellite over the Earth's surface is continuously changed, and if marked on the Earth's surface would be a continuous spiral.

Dutton explains it like this:

> If an imaginary laser beam were to be projected from an orbiting spacecraft towards the Earth's centre, it would mark out an endless spiral on the surface as the Earth rotated beneath it. But if the laser beam were pointed in the opposite direction – at the sky – it would for all practical purposes continuously trace out an unchanging and stationary circle on the celestial sphere. Such a circle would be a Celestial Great Circle.

The prime task was to relate events on the Earth's surface to the starfield. And because of the Earth's constant rotation beneath the stars, it was essential to obtain precise times for UFO events, plus their geographical co-ordinates. Otherwise it would not be possible to relate events to the celestial sphere and discover the directions from which extraterrestrial craft might be approaching the Earth. Times and co-ordinates go together because times are different in different parts or the world and have to be recorded in the model.

These considerations presented problems when Dutton processed the data for the period 1885 to 1971. But the results were intriguing. He found ten favoured orbital angles to the equator and orbital links with sunrise and sunset. He next turned his attention to the geographical distribution of events on the Earth's surface, looking for evidence of spiralled connecting paths which would indicate a type of satellite activity.

For several years Dutton worked away at the data, trying to make sense of the geographical locations and times of the reports by assuming that the objects would be arriving and leaving on natural trajectories, the kind of orbit followed by most satellites. But these efforts were fruitless. 'In the end I decided to let the data distributions suggest their own solution, however improbable the implied orbital period seemed to be!' To his surprise, when he assumed a constant 65.4-minute period and retrograde orbiting (orbits going against the Earth's rotation), everything began to fall into place.

> What fell out of this move was remarkable. I had taken a lot of wrong turnings and ways that led nowhere and at last everything seemed to fall into place. If I had continued to impose *our* practical limitations nothing would have been discovered.

This was the take-off point in Dutton's development of the Astronautical Theory.

## DEVELOPING THE THEORY

The next advance came when some colleagues, computer experts at British Aerospace, devised a program to plot out the identified ground tracks, using a world-graphics program. Dutton explains:

> I had previously processed all the data manually, and had not been able to obtain an overall view of the situation being revealed. The program extended all the identified spiralled arcs to produce, for each case, the track for one complete revolution of the Earth.

The computer produced numerous ground tracks with what appeared to be injection points for orbits at the equator. Its output showed that some arcs converged at the equator while others linked up to form complete orbital sequences. Some changed their angle of orbit at the equator. (See Figures 2 and 3.)

Dutton theorised from this work that extraterrestrial vehicles, perhaps the large cylindrical craft sometimes reported, were keying into orbit at set points on the equator.

> The so-called Mothership vehicles have been reported to sometimes discharge and retrieve surveillance craft whilst hovering in the atmosphere. This may also occur from orbit. Some witnesses have reported objects like satellites which have

Figure 2: Determined orbital tracks marked on the Earth's surface.

stopped abruptly and then have resumed orbital speed again on a different track. My work suggests that these sudden changes of direction may occur over ground track intersections.

Many such reports exist, although they are actually unimportant to the Astronautical Theory. *They are not needed to test it.*

At that time Dutton was using data from over 400 selected reports of close encounters, covering the period from 1885 to 1971. And the tracks on the Earth's surface which these gave related directly to what appear to be 'favoured orbits determined by a few Great Circles on the celestial sphere'.

186

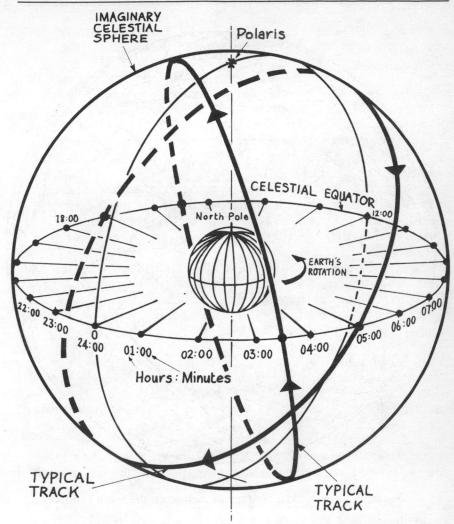

Figure 3: The celestial sphere and favoured track orientations.

Dutton said:

I found that long strings of sightings were linked by some of the ground tracks. And I was able to identify sixty-six key navigational points on the equator. It would seem from all the reports that the craft involved in close encounters never stray far from the established track lines, which, navigationally speaking, makes a lot of sense, especially with an automated program of surveillance.

According to Dutton, UFOs are coming into 'super orbits' from specific tracks in relation to the Sun and the stars.

A large number of Celestial Great Circle arcs became evident, unmistakably linking the close encounter events with the starfield. I found that the identified ground tracks could be linked to three distinct orbital options, and that fixed orbital injection points were spaced at equal intervals of 5.45 degrees round the equator. From each one, orbits having at least ten inclinations [angles] to the equator of between 42 and 76 degrees could be adopted to cover all the inhabited regions of the world. With this set-up there is the possibility of sixty-six multiplied by ten tracks. That is 660 ground tracks in the alien network.

It must be admitted that these tracks do intersect at some interesting places, such as certain well-known areas of UFO activity and places of historical interest. These might be the best places to observe ET's artifacts in high-speed retrograde orbits, given appropriate astronomical equipment. (See Figure 2.)

## DOUBTFUL DATA

A few contactee cases were included in the data base for the Astronautical Theory, but they are not crucial to it. There have been hundreds of such cases, yet not one has provided anything of acceptable scientific interest – say, something on which one could write a paper for *Nature* or *Science*. Until such evidence is produced, I can only view contactee and abductee cases as psychologically generated, particularly as their distribution seems to be linked to national cultures, especially the North American culture, and population density. That the timings and locations of some of these events fit the predictions of the theory is a problem, but, as the co-discoverer of the structure of DNA, Sir Francis Crick, once said about scientific theories: one should worry about a theory where all the facts fit because some of the facts are bound to be misleading.

We should judge a scientific theory by testing it, no matter how unusual it may appear, and the only fully developed theory to come from the study of the UFO phenomena deserves testing. Dutton's theory predicts when close encounters are likely to occur at given locations in the future from the data such events have provided in the past. If a system is in place, programmed and controlled, for monitoring the Earth, then this may be it. Dutton is finding that new credible events, with geographical co-ordinates and precise times, do fall on or near the tracks determined by the theory. It is now up to others to check if this is so or not.

Dutton's theory can be tested, but there are complications which might deter future testers. He agrees that a proportion of his selected close encounter reports may have been misidentifications or hoaxes. These could have distorted results initially, but he points out that the reports used in recent years are much more reliable, so that early distortions will in time be cleared from the model.

## CORN CIRCLE COMPLICATIONS

Corn circles are as contentious a subject as communications with ET and abductions. Some circles do seem to be associated with the tracks, implying that they have been extraterrestrially produced, but this is currently not an acceptable explanation for the science community. Everyone accepts that many circles are the handiwork of hoaxers, but what of the rest? If ET is up there playing with beams of an unknown energy to flatten the corn into patterns for our diversion and mystification, he is doing a good job. But that energy could have effects on the biology of the plants. Research projects at the appropriate level of plant physiology, for which a high degree of laboratory equipment and know-how would be needed, could determine down to the molecular level what the effects are, if they exist. Again, it would be the evidence that we cannot see by a superficial examination of the corn that would be important. At the time of writing (April 1995) only one biological paper has been published in eight years of the study of corn circles, and that paper was written by an American scientist working independently of those who regularly visit and study the cornfields of Hampshire and Wiltshire in southern England. It is hard to understand how such a situation has arisen when there are plenty of plant physiologists in the universities who could quickly think up scientific ways into the problem during coffee breaks. If one suspects biological effects in the corn circles, as some do, then it is no good merely toying with this suspicion. Research at an appropriate level has to be carried out and papers published in the science journals. Progress cannot otherwise be made.

Simple corn circles, where just a thin ring of corn is absent without any flattening, are almost certainly biological in origin – a fairy-ring phenomenon due to fungal growth out from a central point. Research by SEPRA in France has shown how adequately fungi can draw circles. I saw three rings in cornfields by the side of the M4 motorway not long ago and feel certain that they were not produced by extraterrestrials.

Could the flattening within corn circles be caused by atmospheric vortices, or by BOLs of plasma which have been photographed travelling over the cornfields? Atmospheric physicist Terrence Meaden has spent years developing his theories of atmospheric vortices without finding an acceptable explanation. The whole area seems so confused that any suggestion that a proportion of corn circles may be connected with the UFO phenomena is better left on one side until more research is done. There have been only three instances where people have reported seeing a corn circle being formed. There are a few thousand witnesses to close encounters with UFOs.

This intrusion of the corn circles does not, however, affect the Astronautical Theory. It can be tested against the co-ordinates of the most acceptable close encounters reported worldwide, while observational strategies could be adopted to provide additional support. Both lines of testing are needed.

## AMATEURS WANTED

Amateur astronomers around the world could play an important part in such testing, if they were suitably linked by a communications network, which would not be difficult these days. The aim would be to observe satellite-like UFOs, travelling westward at meteoric speeds of about 400 miles a minute in retrograde orbit, so they could not be mistaken for conventional satellites. The task would be to communicate observations so that a string of amateur astronomers around the world could track the UFO. Dutton would like to see suitably equipped observation posts testing the Astronautical Theory, but amateur astronomers might do the job just as well if suitably connected. Let us call it *The Orbital Network*. It could be economically viable and become popular as many amateurs would be interested in testing the theory. (Would Roy Dutton like to hear from any who would like to participate? Yes, he would. See Information Section on page 205.)

It has to be considered that if these super satellites (UFOs) exist, they may have been detected years ago by our defence radar systems. The power and coverage of NORAD should have been enough for the task. But perhaps the evidence acquired has been confusing – the military mind would not easily accept the presence of objects in retrograde orbits moving faster than any known satellite. Or perhaps the UFOs – because of their construction – would be more easily detected in orbit by visual observations.

Critics may say that the model which Dutton presents looks like something which might have been predetermined by him. He staunchly maintains this is not so:

There has been nothing predetermined in my research. It has been an open-ended exercise throughout. What is surprising is that such a comprehensive theory has come out of my spare-time investigations. It was a miracle I discovered anything with the basic methods, quality of data and times of events on the ground that I had to work with originally.

The Astronautical Theory is a complex theory which took many years to develop and which cannot be fully explained in a book such as this. Interested readers should consult the Information Section. Some recent papers are available.

# CHAPTER 16
## *Contact and Cosmic Realism*

It is said that reality is less dangerous than fantasy, but perhaps not for the UFO phenomena. If all reports are no more than fancies and frauds, there would be nothing to worry about but the weakness of the human brain. A negative result, no evidence of extraterrestrials after rigorous and comprehensive research, would still leave things slightly open. But we could come to a conclusion based on evidence, or the lack of it, instead of the gut instinct which most scientists operate on at present when questioned about UFOs.

Whatever the outcome, the psychologists and sociologists would learn a thing or two. And the phenomena of marsh gas, BOLs and ball-lightning, which puzzle all the plasma and atmospheric physicists I have talked to, might be explained. And the ETH? It would remain a hypothesis which groups of radio astronomers could continue to test with some justification. Space travellers in the future could also watch for anything on the Moon or Mars that looked unnatural – possible relics from visits millions of years ago.

But what if irrefutable evidence is found, or theoretical predictions confirmed? Let us see proof that just one of those thousands of reported UFOs is an extraterrestrial artifact and the status of humanity is up for review. Fear might not be our emotion, but most people unfamiliar with the science of SETI would be concerned. They would not be in a position to understand the situation. It would not be like discovering the first pulsar or the neutrino or the structure of DNA. It would confound and confuse human thought far more than the Copernican and Darwinian revolutions did in their time. We would have to adjust our egos, as well as our minds, to a new universal view. Darwin's evolutionary biology gave us monkeys as ancestors and demoted us from angelic status. We have learnt to accept the monkeys as ancestors, but there is still no one

193

above us except God. Finding that there is would shock a lot of people. Undeniable evidence of ET would force us to acknowledge that dynasties of intelligent beings are higher than us on the cosmic scale. We would all be faced with a reality which previously was only a possibility, something we could ignore completely if we were not interested.

We would have satisfied our craving to know. We would have confirmed the universality of life and intelligence. We would know that life on Earth is not the result of a freak event, that we are part of a great universal process, that what biologists have discovered and explained can be only a tiny part of a phenomenon of life and intelligence animating our galaxy and the entire universe of a hundred billion other galaxies. That would be the satisfying part of our discovery, the easy part.

With the ETH of the UFO phenomena confirmed, however, we would have to accept that uninvited visitors are on our doorstep, interested investigators who may have been secretly watching the unfurling of human life and civilisation from its very beginnings. There has been no competition from them, no exploitation, no intentional contact that anyone can confirm. Information about us, the dawn and development of our civilisation, may be the only commodity taken, the only commodity of interest, and this they would gather best without direct contact. And their future observations might not affect us – ever! They have not in the past. Yet with proof of ET's presence, active in the Solar System, our view of ourselves and life and the universe would be changed. Would it be a change for the better? That is the question.

## NO PR FOR ET

Some people who are connected with SETI and ufology are actually making plans for good public relations when the extraterrestrials finally introduce themselves, either by radio or in flying saucers. I would like to point out that the only relationship we would have to consider is *the fact* that ET is within the Solar System, if that were to be established beyond doubt. Only knowledge of *the fact* should affect us.

If all ETs are at least a thousand light-years away, sitting by their radio transmitters, we could relax and anticipate future broadcasts and what they might contain. But if ET is here, even the most relaxed members of society may tighten up a bit. An announcement that we have extraterrestrial visitors would have to be delayed until the public knew enough about the subject to accept that there would be no danger, that we are in a situation, or predicament, that is part of our existence. We just have not noticed it before. Our lives would not necessarily be changed, although nations may become more co-operative. There would be no protocols for extraterrestrial relationships because they would make no more contact in the future than they have in the past. Why should they suddenly make contact after studying us for thousands of years?

## NO MORAL LESSONS FROM ET

Cosmic values are often talked about by people in SETI and by those of a more religious turn of mind in the UFO societies. But do cosmic values exist and could they underlie the behaviour of extraterrestrials?

Who has brought the concepts of value and meaning and purpose to the Earth? We have developed these for our own well-being. They are not outside human civilisation, an intangible part of the universe. Some fellow mammals – the apes and dolphins – may share these concepts with us in their own way, but we do not really know to what extent. And as far as we are concerned, our moral concepts relate exclusively to our advanced primate biology and culture. What was good for human societies was established by tribal customs and religions as 'good'. What was bad for us was 'evil'. Morality for us has been largely species-specific. It is going to be the same for ET.

Extraterrestrials would be different biologically and very different culturally from us, so it follows that their sense of values would be different. One may wonder if the evolution of a large technologically capable brain, one that brings civilisation, automatically acquires an innate sense of values that is benign towards less able species? The ways in which a lot of people treat lesser creatures may not give us great confidence that such a principle exists in cosmic values. There is an insensitive lack of intellectual consistency in the ways we treat mammals less intelligent than ourselves. In Britain we feed and stroke and cuddle cats while in some countries cats are eaten. Yet people in Britain will eat a pork chop without a thought for cosmic values – and pigs are more intelligent than cats. And our fellow primates the monkeys, close relatives and only a few orders of magnitude below us on the intellectual scale, have received appalling treatment at our hands.

Those people in SETI and ufology who are so keen to contact their 'brothers' from the stars seem to ignore the high probability that most ETIs could be a few orders of magnitude above us on the intellectual scale, which might make their attitude to us similar to our attitude towards, say, the monkeys. We would not want to be in that position. So let us hope a higher and more consistent sense of values prevails with greater intelligence.

We cannot know if this is so or not and, from what we have already considered, perhaps we do not need to know. What I would sooner rely on for our protection, if protection is needed, is our great curiosity value. If ETs are here in the Solar System, they are here because they find us extremely interesting. They have come a long way to study us. And you do not destroy what is of great interest.

## A SUPER HUMAN ET?

There is a widespread assumption that ET is going to be some sort of super human, albeit with superficial anatomical differences, but adjusted to our atmosphere and gravity and micro-organisms. He (or she or it) is going to be biologically and culturally like us, although more advanced because he is ahead of us technologically. He will also be wise – because he has been around a long time – and therefore have the best in human values. That cosy assumption cannot be sustained. ET would by necessity be a social creature, but he would not have acquired human values.

So completely are our lives centred on humanity that those of us who wonder about other intelligent lifeforms and other world civilisations initially imagine that they will be like us with slight variations. The popular culture from childhood onwards reinforces this misconception. I was introduced to extraterrestrial life by the films of Flash Gordon who travelled to Mars in a spaceship built in the Professor's back garden. And what did they find on Mars? Tribes of *Homo sapiens* displaying human values – generally the bad ones. That was powerful conditioning for a child who had never had a lesson in biology. If you carry on along that line, watching science fiction on television and never getting around to attending biology lessons, you may grow up to be a UFO enthusiast who believes everything he reads about human-like extraterrestrials who have crossed the Galaxy to bestow their wisdom upon humankind.

## UNIVERSAL PURPOSE

Although ETs must be different from us, they will at least have a sense of purpose. Otherwise they would not send probes to explore other planetary systems or broadcast their cultures across the Galaxy. To explore with interstellar probes would need patience, stability and a sense of value for knowing and understanding the universe – plus extreme longevity to enjoy the results of their work. Studying other life and civilisations could be the most purposeful

196

activity there is, and information the most valuable commodity. So a sense of purpose appears to be a universal value.

Scientists in astronomical SETI have often speculated that we might benefit from a knowledge of cosmic morality. ET's broadcasts or a data bank on the Moon or Mars might tell us something of the ethical systems of the broadcasters or those who left the data bank for the future. But could such ethical systems be relevant to humankind?

Suppose that the octopoids, which were abundant in the seas during the latter part of the Cambrian and in the Ordovician Period (say 500 to 440 million years ago), had been competitive enough to bring the fishes to early extinction. If the story of the vertebrates had ended with the fishes some 450 million years ago, the biosphere would have been very different. The world might then have been dominated by octopoid lifeforms, and our counterpart (had one evolved in an octopoid dynasty instead of a vertebrate dynasty) would certainly have had a different approach to life, and a different morality. I use the octopoid lifeform for our speculation here because there appear to be only two candidates for technological status. It is rather strange: when we look for another lifeform which might make future technologists, given several hundred million years of evolution, there is only the octopoid lifeform. At least, there are only the vertebrates and octopoids on Earth – which leads to an interesting question. Has life on Earth during the past 600 million years tried out all the viable lifeforms that might lead to technologists? If the reply to that is 'Yes', though we cannot give an answer from what we currently know, then all the technologists in the universe are going to be either vertebrates of a kind (not identical with ours) or octopoids, or robots which develop from either group. One can envisage a few problems for extraterrestrial relations if that were the situation.

## WHAT IS BEHIND UFO PHENOMENA?

At this stage we can only speculate from what we already know. What sort of monitoring system a civilisation thousands of years ahead of us might possess we cannot imagine, except that it could be very strange and unexpected, which is what the most interesting aspects of the UFO phenomena are.

The reported behaviour of many UFOs has puzzled us because of their amazing tricks in spaceflight, and some sober people cannot take them seriously because of this. We are as amazed at what *they* do as Darwin would have been to witness Concorde flying overhead. Extraterrestrial technologies could be incomprehensible to us because we lack the scientific understanding on which they would be based and the experience to be able to see them for what they are. Primitive peoples who had never encountered modern civilisation – when there still were such people around – could not appreciate what they were seeing when they witnessed such things as trains. So we should not doubt the veracity of witnesses who cannot understand what they have witnessed. Those weird reported manoeuvrings of flying saucers are less likely to be a product of imagination because the details are inexplicable. Instead we should doubt those who report technologies that are just one jump ahead of our own.

## GREAT EXPECTATIONS

Paul Davies, Professor of Natural Philosophy at the University of Adelaide, is another scientist who has pondered the possible benefits of contact with ET:

> Who can guess what scientific and philosophical insights might be imparted to us from a community with billions of years of contemplative existence? This knowledge and wisdom would surely dramatically change our entire outlook on life as well as the structure of human institutions.[1]

This could be like trying to change the ways of a rabbit by imparting Holy Scriptures. It is not a realistic expectation. If such beings exist they are not going to teach us how to live. And I cannot envisage our understanding anyone a million years ahead of us. Given the evidence of our own current rapid rate of development, we could have a problem understanding ourselves in a century or two.

Someone a billion years ahead of us could be getting rather close to God, but when we consider the numbers involved in estimating the abundance of ETs, each civilisation to emerge in the Galaxy could be separated by about a million years. This could be why the radio astronomers have not received any interstellar broadcasts. If human beings are here in a million years, we might expect them to be able to explore other worlds by direct contact rather than by long-distance communications.

## THE WAY TO SUPER ROBOTS

If the scientists in artificial intelligence are roughly correct in their predictions, then some very accomplished robots will be operating on Earth within a century or two – quite apart from any that may be visiting us. Some scientists and philosophers are saying that this will be a natural development with no social problems, as long as we're not racist with the robots. We could all live happily together. Your best friend could be a robot. What no one seems to confront, because it is not yet a problem, is that intelligent self-reproducing robots would be very different from intelligent self-reproducing human beings. There would be the great gulf in potency between Darwinian evolution, which governs all life on Earth, and Lamarckian evolution which would be automatically followed by the robots. In Darwinian evolution all improvements have to be tested in the environment by natural selection before they are permanently adopted; Lamarckian evolution allows significant improvements to be made with each generation.

We are Darwinian machines who, given a century, may produce the first generation of Lamarckian machines. This would pose a great threat which we might keep at bay for a while. In order to cope with a world of increasing complexity, no one would object to a 10 per cent increase in intelligence with each generation. In ten generations a new species of *Homo* could be in charge of the planet, but it would be a biological *Homo*. But a 10 per cent increase per generation would probably not be enough to keep ahead of Lamarckian machines which might increase in intelligence by a 100 per cent a generation.

Biological beings would have thrust themselves into a race for dominance which they would surely lose. Biological beings, such as ourselves or biological ETs, might not find it difficult to double their intelligence. Currently, some *Homo sapiens* are twice as intelligent as others with exactly the same biological base. But to go much beyond this might need bigger brains which in turn would need additional biological support, such as increased blood supply and stronger skeletal features to support a larger brain. A biological limit could soon be reached beyond which the human race could not go. One cannot envisage such a limit to the development of super robots, once our level of intelligence is achieved in artificial intelligence.

There are scientists outside the discipline of artificial intelligence who believe they know enough to say that this could not happen, that robots with our level and quality of intelligence cannot be produced. But they are in a small minority compared to those scientists in the discipline of artificial intelligence who believe the development is inevitable, simply because many people will be working in this field which has such enormous economic and social potential – at least until the robots take over!

With this future scenario for ourselves it looks possible that a high proportion of ETs will be robots with intellects and abilities we cannot imagine. Such a development makes interstellar travel look a lot easier, even if convenient and unknown ways of beating the light-years do not exist. Robots from a distant world could just switch off for a few thousand years and arrive here in pristine condition.

So our keenness for contact with ET should be tempered by the possibilities which we can already envisage. Even if the robots do become more like biological beings themselves than the metallic machines sometimes portrayed in science fiction, they would still be capable of Lamarckian evolution. That fact would separate us from them far more than their being based on some super organic microchip which is comparable in size and complexity to a living cell. Lamarckian evolution could take the robot to realms to which no biological being can ever go. Many scientists will say 'So what? *Homo sapiens* will be replaced as we replaced *Homo erectus* who replaced *Homo habilis*.' But that was such a slow business that no one noticed and no one was hurt by the process. Robots, in theory, could replace us in a few decades, once they started to reproduce, instead of the million years it took us to replace *Homo erectus*.

There are problems for the theologians here. Not long ago, the Vatican ran a conference to explore the impact that the discovery of extraterrestrial intelligence would have on Christianity. The underlying belief was that if ET were detected, the Catholic Church would try to convert the extraterrestrials to Christianity. Whether this good intention would extend to super robots with their origins in Lamarckian evolution, I do not know. But we have the ironic situation where the theologians are expecting to convert the extraterrestrials while the scientists in astronomical SETI are expecting the extraterrestrials to convert us – for the better, of course. My guess is that if extraterrestrials are out there, be they biological or robotic beings, neither will happen.

## THE WAY TO REVELATION
It may be that some governments know the truth about UFOs, but are deterred from disclosing it at present because they fear a disturbing public reaction. They may feel the time is not yet right. Yet the time may never be right for a blunt official announcement that would shock the world. The best way to reveal our predicament – which would exist if some UFOs are extraterrestrial artifacts – would be to make *no* official announcements. Let the news filter through slowly, so that we all gradually guess the truth of the situation. It may take a long time but it is probably best that way.

Most people would not be prepared to handle the news that ET is here. Members of UFO societies and *Star Trek* watchers might accept it with enthusiasm, but they are not typical of the general population.

One could almost deduce from recent events that such slow conditioning is in progress, judging from the way in which military personnel at Rendlesham and elsewhere appear to be completely free to give convincing evidence on major UFO events. It looks as if they have had official blessing. Then there is the constant pressure from the UFO societies which can be fed the occasional piece of information – nothing too unambiguous, but it will all build up into one big truth in time. 'That's the way to do it,' as Punch used to say – repeatedly!

## SCIENCE TO PREVENT WORRY

Above all in this UFO–SETI business, the science supporting the extraterrestrial hypothesis should become widely appreciated. It provides a very comforting message. It tells us that if ETs are here today they have been here for a very long time – perhaps millions of years. The fact that they have not taken over the world in all that time indicates that they are not likely to start now.

The science of SETI tells us that planets with flourishing biospheres are not suitable places for alien biologies to set up home. So exploration, *yes*; colonisation, *no*. Our political leaders, who have not yet had a chance to catch up on the science, need not worry about top-secret reports that ET is here. Though they should prepare public awareness before making any announcements.

Most people do not realise how interesting we would be to old civilisations in the Galaxy. If they exist, we are currently front-page news in the *Galactic Times*, the latest technological intelligence to evolve on a blue planet. That will not be happening very often, perhaps once in a million years if our sums are correct; and if it is possible to document the process it will be done without disturbing the subject of study – us!

Broadcasts across the light-years which propagate the culture and knowledge of an advanced civilisation would be contaminatory, if received by less advanced civilisations. But sending probes to investigate the latest civilisation to arrive on the galactic scene need not contaminate. We should therefore not expect gifts of knowledge to advance our science and cure all our ills, most of which are specific to us anyway. We may know that other beings are out there, and that is about all – no guidance to revolutionary technology, no

201

profound insights into cosmic values. Yet we would have confirmed the most fundamental hypothesis in the history of science and philosophy. We would have confirmed that life is a universal phenomenon.

# REFERENCE SECTION

*Chapter 1*
1. 'UFO lands in Suffolk – and that's Official', Ralph Noyes, published in *The UFO Report 1990* (ed. Timothy Good).

*Chapter 3*
1. 'Brave New Horizons', Peter Sturrock, *New Scientist*, 24 December 1988, pp. 49–51.

*Chapter 6*
1. 'Investigating the UFO', V. J. Ballester Olmos, *UFOs 1947– 1987*, published by Fortean Tomes for the British UFO Research Association.
2. 'Scientific Approach and First Results of Studies into Unidentified Aerospace Phenomena in France', J. J. Velasco, presented at AIAA conference, Los Angeles, 19 April 1986, and 'Biochemical Traumatology as a Potent Tool for Identifying Actual Stresses Elicited by Unidentified Sources: Evidence for Plant Metabolic Disorders in Correlation with a UFO Landing', Michael C. L. Bounias, *Journal of Scientific Exploration*, 1990, vol. 4, no. 1, pp. 1–18.
3. 'The Delphos Case: Soil Analysis and Appraisal of a CE-2 Report', Erol A. Faruk, *Journal of UFO Studies*, 1989, vol. 1.

*Chapter 9*
1. *Is Anyone Out There?*, Frank Drake and Dava Sobel, Delacorte Press, New York, 1992.

*Chapter 10*
1. Drake and Sobel, op. cit.

*Chapter 11*
1. References to all Frank Tipler's SETI papers are given here because of their importance to the subject: 'Extraterrestrial Intelligent Beings do not Exist', *Quarterly Journal of the Royal Astronomical Society*, 1980, vol. 21, pp. 267–81; 'A Brief History of the Extraterrestrial Intelligence Concept', *Quarterly Journal of the Royal Astronomical Society*, 1981, vol. 22, pp. 133–45; 'Additional Remarks on Extraterrestrial Intelligence', *Quarterly Journal of the Royal Astronomical Society*, 1981, vol. 22, pp. 279–92; 'The Most Advanced Civilization, in the Galaxy Is Ours', *Mercury*, January–February 1982, pp. 5–37, 'Extraterrestrial Intelligence: the debate continues' (a comprehensive review paper with several contributors), *Physics Today*, March 1982, pp. 27–38.

*Chapter 13*
1. 'Analysis of a UFO Photograph', Richard F. Haines, *Journal of Scientific Exploration*, 1987, vol. 1, no. 2, pp. 129–47.
2. 'A Large Stationary Object Above Montreal', Richard F. Haines and Bernard Guénette, *Alien Update*, Arrow, Random House, London, 1993.

*Chapter 14*
1. 'Effects of UFOs on People', James McCampbell, *UFOs 1947–1987*, published by Fortean Tomes, pp. 200–210.
2. 'The UFO Propulsionists', Ken Behrendt, *UFOs 1947–1987*, pp. 255–63.

*Chapter 16*
1. *Are We Alone?*, Paul Davies, Penguin, 1995.

*Photograph 1*
Richard F. Haines and Jacques F. Vallee, *Journal of Scientific Exploration*, 1989, vol. 3, no. 2, pp. 113–31, and 1990, vol. 4, no. 1, pp. 71–4.

# INFORMATION SECTION

*Alien Update*, published annually by Arrow, edited by Timothy Good, provides a useful source of UFO news.

Astronomers (advanced amateurs and professionals) interested in investigating the Astronautical Theory should write to: Roy Dutton, c/o 545 Babbacombe Road, Torquay, Devon, TQ1 1HQ.

BUFORA (British UFO Research Association), B.M. BUFORA, London, WC1N 3XX. Publishes the *UFO Times*, a bimonthly magazine.

Contact International (UK), 11 Ouseley Close, New Marston, Oxford, OX3 0JS. Publishes a bimonthly magazine.

Fund for UFO Research Inc., PO Box 277, Mount Rainier, Maryland 20712, USA. One of the leading UFO associations in the United States, it provides financial support for scientific research and investigations of the UFO phenomena.

The J. Allen Hynek Center for UFO Studies, 2457 West Peterson, Chicago, Illinois 60659, USA. Probably the leading UFO association in the world, CUFOS is not a membership organisation and functions more like a scientific institute. It aims to be a reliable source of information about UFOs and publishes a magazine, technical journal and specialised monographs.

Operation Right To Know was launched in the USA during 1992 to present a public approach to the problem of UFO secrecy on the part of governments. Its aim is to raise public awareness of the available evidence of the UFO phenomena and to help foster international co-operation amongst researchers and organisations. It publishes a regular newsletter and other documents. Address in the UK: 20 Newton Gardens, Ripon, North Yorkshire, HG4 1QF.

'Project Delta: A Study of Multiple UFO' by Richard F. Haines. Published by LDA Press, PO Box 880, Los Altos, California 94023-0880, USA, a recent review of more than 400 reports by one of the leading scientists in ufology.

Project Hessdalen, Bukkholmvelen, Ulleroy, N-1747 Skjeberg, Norway. It has a permanent research centre staffed by personnel from Østfold Engineering College. It is active in running conferences for physicists and establishing an automatic field station.

Quest International Publications Limited, First Floor, 66 Boroughgate, Otley, Leeds, LS21 1AE, publishes *UFO Magazine*, the leading magazine in the UK with an international distribution. The policy of the magazine is to accept no single hypothesis, but to cover new and historical information in a scientific manner. Quest's research group has more than a hundred active investigators in the UK and abroad. A free UFO Directory is available, offering a wide range of official documents, videos of UFOs, audio tapes and slides.

*SETI News*, a quarterly magazine for everyone, published by the SETI Institute, 2035 Landings Drive, Mountain View, California, 94043, USA. The Institute runs the world's major program in astronomical SETI.

# INDEX